THE JOHNS HOPKINS UNIVERSITY STUDIES IN HISTORICAL AND POLITICAL SCIENCE

SERIES LXXXIV (1966) NUMBER 2

EIGHTY-FOURTH SERIES (1966)

1. Search and Seizure and the Supreme Court: A Study in Constitutional Interpretation
   BY JACOB W. LANDYNSKI
2. Money and Conquest: Allied Occupation Currencies in World War II
   BY VLADIMIR PETROV

MONEY AND CONQUEST

Allied Occupation Currencies in World War II

MONEY AND CONQUEST

Allied Occupation Currencies in World War II

By
VLADIMIR PETROV

BALTIMORE
THE JOHNS HOPKINS PRESS

Baltimore, Maryland 21218
Printed in the United States of America
Library of Congress Catalog Card No. 66–26685

The book is published in cooperation with The Institute for Sino-Soviet Studies of The George Washington University.

For

JEAN

ACKNOWLEDGMENTS

I would like to express my sincere gratitude to several Yale professors who offered helpful comments and critiques in the early stages of this study: Samuel Flagg Bemis, John Morton Blum, David Nelson Rowe, Hajo Holborn, Robert Triffin, John M. Montias, Frederick C. Barghoorn, and, particularly, H. Bradford Westerfield. Outside of Yale, I am greatly indebted for advice and encouragement to Dr. Stefan T. Possony, Director, International Political Studies Program, the Hoover Institution, Stanford University; and to John A. Thomas, University of Essex, England, for his friendly assistance. None of these men, obviously, bear direct or indirect responsibility for the final product.

May, 1966
Washington, D. C.

VLADIMIR PETROV
Institute for Sino-Soviet Studies
The George Washington University

CONTENTS

MONEY AND CONQUEST

Allied Occupation Currencies in World War II

CHAPTER I

INTRODUCTION

During the prolonged siege of Tyre in the year 1123, the Doge Domenigo Michieli exhausted his treasury chest. Because his brave Venetians clamored for pay and some reportedly contemplated desertion, the resourceful Doge had leather coins struck and used them to pay his troops. The issue of this "money of necessity" was accompanied by a solemn promise that it would be redeemed at full face value upon the return of the fleet to Venice. Historians did not record the reaction of the crusaders to this early substitute for good gold, or indeed whether Domenigo Michieli, noted for his shrewdness as well as his ferocity, actually honored his pledge.[1] But in all probability these leather coins were the first issue of what has eventually come to be called military currency. Although the evidence is meager, it seems that throughout the Middle Ages and on into the modern period, such currencies were used from time to time, serving a single limited purpose, that of paying troops when supplies of regular money were inadequate or non-existent; they bore no relation to the currencies of the occupied enemy territories.

In the nineteenth century military currencies assumed a new and important role: they were used not only to pay troops but also as a means of paying the people of an occupied territory for supplies requisitioned by the occupying army. This practice was pursued by the North in the American Civil War; by the Prussians in the Seven Weeks' War (1866) and in the Franco-Prussian War (1870–71); by the Russians in the Balkan War (1877–78) and in the Russo-Japanese War (1904–5). Depending on its policies, the occupying power could either redeem military notes or make

1. W. Carew Hazlitt, *The Venetian Republic, Its Rise, Its Growth, and Its Fall, A. D. 409–1797* (4th ed.; London: Adam and Charles Black, 1915), I, 174.

them a liability of the defeated state as a part of the peace settlement. It should be noted that the enlightened practice of paying the population of the occupied territories was recognized in the Hague Rules of 1907 respecting the laws and customs of war on land. Article 46 states that " private property cannot be confiscated," and Article 47 adds that " pillage is formally forbidden."

Until World War II military currencies served as legal tender only in a limited sense. The people living in the occupied territories were forced to accept military promissory notes in lieu of payment for requisitioned supplies and services, but these notes did not replace or supplement the indigenous currency. Although they changed hands, their value was usually below that of " regular " money because the terms for their eventual redemption were unknown and depended on the outcome of the war.

During World War II military currencies were used by all the major powers and to a much greater extent than ever before. In addition to paying the troops and compensating the owners of requisitioned property, military currencies also served as a major means of manipulating the economies of occupied territories. These currencies were proclaimed legal tender alongside the indigenous currencies; their circulation was enforced, and no discrimination against them was tolerated. Their impact upon the economies of conquered territories was considerable. Consequently, they came to be viewed more as an aspect of occupation policy than merely as a temporary military expedient.

The extent to which military—or occupation—currencies were used varied greatly from place to place and depended on the economic aims of the occupying powers. Military currencies offered a very effective means of regulating monetary circulation. And the power to issue these currencies in many instances proved to be a much more effective means of regulating the economies of occupied countries than decrees and regulations, which were often difficult, if not impossible, to enforce.

Like all other instruments of control, the monetary policies of occupation reflected the general attitudes of the victor toward the vanquished. These policies were not always clear-cut and sometimes they were affected by such extraneous factors as the particular interests of the military. In addition, their success was limited by a number of factors. First, there was the erratic response of war-torn and unstable economies to decrees affecting money and banking. Second, the execution of these monetary policies was frequently characterized by inconsistency, ineptness, improvisation, and ignorance of local economic and political conditions. Finally, in many instances, the professed goals of monetary policies proved to be unattainable because of the confused and contradictory nature of the occupation directives and lack of coordination between the various levels and branches of the army and the military government. Although occupation monetary policies were intended to further the interests of the victors, in the end they frequently failed to fulfill the planners' expectations.

The monetary policy experiences of the various occupying powers in World War II have little in common, and it is difficult to work out a general pattern. Even in the case of the German occupation of Europe—which was the best thought out and best organized—policies differed widely from country to country. These differences were predicated by a number of factors, political as well as economic, and accounted for a flexibility which turned out to be a definite asset to the occupied countries. By contrast, the most rigid pattern of all, that of the Soviet occupation of East and Central Europe, had by far the most disastrous economic consequences. The Soviet experience also showed that occupation currencies did not have to be of a special design, or be issued on the conqueror's titular authority, in order to function as such: all that was required was an actual assumption by the occupation authorities of full control over the issue and circulation of currencies.

Despite the fact that occupation monetary experiences in World War II seem to consist of seemingly unrelated episodes, in all cases, regardless of the specific conditions in the occupied country and of the policies of the occupying power, the administrative, economic, and financial problems of occupation were essentially the same. Depending on a number of factors, such as the objectives of the occupying power, the competence of its administration, or the responsiveness of the population to the military government, these problems could be aggravated or alleviated, but never eliminated.

This book is primarily concerned with Allied monetary policies and experiences of occupation in World War II in Europe, with a particular emphasis on American policies and experiences, beginning with the landing in North Africa and ending with the abolition of the Allied military mark currency in Germany in 1948. German policies and experiences are presented in Chapter 2 as a background against which to view Allied monetary practices. A discussion of the Pacific Theater is left out, in part because of the paucity of data and in part because, for a variety of reasons, monetary experiences there differed vastly from those in Europe.

There are further limitations in this book. Policies and practices of the United States remain central throughout, while those of Great Britain, the Soviet Union, and France are described only cursorily. In addition, with the exception of one chapter, the book deals with occupation of the major "enemy" as distinct from "liberated" countries. This categorization is somewhat arbitrary. The Allied attitudes and policies toward "liberated" Europe differed markedly from country to country; the treatment of France or Greece had little resemblance to that of Norway or Holland; Austria had been declared a "liberated" country, yet it was subjected to a fullfledged occupation for ten years.

Equally different were the occupations of Italy and Germany, which represent the bulk of this study. The Italian government, which was given a status of "co-belligerent" shortly after the armistice, played, or attempted to play, a role in the politics and economics of occupation. Germany, on the other hand, had no government and remained strictly an object of occupation; all the policy conflicts resulting from the occupation were among the occupying powers, not between the occupying powers and the Germans.

A study at this time of occupation experiences is justifiable on several grounds. In the first place, such a study permits a certain insight into the policies and mechanics of occupation in modern war. Second, it is important to understand the place which monetary policy has been assigned within the whole occupation policy framework. Third, the differences between "regular" money and occupation currencies and the inherent properties and functions of the latter deserve greater attention than has previously been paid to them. Finally, the impact of troop spending on the economies of the economically weak countries is not a problem which is limited to wartime; it is a problem to which we have yet to find a satisfactory solution and which needs to be at least clearly defined.

Of no lesser concern is the eternal question of the reconciliation of the victors and the vanquished after the hostilities end. There is no doubt that the roots of many of our present difficulties with Europe go back to the period when multitudes of soldiers and officials in strange uniforms came in direct contact with, and imposed their presence and will upon, the native populations of the occupied lands. In the minds of the Europeans, the Anglo-American victory was associated with the restoration of national independence, human dignity, liberty, and a prosperous peaceful life. These hopes and expectations were not a mere product of effective propaganda. They were as deep as they were spontaneous and even the sight of many cities destroyed by Allied bombers did not seem greatly to affect such popular sentiments. This was true throughout the continent. To some extent it was true even in Germany, where a great many people hoped that somehow the might of the United States would save them from the frightening specter of Soviet domination.

Yet within a few short months after the fighting had stopped very little remained of this goodwill for the Americans in the countries they entered as liberators or conquerors. Even in Western Europe, where the nations regained their national independence thanks to the Allied victory, the initial warmth, gratitude, and enthusiasm for the Americans and the British quickly disappeared under the harsh realities of military occupation and direct encounter. Disappointment and even resentment spread rapidly, contributing to a trend which greatly affected international relations in the postwar world.

This development needs to be understood. It is inadequate to argue that the European's expectations were unreasonable and that military occupation was destined to cause hardships regardless of Allied intentions. Even at the time, it was fairly clear to some of the key participants in the events that many of the hardships that the occupied nations suffered were unnecessary and that conditions might have been much improved had the Allies adopted a more realistic and enlightened approach.

One of the many myths that have grown up in the United States with regard to the liberation of Europe involves the "benevolent" nature of the Allied occupation. Benevolence is a matter of degree and of perception. Clearly, the Americans and British had neither Gestapos nor extermination camps, nor did they terrorize their opponents as the nazis and their quisling allies had done during the war. What tends to be overlooked is that to appreciate fully the impact of the Allied occupation and the reaction to it, their occupation practices must not be measured against those of the Axis powers but against the hopes and expectations of the occupied nations. And in any case there were aspects of Anglo-American occupation which were not benevolent by any standards. In a sense, this is a story of the dissipation among Europeans of an enormous amount of goodwill for the United States which existed toward the end of World War II.

The books which have been written about the Allied occupation in Europe during the postwar years can be divided into three groups: (1) official studies of the mechanics and policies of occupation, (2) descriptions, often emotional, of the miseries of life under the Allied rule, and (3) various politically motivated accounts. It is my intention to attempt to merge the experiences of the rulers and the ruled and to analyze their interrelationships in a systematic way. This intention accounts for the focus on occupied countries and the victors' attitudes toward them rather than on experiences of particular occupation administrations. Without such a format it would have been impossible to relate the victors' objectives and practices to the reactions of the vanquished.

While concentrating on occupation monetary policy, this study is also a political analysis. The subject is sufficiently restricted yet broad enough to reflect the interdependence of the many aspects of military occupation. In order to recreate as full a picture as possible it was necessary to draw upon a wide variety of sources, none of them fully adequate: official documents and statistics, the published memoirs of the principal actors, and the various relevant scholarly contributions. Yet it would be very difficult to present a coherent picture of the monetary policies and practices by relying entirely on published materials. It has therefore been necessary to supplement these sources with material derived from numerous extended interviews with individuals who actually took part in the planning, formulation, and execution of United States occupation policies in Italy and Germany. These interviews not only provided me with a good deal of corroborating evidence, but also, perhaps more importantly, helped me integrate and evaluate the material which was already available.

The following persons provided me with information regarding developments in Washington: Ambassador Loy W. Henderson;

the late Vice-President of the United States Henry A. Wallace; General John H. Hilldring, former Chief of the Civil Affairs Division of the War Department; Hajo Holborn, one of General Hilldring's aides; William Henry Taylor, former Assistant Director of the Division of Monetary Research of the Treasury Department; and Philip E. Mosely, former United States representative on the European Advisory Commission. On the financial aspects of the Allied occupation of Italy, more useful information was provided by former Financial Adviser, G-5, AFHQ, Frank A. Southard, Jr.; Victor Sullam, consultant to The Board of Economic Warfare; and Colonel Philip J. Corso, former Chief of the C. I. C., Rome. On the occupation of Germany, of great help were Ed Tenenbaum, former Special Assistant to the Finance Adviser of the OMGUS; Ralph McCabe, former Chief of the Financial Institutions Branch, OMGUS, and in particular his deputy, A. J. Warner. With regard to a number of general policy developments related to Germany, conversations with General Lucius D. Clay and Ambassador Robert E. Murphy were enlightening. There were also several other knowledgeable officials who, for various reasons, prefer to retain their anonymity; among them were former officials at Karlshorst, the Soviet headquarters in Germany.

On balance, I cannot claim this as a "definitive" study. There are still many gaps in the record which can be filled only after many more official and private collections of documents become open for study, and there are some gaps which are likely to remain open forever.

There is an additional problem. The subject of the Allied military occupation in World War II is still a touchy one, in spite of the intervening two decades, with many people who directly or indirectly (even if only emotionally) were involved in the memorable events of those years.

Finally, there was the problem of balancing the picture. Quite obviously, occupation currencies were only one—although a major—factor contributing to inflationary developments and economic collapse in occupied lands. Others included damage to the physical plant resulting from military operations; disruption of trade; drastic political, administrative, and social dislocations; and even purely psychological difficulties experienced by the vanquished in adjusting to the peculiarities of life under alien rule. These factors are recognized in this study and brought to the reader's attention whenever it seems warranted. Yet there is no way of measuring to what extent each of the factors affected a given situation. Since it is the purpose of this work to focus attention on occupation currencies (and their political background), it is all but inevitable that this particlar element of the whole picture will seem to be overemphasized at the expense of the others.

CHAPTER II

UNDER GERMAN RULE

From 1939 to 1944 the major part of continental Europe was controlled politically and economically by the Third Reich. It was upon this base that Hitler built up the powerful war machine which the Allies finally crushed in 1945. For the most part, this period has been studied from the military point of view; relatively little attention has been paid to the complex international relations involved in German-dominated and war-torn Europe. Yet World War II cannot be understood simply in terms of armies, strategies, victories, and defeats. Germany's military power was necessarily based on the exploitation of European resources; it involved the economic and political integration and control of an entire continent. This chapter is concerned with some of these problems and the way in which the Third Reich dealt with them.

Germany's relations with individual countries were far from uniform, depending on a series of factors of which the conduct of war was only one. There was a group of " neutrals "—Switzerland, Sweden, Turkey, Spain, Portugal—whose neutrality was recognized by the Reich government, and who were often subjected to pressures both from Germany and the Western Powers. There was a group of " friendly " countries—Italy, Finland, Hungary, Rumania, Bulgaria—which maintained a large degree of independence in domestic and even in foreign affairs throughout the war, and there were the much less independent but not less " friendly " Croatia (which broke from Yugoslavia) and Slovakia, the remnant of Czechoslovakia. There were also " occupied " countries under German military and sometimes civilian control but at the same time ruled by quisling regimes. These sometimes had considerable autonomy (depending on the security conditions), but all were in various degrees incorporated into Hitler's

New Order. Denmark was ruled by the Danish government, with minimal German intervention through the greater part of the war. Norway had a nominally independent native government which closely collaborated with the Reich but which was nonetheless supervised by the German occupation authorities. Holland was administered by the Germans but received relatively benevolent treatment because Hitler considered the Dutch "Germanic" people. Belgium was under German military administration, but local authority remained in Belgian hands.

France, the largest of the German-dominated countries, was governed by the Vichy government, which cooperated with the nazis; it possessed a degree of independence in its foreign affairs—and full independence in internal affairs in the unoccupied part of the country, the so-called Vichy France. Elsewhere, the local French administration, although directed from Vichy, had to carry out the orders given by the German military authorities. After the Anglo-American invasion of French North Africa in November, 1942, the whole country came under the German military occupation, and the Vichy government's policies were virtually dictated from Berlin.

Greece was divided into three parts: one was occupied by Bulgaria; one was under German military administration; and one was ruled by the Greek government, with Germans and Italians, particularly the former, retaining control over all the more important economic and strategic matters. Parts of Yugoslavia were given to Bulgaria, Hungary, and Italian-ruled Albania; and, as Croatia became independent, Serbia was put under German military administration with a Serbian civil government.

There were also two "protectorates" in Europe—Bohemia-Moravia and the "Governor-Generalship" (eastern Poland)—ruled directly from Berlin. Finally, there were three *Reichskommissariats*—Ostland, Belorussia, and Ukraine—under the Reich's Ministry for the Occupied Eastern Territories as well as vast "unorganized" areas to the east which were war zones in the strict sense of the word and which were under direct military rule.

The economic aspects of European life during these years have received even less attention than political ones. Although Europe's economy was dominated by Germany's war needs, this is not the whole story, for despite wartime abnormalities, Berlin wanted to use economic relations as a means of integrating Europe. It is worth remembering that Germany did not expect to lose the war, and that while they were fighting, Reich leaders were also trying to lay foundations for the future. The European system envisaged by them was to be dominated by Germany; but at the same time it was to be a multiple system, not simply an enlarged Germany.

The immediate needs of waging the war severely limited Germany's ability to develop this system. The Third Reich started the war with inadequate means. After Hitler failed to secure peace following the Polish campaign of 1939 and failed to defeat the British in 1940, it became obvious that the continuation of war would require the mobilization of the resources of all the defeated and occupied countries of Europe. The Soviet Union tried to help during the years of Nazi-Soviet friendship, but even then, while Germany's needs were relatively small, it could not fulfill them. The invasion of Russia in 1941 opened opportunities to exploit Russian resources more fully, but by then German requirements had also greatly increased.

As things stood halfway through the war, Germany (including Austria, Danzig, Sudetenland, western Poland, Memel, Luxembourg, and the two "protectorates") remained the principal base of the Reich's war economy. Extensive planning and an elaborate system of controls, combined with the efficient administration and the discipline of the German people, made Germany a highly productive industrial country. But to assure Germany's final victory, its resources had to be supplemented by those of other European countries.

Indiscriminate looting of the occupied countries was no answer. The Germans resorted to it in Poland and in Russia, which Hitler envisaged as the future *Lebensraum* for the German race. A great deal was extracted from the eastern territories through requisitions and confiscations, but these were essentially one-shot affairs; the productivity of the occupied areas of Russia fell sharply in a very short time.[1] When the war in Russia did not end quickly, the

1. Whatever Hitler's long-range plans for incorporation of Russia into the Reich, they were made subordinate to the urgent demands of the war, and his orders for the east provided for "immediate and maximum exploitation of the occupied areas in favor of Germany." For a discussion of German requisitioning in Russia, see Alexander Dallin, *German Rule in Russia, 1941–1945* (London: Macmillan, 1957), Chapters XV–XVIII. It is clear the amount of goods which Germany exported from the occupied areas of Russia would have been greater if it had not attacked the Soviet Union and continued to receive Soviet deliveries on

need for a sustained support of the Reich's war effort became overwhelming. This support had to come from the "friendly" and "occupied" countries of Europe. It could come only if production everywhere was kept at the highest possible level. Moreover, it could come only through organized trade and not as a result of sheer political-military pressure for deliveries of food, raw materials, and manufactured goods. Such pressure would have led inevitably to curtailment of production, shutdowns, and ever-greater discontent, with the resulting spread of resistance.[2]

Part of the problem was solved by levying direct occupation costs on the occupied countries. German political and military pressure was brought upon quisling governments to make them pay the bills for various supplies and services, billeting of troops, transportation, and the like.[3] Similar arrangements were made in "friendly" countries where German contingents were stationed. The difference was that "friendly" governments charged the costs to Germany, whereas the governments of the occupied countries had to pay the costs out of their own budgets. The latter often collaborated wholeheartedly. They could reason that no matter how high the costs of occupation were, they would have been much higher—both in material and human terms—had their nations chosen a course of total resistance. Perhaps typical was the position of the Vichy leaders Laval and Darlan, who were "deeply convinced that Germany would win. The thing was for France to be in the good graces of the Fuehrer and secure a leading position in his new Europe of the future. . . . Both for themselves and for their country, they were intent on being on the winning side."[4]

---

the 1940 scale. The costs of waging war in the east, in equipment, supplies—and human lives—had, of course, to be borne by Germany entirely. From the standpoint of immediate economic advantages to Germany, Hitler's war in the east made no sense.

2. In one area, however, the Reich leaders had to take risks: importation of foreign labor into Germany was absolutely essential to the war effort. See Royal Institute of International Affairs, *Occupied Europe* (London: 1944), p. 19.

3. Initially, the occupation costs were not related to what the German military spent in the occupied country, but were fixed on the basis of the maximum war budgets of the country prior to German conquest. Later they were scaled down, but in the meantime Germany accumulated substantial credit balances soon to be offset by her growing indebtedness in European trade. See Thomas Reveille, *The Spoil of Europe* (New York: Norton, 1941), p. 91.

4. William L. Langer, *Our Vichy Gamble* (New York: Knopf, 1947), p. 386.

The price for "being on the winning side" was quite stiff. By September, 1944, the total amount of occupation costs paid by the European governments added up to 84 billion marks. France paid 35.25 billion marks; Holland 8.75; Belgium, 5.70; Denmark, 2; and Italy, 10. The occupation costs in Italy accrued in 1943–44, during the rule of the Republic of Salò in Northern Italy, after Germany assumed the whole burden of waging the war against the Allies. The rest was paid by the governments of Norway, Greece, Croatia and Serbia, and by the "protectorates" and *Reichskommissariats* in the east.[5]

Yet occupation levies (and outright seizures) could not satisfy all Germany's needs: the annual rate of payments by the "occupied" countries was equivalent to some 16 billion marks as compared with a German war expenditure of about 120 billion.[6] Since the mobilization of Germany's internal resources could not make up the difference, the Reich government considered it imperative to open up normal trade channels to assure a maximum inflow of the badly needed goods. But this posed a problem because trade required financing and the Reich government could not export enough to pay for Germany's imports. The gold and currency reserves of the Third Reich had never been high. They were supplemented to some degree by the confiscated assets of aliens and Jews, and as the German conquest progressed, private citizens in all occupied countries were ordered to surrender (either directly to the conquerors or to local central banks) those of their assets which could be converted into hard currencies.[7] Yet these resources could pay for only a fraction of Germany's trade deficit, which increased rapidly after 1941.[8]

5. Bank for International Settlements, *Fourteenth Annual Report* (Basle, 1944), pp. 161–63. These figures do not include direct requisitions. Some interesting—although highly emotional and statistically unsupported—observations on German requisition practices can be found in Paul Einzig, *Europe in Chains* (New York: Penguin, 1940), *passim*.

6. Royal Institute of International Affairs, *Occupied Europe*, p. 34.

7. *Ibid., passim.* One estimate put the amount of publicly owned gold thus collected at 1.2 billion—obviously not a conservative estimate. Reveille, *The Spoil of Europe*, p. 135.

8. During 1939–40 Germany had a significant trade surplus due to the decline of imports from European countries and the necessity to intensify exports to the countries which had become economically dependent on Germany. See Bank for International Settlements, *Eleventh Annual Report* (Basle, 1941), pp. 27–28; cf. *Twelfth Annual Report* (Basle, 1942), p. 47.

The position of Western European countries involved in inter-European trade was often worse. The fleeing governments of Belgium, Holland, and Norway had successfully transferred their gold reserves abroad. A large part of the huge gold reserve of the Bank of France had been shipped to the United States; another part was evacuated to one of the French African colonies and was beyond the reach of the Germans.[9] All German assets, as well as the assets of governments ruled by quislings, were frozen in the United States, Great Britain, and other Allied nations.[10] In these circumstances, the trade balances of the European countries had to be settled in other than traditional ways.

Even before the war the Reich government had refused to allow the shortage of financial resources to interfere with production or trade. According to nazi theory, production was to be determined only by the amount of raw materials, labor, and industrial capacity available; if some countries also needed capital, such capital would be supplied by Germany. Trade among European countries drawn into the German orbit was to be financed through a multilateral exchange clearing system, with Berlin as the financial center of the continent.[11] Under this system the member countries could trade without having to provide foreign exchange in settlement of their trade balances. The adverse balances would be offset against each other by the central clearing office in Berlin. The currencies of all countries would be stabilized in relation to the reichsmark which, in turn, would be kept stable in relation to gold or the dollar.[12]

9. Einzig, *Europe in Chains*, p. 89. There is no record that the Germans ever tried to get the French gold from the Vichy regime. See Robert Murphy, *Diplomat among Warriors* (Garden City, N. Y.: Doubleday, 1964), p. 74.

10. For a discussion of foreign assets in the United States, and of the Morgenthau-Hull-Roosevelt positions on freezing these assets, see Judd Polk, " Freezing Dollars against the Axis," *Foreign Affairs*, XX, No. 1 (October, 1941), and John Morton Blum, *From the Morgenthau Diaries: Years of Urgency* (Boston: Houghton Mifflin, 1965), pp. 326–43. Cf. Bank for International Settlements, *Thirteenth Annual Report* (Basle, 1943), p. 46.

11. See Paul Einzig, *Hitler's " New Order" in Europe* (London: Macmillan, 1941), Chapter IX. Although factual, this book is full of wartime propagandistic overtones and is devoid of figures and limited to general observations. Those interested in the Far Eastern developments might profit from Einzig's *The Japanese " New Order" in Asia* (London: Macmillan, 1943).

12. After two years of war, Germany abandoned the latter part of this operation, limiting the stabilization of the currencies to their relation to the reichsmark only. See Bank for International Settlements, *Thirteenth Annual Report*, p. 40.

The system of multilateral exchange clearing, first introduced by Germany in 1931 with the beginning of the great financial crisis, served before the war as an instrument of German economic expansion, particularly in southeastern Europe.[13] But it was during the war that it acquired its maximum dimensions and turned Berlin into a major world financial center. This arrangement was eventually joined by neutral Sweden and Switzerland; only Turkey, Spain, and Portugal, jealous of their economic independence (and having more extensive contacts with the outside world), did not participate in the clearing system.[14]

Germany benefited from this system of trade financing more than any other country. Since its imports after 1941 considerably exceeded its exports, it soon accumulated substantial debit balances in relation to all the conquered countries. But all debit balances were declared frozen until after the war; no deficit in the balance of payments interfered with the flow of trade, and Germany could continue to draw on European resources.

The drawback of such a system was that producers and exporters in various countries could not wait for payment indefinitely. As a consequence, they were financed by central banks of their own countries which had little choice but to provide the necessary credit. The resulting overexpansion of credit did not disturb the Reich Ministry of Economic Affairs. Production retained priority; financial matters had to take care of themselves as best they could. The results of this overexpansion of credit were the growth of inflation, economic dislocations, excessive exports, and, in some countries, heavy occupation costs. Because Europe's economy was now more integrated, there was greater danger that inflation would engulf the whole continent.[15] The Reich government was acutely aware of this. Therefore its expansionary monetary policy was accompanied by a number of measures aimed at controlling inflation.

Within Germany proper this control was achieved by virtually

13. See, for example, Antonin Basch, *The Danube Basin and the German Economic Sphere* (New York: Columbia University Press, 1943).

14. Henry Simon Bloch and Bert F. Hoselitz, *Economics of Military Occupation* (Chicago: University of Chicago Press, 1944), p. 16.

15. According to Bank for International Settlements, *Thirteenth Annual Report*, p. 61, the percentage of trade with Germany in total turnover increased between 1938 and 1942 as follows: Belgium from 12 to 65, Bulgaria from 56 to 65, Denmark from 22 to 70, France from 7 to 50, Hungary from 28 to 53, Italy from 23 to 60.

freezing prices and wages at the prewar level and by securing the supply of essentials at fixed prices through a system of rationing.[16] But although rationing and wage-and-price controls existed in all countries, their effectiveness was uneven; it depended on many local factors and never matched that of Germany.[17] A continuous rise in prices, especially outside of Germany, resulted. As compared with the increase of 8 per cent in wholesale prices in Germany during the 1939–42 period, the corresponding increases for other European countries were as follows: [18]

Bulgaria	+ 101	
Denmark	+ 95	
France	+ 122	
Hungary	+ 88	
Norway	+ 79	
Rumania	+ 252	(retail prices)
	+ 74	(cost of living)
	+ 374	(cost of living)

In order to cope with the problem of rising prices and keep the cost of imports down, the Reich government attempted to arrest prices of the goods entering foreign trade, and in 1942–43 most of Germany's new clearing and commercial agreements with its trade partners had clauses fixing the prices of the more important commodities exchanged.[19] At the same time, Germany made assurances that after the war it was going to pay its debts " in marketable manufactures at rates of exchange corresponding to purchasing power parities at the time when balances were accumulated." [20]

Under the system of multilateral clearing, the rates of exchange of European currencies were tied to the reichsmark and effectively controlled by the Reich. However, the advantages of controlling

16. Between 1939 and 1942 the wholesale prices in Germany increased by 8 per cent, the cost of living by 8 per cent, and hourly wages by 2 per cent. *Ibid.*, p. 85. On nazi price policies, see Ladislas Farago (ed.), *The Axis Grand Strategy: Blueprints for the Total War* (New York: Farrar & Rinehart, 1942), pp. 518ff.

17. Pointing out that the populations of the occupied countries were not nearly as disciplined as the German people, Einzig wrote that price controls (like other measures adopted under dictation from Berlin) were regarded " as part of the measures imposed upon the oppressed nations by German tyranny," and for this reason it was " considered patriotic to evade it."

18. Bank for International Settlements, *Thirteenth Annual Report*, pp. 87–91.

19. *Ibid.*, pp. 87–91.

20. Richard A. Lester, *International Aspects of Wartime Monetary Experience* (Princeton: Princeton University Press, 1944), p. 17.

the rates of exchange proved to be largely illusory because Germany had no way to regulate the purchasing power of local currencies. The relatively modest overevaluation of the reichsmark following occupation gave German importers some initial advantage,[21] but this advantage was wiped out as the prices for imported goods started their sweep increase. To counteract this trend—which was most pronounced in the early years of the war—Germany negotiated further changes in the rates of exchange which would secure the continuous advantage of the reichsmark. These changes affected the currencies of both the "occupied" and "friendly" countries as follows: [22]

(in units of national currencies)

"Occupied" countries	5/9/40	4/1/41	1/1/42
Norway	1.76	1.76	1.76
Denmark	2.07	2.07	2.24
Holland	0.75	0.75	0.75
Belgium	2.39	2.50	2.50
France	17.84	20.00	20.00
"Friendly" countries	7/1/40	4/1/41	4/1/42
Bulgaria	32.75	32.75	32.75
Greece	46.50	48.50	60.00
Hungary	1.62	1.66	1.66
Rumania	49.50 *	59.50 *	59.50 *
Yugoslavia (Serbia)	14.40	17.82	20.00

* For oil and timber exported to Germany a rate of Lei 44.75 to 1 RM was maintained.

Neither the fixing of prices nor the overevaluation of the reichsmark arrested the growth of the Reich's indebtedness in its clearing accounts, which was primarily caused by its increasing trade deficit. By September, 1944, this indebtedness reached 40 billion marks—as compared with 3 billion in December, 1940.[23] After 1942 the

21. According to one calculation, the overevaluation ranged from 19 per cent in the case of Slovakia to 71 per cent in the case of Greece—where inflation was quite advanced at the time of German conquest. See Bloch and Hoselitz, *Economics of Military Occupation*, p. 36. An overvalued rate of exchange made German exports dearer and imports cheaper, thereby creating a larger import surplus. Therefore, in the long run, the overvaluation of the reichsmark contributed to the increase of German foreign indebtedness.

22. Bank for International Settlements, *Fourteenth Annual Report*, p. 163.

23. Bank for International Settlements, *Tenth Annual Report* (Basle, 1940), pp. 28–30; *Twelfth Annual Report*, p. 26; *Thirteenth Annual Report*, p. 40.

Reich government chose not to try to revise the rates of exchange any more, and they remained the same for the duration of the war. German financial leaders apparently preferred to accept a greater debt rather than to risk the consequences of further depressing European currencies.

It is hard to say what would have happened if the war had lasted longer or how the debt would have been settled had Germany won the war. As it was, this debt has remained unsettled because no successor government emerged after the war which could have legally assumed the Reich's international obligations. However, in spite of many difficulties, the system of international finance in Europe instituted by Germany worked out better than most observers expected. Years later, and under entirely different conditions, the Reich's experience was utilized by the founders of the postwar European Payments Union and of the multilateral clearing system of the communist bloc.

In its monetary policies the Reich government consistently followed a conservative approach. It was very sensitive to the dangers of currency inflation, probably more so than to other kinds of inflation. It was aware that monetary circulation was easier to control than other economic factors. This was true within Germany. It was even more true in the case of German military currency circulating in occupied countries where other factors were much less controllable.

The financial needs of the German military and military government agencies outside of Germany were, from the start, taken care of by special banks, the *Reichskreditkassen*, which issued military currency, the *Reichskreditkassenscheine*, denominated in reichsmarks. This currency, backed by loan to the Reich and occupation costs accounts, was first put into circulation in Poland in 1939. In 1940 it appeared in Denmark, Norway, Holland, Belgium, and France; in 1941, in the Balkans and in Russia. The *Reichskreditkassenscheine* was for a while legal tender throughout German-occupied Europe.[24] At its peak in November, 1943, its circulation reached 3.35 billion marks.[25]

24. In addition, Germany used special *Wehrmachtsverpflichtungsscheine*, or military promissory notes. These were issued in denominations of 50,000 reichsmarks and over and were used for big purchases. While also representing obligation of the Reich, they were not legal tender in the accepted sense. See Bank for International Settlements, *Twelfth Annual Report*, p. 129.

25. By the end of 1943, it was down to 2.9 billion due to withdrawals from

The original purpose of issuing special military currency was to assure that the financial needs of the army—including the payment of the troops—were met, without at the same time adversely affecting the monetary situation inside Germany. German authorities quickly realized, however, that military currency had significant drawbacks. First, as conceived, military currency was in fact a *German* currency; it represented a German debt in clearing accounts with occupied countries. Since it was scarcer than the local currency and had the prestige of being denominated in reichsmarks, it was often preferred to the local currency and tended to acquire a premium or to be hoarded, thus creating hidden claims against Germany. This hoarding would have been of minor significance if most of the *Reichskreditkassenscheine* had remained in private hands as a form of personal savings; that kind of claim could have been dealt with, one way or the other, after the war. But it was inevitable that substantial amounts of *Reichskreditkassenscheine* would end up in banks, thereby immediately and automatically increasing the claims of the occupied country against Germany and adversely affecting the already negative German balance of payments.[26] In addition, because German notes were in effect an all-European currency, they had an exceptional attractiveness in black market and smuggling operations. This made *Reichskreditkassenscheine* a very mobile currency internationally and created a significant problem of currency traffic controls.

Second, despite strict limitations imposed on the redemption of *Reichskreditkassenscheine*, soldiers and foreigners entering Germany were allowed to transfer their savings home, and a great majority of them took advantage of this opportunity, thus increasing the money in circulation in Germany. On the other hand, German authorities found it equally undesirable that the troops should spend all their money in the countries where they were

circulation in France and Italy. Bank for International Settlements, *Fourteenth Annual Report*, p. 160.

26. Germany did not use *Reichskreditkassenscheine* to transfer occupation costs to the occupied countries. Cf. Walter Rundell, Jr., *Black Market Money: The Collapse of U.S. Military Currency in World War II* (Baton Rouge: Louisiana State University Press, 1964), pp. 46, 82. Once the *Reichskreditkassenscheine* reached central banks of the occupied countries, they became part of Germany's recognized debt. The nearest parallel to the *Reichskreditkassenscheine* were the so-called yellow-seal dollars used by the United States in the Mediterranean Theater after the landing in North Africa.

stationed. Troop spending turned out to be a major inflationary factor, pushing prices up wherever large military units were stationed. This was so even in the more prosperous countries in Western Europe where a German soldier's pay was not relatively high and where goods long unavailable in Germany could be bought. But it was even more of a problem in the poorer areas of the Balkans and Eastern Europe, where the German soldier's pay-scale was much higher vis-à-vis that of the local population and where consumer goods were scarce.[27] As the scarcities increased and the prices went up, discontent and resentment against the Germans grew. In some cases, especially in the occupied countries in the east, where local public opinion was of secondary importance to them, German authorities could disregard the political consequences of troop spending. Economic effects were another matter; they were carefully watched by the powerful Ministry of Economic Affairs. No less important perhaps was the attitude of the military command: the *Wehrmacht* considered excessive purchasing power harmful to the soldiers' morale.

The third drawback of military currency was relatively minor. Because of the unevenness with which inflation progressed in various European countries, there appeared a necessity in certain instances to protect the interests of the German troops. The soldier's pay which looked adequate in some countries had a much lower purchasing power in others. In order to satisfy the soldiers in the situations where their complaints seemed justified, German authorities provided special bonuses to the basic rate of pay, adjusting them in accordance with the price levels in the different countries.[28]

The fourth problem was much more complex. It stemmed from the fact that the *Reichskreditkassenscheine* used for troop pay were denominated in marks and thus bore a fixed relation to the local currencies. There were no special military rates of exchange, but for all practical purposes *Reichskreditkassenscheine* were as good as reichsmarks, or better. However, because the rise in prices varied from country to country, there was a corresponding variation in the purchasing power of *Reichskreditkassenscheine* which led to their gravitation toward the countries where their

27. Bloch and Hoselitz, *Economics of Military Occupation*, pp. 82–83.

28. Frank A. Southard, Jr., *The Finances of European Liberation, with Special Reference to Italy* (New York: King's Crown, 1946), p. 116.

purchasing power was highest. The traffic of military currency went from the east of Europe toward France, and *Reichskreditkassenscheine* developed into a form of traveler's money, or clearing currency, not only for the German troops but also for civilians.[29]

This traffic was largely spontaneous and could not be controlled effectively. It created numerous problems in monetary transactions. It also opened possibilities for German participation in local black markets, including the currency market. Because of the strict discipline of German soldiers, this participation was, for the most part, negligible, although from time to time some more enterprising officials (usually belonging to auxiliary German organizations) were caught in large-scale operations. Nevertheless, the danger was there and had to be watched for.

There were no simple and easy solutions to these problems, and to keep their monetary house in order the German authorities carried out a variety of measures. Probably the most significant of these was a maximum reduction of the *Reichskreditkassenscheine* in circulation. Their withdrawal was conducted in stages, country by country, as conditions permitted. The notes which had accumulated in central banks were surrendered to Germany, and the amounts were added to the latter's clearing debt.

In Poland, military currency was replaced by the zloty, issued by the German Governor-Generalship, by the end of 1939.[30] In Western and Northern Europe, where the speed of German conquest left the existing financial systems and facilities virtually intact, the local governments, after a short period of confusion, assumed the responsibility for supplying occupation authorities with local currency for troop pay. Although *Reichskreditkassenscheine* retained their legal status, they were completely withdrawn from circulation in the west by the end of 1943. Soldiers received their pay in local money, except for that part of it which they chose to remit home as savings. Under the threat of punishment, they largely refrained from making money on the black market;

29. Bank for International Settlements, *Fourteenth Annual Report*, pp. 159–61.

30. Old zloty notes of the Bank Polski were also exchanged into the new currency. This operation was used, in part, to dispossess the more well-to-do Poles, in line with the general oppressive policy of the nazis in the east. See Reveille, *The Spoil of Europe*, pp. 122–23. In Poland, as well as in the occupied territories of the Soviet Union, inflation was allowed to reach a very high level; artificially created shortages of commodities made black market prices soar higher than elsewhere in Europe.

their pay was low and, in any case, they had little to sell. In the case of transfer to another country, they had to get rid of the local currency left in their pockets locally; no exchanging was allowed.

In order to discourage troop spending in " friendly " countries, German authorities resorted to the ingenious device of special " canteen money " (*Wehrmachtsbehelfgeld* and *Verrechnungsscheine*), which was expressed in marks but had a value ten times greater than its face value if spent in army canteens or remitted home as savings. There was no danger of hoarding: the " canteen money " was not legal tender and therefore had no attraction to local populations. This money was used in Hungary, Rumania, Bulgaria, and Slovakia. It hurt the German treasury but achieved its purpose: troop spending did not add to the inflationary pressures in the satellite countries or to Germany's debt.[31]

Finally, the function of *Reichskreditkassenscheine* as universal travelers' money ended when, by the decree of October 13, 1944, it lost its status as legal tender and was replaced by the *Verrechnungsscheine fuer das Deutsche Wehrmacht*, a sort of military traveling voucher which was not legal tender and could not be used by civilians. By then, of course, the number of foreign countries under German domination had been greatly reduced.

At all times, military currency was kept separate from the currency used in Germany, and " stringent foreign exchange regulations were imposed to prevent the issue of *Reichskreditkassenscheine* from adversely affecting the value of Reichsbank notes in Germany." [32] This goal was pursued consistently and with apparent success. The Reich government did not allow war conditions to interfere with its standing objective of preserving overall financial stability.

One peculiar episode throws light on the German preoccupation with the normal functioning of European finances. Early in the war, the Reich Secret Service came up with a fantastic scheme which, they thought, would ruin the financial foundation of the British Empire. Himmler's deputy, Reinhard Heydrich, conceived an idea to produce perfect notes of the Bank of England and to distribute them in such a way and in such quantities that the Bank's bankruptcy would be inevitable. Such notes were, in fact, pro-

31. Without the inducement of extra purchasing power, the " canteen money " had its parallel in Allied experience in the form of the scrip money or Military Payment Certificates introduced in the fall of 1946.

32. Bank for International Settlements, *Thirteenth Annual Report*, p. 186.

duced, but the grandiose scheme ran into a number of insurmountable obstacles and finally had to be abandoned.

The Secret Service then decided to use the counterfeit notes as a source of financing various intelligence operations and purchases of raw materials in neutral countries. But even this more modest project required that the bogus money first be marketed and turned into real currency. Through its own network, the Secret Service tried to distribute the fake notes in Paris, Athens, and in some other capitals. This operation soon came to the attention of Walter Funk, Minister of Economic Affairs of the Reich, who immediately instructed the Secret Service that "in no circumstances would it be allowed to operate [with the fake notes] in any part of Europe under German occupation, as it would upset currencies which he was endeavoring to stabilize."[33] Funk's orders reduced the possible utilization of the pound notes further, but this episode helps to illustrate that in their efforts to maintain a sound monetary system in Europe the German government meant business.

The way in which the Germans directed European finances reflected their over-all objectives. The Reich government started the war in order to build a New Order in Europe designed to assure the dominant position of Germany for a millenium to come. This predetermined a peculiarly constructive element in German monetary policies—an element, as we shall see, almost totally absent in the subsequent Allied practices.

There was another essential difference in the two approaches to financial problems of occupation. The Reich policymakers were acutely aware of the interdependence of the economies of the European countries. They knew that the solvency and prosperity of Germany was inextricably linked to that of the rest of Europe. Even while taking full advantage of European resources in order to assure victory in the war, German leaders kept their eyes on the future and tried to avoid excessive economic dislocations. The only exception was in the east, in Poland, and in the occupied areas of the Soviet Union, where the nazi leaders felt free to subordinate long-range considerations to the immediate needs of the Reich.

33. Wilhelm Hoettl, *Hitler's Paper Weapon* (London: R. Hart-Davis, 1955), p. 49.

Finally, there was a powerful psychological factor behind the German approach. The German leaders were constantly haunted by the specter of a runaway inflation of the kind which had engulfed Germany after World War I. Few people outside of Germany knew—or cared—much about it, but to the Germans it was a very real thing. "To all who still remember it," wrote Hjalmar Schacht, the man who has been credited more than anyone else for restoration of the German economy,

> "the period of inflation" stands for the hunger blockade; the surrender of real values to foreign powers; political outlawry; regrouping of the population; the rise of obscure figures to sudden wealth. To hitherto wealthy classes it meant loss of capital, to the well-to-do, the moderately comfortable and the small man, it spelt ruin. In Government and official circles it signified corruption; political jobbery between the Parties, the *Wehrmacht* and the Ministries; increase in child mortality, and in crime; the young crippled with rickets, the old dying before their time.[34]

While the causes of the 1920–23 inflation in Germany were multiple, the oversupply of money due to deficit financing was a key factor. The deluge of marks was much more than a monetary disaster. The time arrived when the Reichsbank "was finally reduced to making apologies for its inability to provide for a weekly output of more than several billion (or trillion) of marks of the required denomination and to an expression of hope that this situation would be quickly remedied by an improvement in the speed of the printing presses! The printing presses did their bit. By the end of the inflation the daily output of currency was over 400,000,000,000,000,000 marks."[35] In 1913 the mark was solidly based on gold; in 1923 its value was, as the same writer put it, "something more ridiculous than zero."

In time the economic conditions improved, but the social changes caused by the inflation turned out to be irrevocable. Moreover, "the drama, and particularly the tragedy, of the time left an indelible impression of the evils of inflation on the minds of

34. Hjalmar Schacht, *My First Seventy-Six Years* (London: Wingate, 1955), p. 163.

35. Frank D. Graham, *Exchange, Prices and Production in Hyper-Inflation: Germany, 1920–1923* (Princeton: Princeton University Press, 1930), p. 35.

the generation which lived through it."[36] And although the Nazi Party came to power largely owing to the conditions created by the Great Depression, its political outlook as well as the peculiar mentality of its leaders had been marked by the Great Inflation. In fact, Hitler's *putsch* in Bavaria in November, 1923, took place at the moment when the inflation was at its severest, and much of the future Fuehrer's demagogy centered on its disastrous consequences.[37]

As often happens with regimes that come to power by revolutionary means, the Reich leaders were always haunted by the specter of another social and political upheaval. Those in charge of Germany's economy had learned the lesson of hyperinflation well. Men like Schacht and Funk kept bending over backward in their efforts to prevent inflationary trends generated by the war from getting out of hand.[38] Knowing that Germany could not be insulated from developments in the rest of Europe they aimed at preserving monetary stability everywhere, sometimes sacrificing immediate gains for the Reich to the long-range requirements of what they considered to be sound finance. At no time did Germany attempt to turn "cheap" military currency into a means of its enrichment—or into a weapon against the occupied countries. The New Order which Hitler sought to establish ruled out a monetary policy which would have led to economic, social, and political chaos, and consequently it made his task of ruling Europe more difficult.

The facts concerning the German occupation experience and the management of economic and financial matters were available to the wartime Allied planners: Allied intelligence in Europe worked very well. Yet in planning the finances of liberation—and the occupation of the enemy countries—Allied officials completely ignored this experience.[39]

36. *Ibid.*, p. 14.

37. See for instance John W. Wheeler-Bennett, *The Nemesis of Power: The German Army in Politics, 1918–1945* (New York: St. Martin's Press, 1954), p. 58. Cf. William L. Shirer, *The Rise and Fall of the Third Reich* (New York: Simon and Schuster, 1960), pp. 61–62.

38. See Indexes of Note Circulation in various countries during the war in Bank for International Settlements, *Fourteenth Annual Report*, p. 272. Cf. V. P. Komissarov and A. N. Popov, *Den'gi kredit i finansy evropeiskikh stran narodnoi demokratii* (Moscow, 1960), p. 12, for the postwar years.

39. Of course, references to German practices were frequent but they always had an all too familiar propaganda ring. This was true of even serious studies.

Several factors were responsible for this situation. One was the overwhelming concentration on the immediate goal of winning of the war. The intense desire to crush the enemy permeated all aspects of Allied planning and activity to a degree that almost any subject not clearly and directly related to the war effort was denied consideration. Second, the unprecedented lavishness in military expenditures was accompanied in Washington by parochial attitudes deeply rooted in prewar isolationism. This parochial thinking accounted for the lack of interest in the general economic well-being of even the Allied and friendly nations, let alone in such " abstract " notions as economic interdependence of European countries in the postwar era. Third, many influential men found it unthinkable that after the war Germany and Italy would still exist as national and economic entities; rather they were seen as vacuums to be filled by yet to be determined new contents. This expectation created a strange aberration that everything created by the Axis governments was transitory and ephemeral, doomed to vanish on the day of victory.

But perhaps decisive for the Allies' deliberate refusal to learn anything from German experience was the highly emotional climate which prevailed in Great Britain and, especially, in the United States. To study German occupation policies and practices would have required the admission that the Third Reich and the Allies had *some* similar objectives; that Reich officials were not uniformly the madmen they were depicted to be by wartime propaganda; that in fact there were among them rational and intelligent men capable of conceiving rational and intelligent economic programs for the occupied countries; that in spite of the tragic and inhuman aspects of its rule in Europe, Germany was capable of a constructive role in human civilization.

For instance, Randolph Paul, in his learned study, " Re Opinion on the Legality of the Issuance of AMG Currency in Sicily," which in December, 1943, was accepted by the Treasury Department as the legal foundation for military currency matters, says: " The vice of the German practice is not in the use of [military] currency but in the excessive issue of valueless currency as a device of stripping the occupied areas of its goods and its labor for the benefit of Germany." U. S. Congress, Senate, *Hearings before the Committees on Appropriations, Armed Services and Banking and Currency*, 80th Congress, 1st Session, June 17–18, 1947, p. 82. Paul's document was presented to the Senate investigators in 1947, by which time the Treasury had become fully aware of the fact that the " viciousness " of Allied financial practices had left that of the Germans far behind.

Such an admission was psychologically beyond the capacity of the Allied planners who regarded Germany as totally evil. Related to this mental bloc was the peculiar phenomenon where almost everybody, from the White House down, believed that after victory the United States would be able to avoid any responsibility for the fate of the defeated nations. This attitude was reflected in almost childish talk about withdrawing from Europe almost immediately after the war, talk which seemed to make serious planning of administrative, economic, and financial measures for European occupation wholly unnecessary. All that American officialdom was capable of were makeshift arrangements, tailored to satisfy only the most pressing immediate needs of the military. Germany's failure and accomplishments in the techniques of governing the occupied areas were of no interest to anyone.

This was unfortunate. The Allies came to a Europe devastated by war, and they had to operate in conditions much more difficult than those which faced the Germans. Every bit of advance knowledge of the problems of occupation and of their possible solutions would have been of significant value. Instead, the Allies had to learn exclusively through their own errors, thus turning their occupation of European countries into an extremely costly economic and political liability.

Chapter III

ALLIES IN NORTH AFRICA AND FRANCE

North Africa

The Allies' occupation policies faced their first test in North Africa. As was the case in the other countries that they occupied subsequently, their policies in North Africa were more a function of *their* emotions, national attitudes and habits, rules and regulations, and the structural characteristics of their administrative machinery than they were of the actual political and economic realities in the occupied territory. Monetary and economic policies, always an integral part of general occupation policies, were determined by short-term pragmatic needs (everywhere except Germany), with some on-the-scene variations.

The problems which the Allies had to resolve were posed by the inevitable decline of economic productivity and by the political-administrative void in the conquered areas. To a very large extent these problems were created by the occupation itself. Peculiarly interwoven as they were, they formed a complicated but nonetheless discernible pattern which repeated itself in every country the Allies occupied. There were of course differences between the "liberated" and "enemy" countries, and between the countries which had a very independent government bent on asserting its own particular interests as distinct from those of the Allies and the countries with weak and dependent governments or no governments at all. There were also differences in the scope of the occupation, and, in political terms, the countries of Western Europe could not even be called "occupied." But insofar as economic and monetary experiences were concerned, these differences were greatly overshadowed by similarities created by the mere presence in the country of a large and self-contained body of foreigners who enjoyed a distinctly privileged status. The difficulties in solving some of the problems of the military occupation were precisely in that they were of the victors' own making. These problems were eventually solved—not without leaving a certain political residue—but they were solved by native forces, after the occupation itself had essentially ended.

Although the Allied experience in the occupation of "liberated" North Africa and France was, in a sense, incomplete, it will be useful to survey briefly its relevant aspects, if only to demonstrate its similarities with the experience in the "enemy" countries, Italy and Germany.

Before the Anglo-American landing in North Africa in November, 1942, no military currency had been used by the Allies. The scale of military operations had been relatively small; no protracted occupation of enemy territories had been involved. The British had fought in the Middle East and in North Africa, with the bulk of their troops stationed in former imperial possessions. American active participation in the war had been limited to the Pacific Theater and the Americans had not yet had an opportunity to occupy foreign lands. In the Pacific, the United States forces had used regular dollars with the word "Hawaii" printed on them.[1]

Despite the relatively defensive nature of the British military operations in the Middle East and North Africa prior to the landing in North Africa there were nevertheless administrative and financial problems of staggering complexity. The military administration had to deal with a wide variety of currencies: British pounds sterling, Egyptian pounds, Indian rupees, various Middle Eastern currencies, East African shillings, Ethiopian Maria Theresa silver dollars, Tripolitanian lire. All had some value and all were in simultaneous circulation throughout North Africa, subject to fluctuations in rates of exchange and a lively traffic from country to country which depended on economic and military developments.

The British army itself made use of British and Egyptian pounds and Maria Theresa dollars. This latter currency, adopted out of

1. The use of the Hawaiian overstamp dollars was not strictly enforced. The Navy and the Seventh Air Force successfully resisted the very modest restrictions which this currency implied, on the grounds that their personnel had "transient status."

political considerations, proved to be a great nuisance. When the British entered Ethiopia, they discovered that the population would accept no currency except the familiar Maria Theresa dollars, which before the war had been minted in Trieste. Besides the disadvantage of not having any fractional coin, these dollars were bulky and difficult to handle: one ton of coin (excluding packing) was worth only about £3,000. However, because the liberation of Ethiopia was politically important, the British had no choice. In all, nearly £3 million worth of the dollars were struck from the dies in London (all of the traditional tenor of .833 fine) and brought to East Africa.[2]

When the British troops entered Italian colonies, the occupation authorities at first recognized the indigenous lire and fixed the rate of exchange at 480 lire to £1. Although this rate greatly overvalued the pound and hurt the local population and Italian interests, according to Lord Rennell of Rodd (who was in charge of civil affairs in North Africa), "the effect of this decision in the bazaar markets of Cairo and Levant . . . was most satisfactory. The decision was a good piece of political and economic warfare."[3] The overvaluation of the pound allowed the British to reap substantial benefits in former Italian colonies and at the same time raised the standard of living of the British military and civilian personnel who had been fighting and living under conditions of considerable austerity. On the other hand, the increase in the purchasing power of the troops created strong inflationary pressure. Inflation produced some fortunes, but it also aggravated the general poverty in the occupied areas. Despite these difficulties, however, and despite the maze of currencies they had to handle (an accounting nightmare), the British managed their monetary affairs quite well. This success was chiefly a result of the elaborate system of currency control, reserves, and supply machinery which they instituted.

A proposal to create a special military currency for the needs of the Army was debated in the War Office in London as early

2. Lord Rennell of Rodd, *British Military Administration of Occupied Territories in Africa* (London: H.M. Stationery Office, 1948), p. 367. The dies of the Maria Theresa "thalers" were ceded by Austria to Italy during the Italian-Abyssinian war (1935–36) for the specific purpose of manufacturing new coins for use in Abyssinia. The British apparently forged the dies. See Arthur Nussbaum, *Money in Law, National and International* (Brooklyn: Foundation Press, 1950), p. 315.

3. Lord Rennell of Rodd, *British Military Administration*, p. 369.

as March, 1941. It was, however, only after the invasion of Tripolitania in the spring of 1943 that the British Military Authority (BMA) currency was actually introduced as legal tender in North Africa. This currency was well printed from engraved plates and denominated in the traditional British units; the rate of exchange of 480 lire to £1 was preserved. BMA currency was purely a fiat money, a true occupation currency, but for the British troops it was redeemable in pounds. Its use simplified accounting and served to reduce the cost of the war and the occupation for the British government. However, it turned out to be a mixed blessing. One difficulty of BMA currency was that the lowest denomination used was the one shilling note, which tended to become the minimum price unit for all transactions, pushing up the local price level. Another problem was more important: BMA currency immediately started drifting from Tripolitania to Cyrenaica, Egypt, and even to Tunisia, where its purchasing power was higher. The British authorities soon discovered that the prevention of currency trafficking, including trafficking by the troops, was of paramount importance if price levels within each territory were to be stabilized. They were aware that the only effective way to combat this traffic was to maintain all the currencies stable *inter se*, even Italian (i.e. "enemy") currency vis-à-vis the British currencies. This task proved to be largely beyond their power.

One remedy, although it was only partially effective, was found in extraordinary control measures. Lord Rennell relates that "the watch kept on the black and bazaar markets of the Middle East, and notably those in the occupied territories, was close and continuous; within the limits of what could be done . . . trafficking was very considerably checked."[4] However, his contention that "the fact that watch was kept the whole time maintained illicit currency transactions by the troops well within bounds" can be accepted only with reservation. Compliance with the often unenforceable regulations depended on the discipline and conscience of the individual soldier. Evidence abounded that many British personnel succumbed to the temptation to make a quick profit by selling the currency to local operators.[5] The currency traffic inten-

4. *Ibid.*, p. 380.

5. The currency traffic was not limited to BMA notes. The attraction of high profits prompted a number of servicemen, including Americans, to smuggle British pounds out of England on their flying trips to North Africa. See Walter Rundell,

sified after the landing in Sicily in July, 1943, where BMA notes were used as a " spearhead " currency. By this time the monetary situation was growing so chaotic that the British decided to abandon the experiment altogether, and by the end of the war the BMA currency was called in everywhere.[6] In North Africa it was exchanged for the existing local currencies (for Tripolitania the British created a new military authority lire), in Sicily and Italy, for the Allied military lire.[7]

The American forces in North Africa made no use of military currency. The invasion was organized with considerable neglect of civil affairs, which were largely left up to the imagination and improvisation of the officials on the spot. Although the U.S. Treasury Department raised the question of printing a special military currency in July, 1942, no action was taken because of the objections from the War and State Departments.[8] In the end, the troops were supplied with dollar currency. These notes were not regular silver certificates but the equivalent of the Hawaiian overstamp dollars used in the Pacific. Known as the " spearhead " currency, they bore a special yellow seal and were used by the American troops in Africa and later in Sicily. As the Treasury Department explained, this distinctive mark was adopted " partly

---

Jr., *Black Market Money: The Collapse of U.S. Currency in World War II* (Baton Rouge: Louisiana State University Press, 1964), p. 20.

6. Earlier in the spring the British considered replacing the lira currency in Tripolitania with BMA notes which would bear an appropriate overprint, but these plans met opposition in the U.S. State Department which objected to any but local currencies. See Secretary Hull's correspondence with Under Secretary of the Treasury Bell in *Foreign Relations of the United States, 1943* (Washington: U.S. Government Printing Office, 1963), I, 1037–39. Hereinafter referred to as *1943 Papers.*

7. Under quite different circumstances, BMA currency appeared in Greece after the British landed there in October, 1944. The indigenous drachma currency had deteriorated to an extraordinary extent. In most areas outside of Athens drachmas were simply not accepted; the population used gold sovereigns for currency, of which about 2 million had been put in circulation by the Germans in an attempt to stabilize the monetary market. Barter trade was widespread. The new Greek government asked the British to use BMA notes until the Bank of Greece could provide the military authorities with a stable Greek currency. The British government agreed and promised to reimburse the Bank of Greece for all BMA notes spent by British forces for military purposes. A U.S. military establishment in Greece also used BMA currency which it received by special arrangement, directly from the British. See Frank A. Southard, Jr., *The Finances of European Liberation, with Special Reference to Italy* (New York: King's Crown, 1946), pp. 41–44.

8. Secretary Hull's memorandums to Secretary Morgenthau and President Roosevelt, *1943 Papers*, I, 1029–31.

for security reasons to permit the isolation of the currency if it fell into enemy hands, partly to prevent the influx into the area of dollar currency already in the hands of the enemy, and partly to facilitate its entry into the United States by freeing it from present restrictions on ordinary U.S. currency." [9] In other words, the intention was to stop the circulation of yellow seal dollars wherever the enemy would get hold of large amounts of them in the course of military operations; to prevent the enemy agents from flooding the American-occupied areas with regular silver certificates, presumably for subversive purposes; [10] and to allow the soldiers returning to the United States to bring back their savings in identifiable notes—a privilege denied civilians during the war.[11]

The experience in North Africa indicated that the use of yellow seal dollars by the American troops had certain disadvantages. For one thing, like the *Reichskreditkassenscheine* of the German occupation, they were a genuinely stable currency with a significant hoarding value. For another, the accumulation of dollars in the hands of local populations tended to undermine local currencies, with some unfavorable political repercussions. It also led to a creation of dollar claims against the United States which traditionally were considered detrimental to the American interest.

The search for a different solution was also stimulated by another development. It was soon discovered that many soldiers were making profits on the black market by selling their possessions, yellow seal dollars, and PX rations. Because of lax controls over remittance procedures, army finance officers ended up receiving from soldiers for remittance home greater sums—in local currencies—than they in fact paid out to them.[12] So long as total

9. Treasury Department Press Release No. 38–10, August 17, 1943.

10. This particular apprehension was quite groundless; neither Germany nor Italy would contemplate using their very limited dollar reserve for any large-scale subversion in the Allied-held territories. In 1942, the German Secret Service had only $50,000 in American currency at its disposal for all intelligence and other operations in the enemy-held areas. See Wilhelm Hoettl, *Hitler's Paper Weapon* (London: R. Hart-Davis, 1955), pp. 50ff.

11. American merchant seamen, making money on the black market in African ports, insisted on being paid in yellow or blue seal dollars for their merchandise because they were not allowed to convert local currencies into dollars at official rates of exchange.

12. U.S. Congress, Senate, Testimony of William Henry Taylor, *Hearing before the Permanent Subcommittee on Investigations of the Committee on Government Operations*, 84th Congress, 2d Session, October 19, 1953, pp. 66, 69.

" savings " did not exceed total troop pay, this did not worry the accountants. Yet some officials were becoming aware that such profitable black market operations could result in an overdraft of funds appropriated by Congress for troop pay. As it will be seen, for a variety of reasons this danger was largely ignored for at least three years after the landing in North Africa.

The decision in the spring of 1943 to do away with dollars in occupied areas took into account the threat of economic disorder and the adverse effects of the currency black market, but it was dictated primarily by political considerations. The Allies felt that both " enemy " and " liberated " countries should pay a part of the costs of conquest or liberation, whichever was the case; [13] Ethiopia and Greece were the only exceptions. The Allied experts decided that the transfer of such costs could be accomplished best if the currencies used by the fighting forces were denominated in the traditional units of the occupied countries.

A delicate political problem was posed by the need to assure the armies invading " liberated " countries of Europe with an abundant cash supply. The U.S. Treasury Department proposed to print enough notes (of different design but denominated in terms of local units) and to issue them on the United States military authority. This procedure was opposed by the British and by the State Department. The British government pointed out that " the Allied Governments-in-exile would object to the use by friendly invading forces of any currency other than the currency they were preparing or local currency," [14] and Secretary Hull agreed that " the fullest and most careful consideration " should be given to the views of these governments. While the Treasury Department wanted to avoid any advance consultations on this issue—and favored arbitrarily established rates of exchange—the State Department insisted that such consultations be held as early as possible.[15]

13. Morgenthau to Hull, March 30, 1943, *1943 Papers*, I, 1035. Cf. Phillips to Bell, February 6, 1943, in Harry L. Coles and Albert K. Weinberg, *Civil Affairs: Soldiers Become Governors* (Washington: Department of the Army, 1964), p. 687.

14. Bell to Hull, April 24, 1943, *1943 Papers*, I, 1038.

15. Morgenthau to Hull, March 30, 1943, and Hull to Morgenthau, March 31, 1943, *ibid.*, I, 1036. The Treasury lost on this issue. The rates of exchange thus established corresponded generally to the prewar rates. See *Secretary of the Treasury Annual Report: 1944–1945* (Washington: U.S. Government Printing Office, 1946), pp. 387–88.

During the spring and summer of 1943 talks were held in Washington with representatives of the Belgian, Dutch, and Norwegian governments, and satisfactory arrangements were apparently worked out regarding the rates of exchange and the sovereign right of these governments-in-exile to control monetary circulation in their countries after the Allied invasion.[16] However, no clear over-all financial policy toward the " liberated " countries emerged from these discussions, partly because of a very special situation which was developing in one, already " liberated," territory—French North Africa.

A major factor which influenced the formulation of the Allied economic policies in " liberated " French North Africa was the peculiar situation of that territory: until the invasion it had been ruled by the quisling government of Vichy, the government with which the United States had maintained diplomatic relations.[17] Unlike other nations of German-dominated Europe which were represented in the Allied camp by governments-in-exile (located in London and Cairo), France had no such representation. The only significant French force on the Allied side was the Free French movement, led by General Charles de Gaulle, which was supported by the British but essentially ignored by the United States government. A key element in the American attitudes was a deep-seated and highly personal dislike which President Roosevelt had developed toward the French leader and his claims to represent the interests of Free France. Largely because of this attitude, Roosevelt preferred to treat French North Africa not as a " liberated " but strictly as an occupied territory. Shortly after the landing, he wrote Churchill:

> We have a military occupation in North Africa and as such our Commanding General has complete charge of all matters civil as well as military. We must not let any of our French friends forget this for a moment. By the same token I don't want any of them to think that we are going to recognize

16. See the correspondence between the Treasury and State Departments and other memorandums on the subject in *1943 Papers*, I, 1031–34, 1039–43.

17. On United States policy toward Vichy, see William L. Langer, *Our Vichy Gamble* (New York: Knopf, 1947); William D. Leahy, *I Was There* (New York: McGraw-Hill, 1950); and the illuminating account by Robert Murphy, *Diplomat among Warriors* (Garden City, N.Y.: Doubleday, 1964).

> any one of any committee or group as representing the French Government or the French Empire. The people of France will settle their own affairs after we have won the war. Until then we can deal with local Frenchmen on a local basis wherever our armies occupy former French territory. And if these local officials won't play ball we will have to replace them. . . . Why doesn't De Gaulle go to war? Why doesn't he start North by West half West from Brazenville? It would take him a long time to get to the Oasis of Somewhere.[18]

De Gaulle did not want " to go to war." In the matters of military strategy he accepted Anglo-American supremacy, and for the time being did not insist that the French troops, fully dependent on the Allies for their supplies, play an independent role. Instead, he devoted his attention to the creation of unity among the French and on laying the foundation for a resurrected France. As Robert Murphy, who was then United States Minister-Resident in North Africa, points out, the General's thoughts " were two jumps ahead of everybody else's. . . . De Gaulle correctly calculated that Allied victory was certain and that France would share in that victory regardless of what French soldiers accomplished or failed to do. This politically minded General decided that it was his function to concentrate upon restoring France as a great power." [19]

Instead of taking into account de Gaulle's growing popularity among the French in North Africa and the resistance movement in France proper, and instead of recognizing this insurgent nationalistic spirit, Roosevelt antagonized the French further by his constant efforts to prevent the General from consolidating all

18. Roosevelt to Churchill, January 1, 1943, *1943 Papers*, II, 23–24. Within the United States government, the opposition to de Gaulle and his Free French centered in the State Department, which was committed to the maintenance of relations with Vichy France as well as to the traditional forms of diplomacy which excluded a possibility of dealing with both antagonists simultaneously. But this commitment does not explain the highly emotional reaction to de Gaulle displayed by President Roosevelt, Secretary Hull, and a number of other high officials, especially after de Gaulle's seizure of Saint Pierre in December, 1941. For an enlightened study of the Allies' relations with de Gaulle, see Dorothy Shipley White, *Seeds of Discord* (Syracuse: Syracuse University Press, 1964), esp. Chapters IX, XIX, XX, and XXI.

19. Murphy, *Diplomat among Warriors*, p. 177.

antinazi elements under his leadership. He resented the formation of the French Committee of National Liberation (CLN), which was formed in Algiers on June 3, 1943, and of which de Gaulle was a ranking member. On June 17, 1943, he wrote to General Eisenhower, Supreme Commander of the Allied Forces in the Mediterranean, that "during our military occupation of North Africa, we will not tolerate the control of the French Army by any agency which is not subject to the Allied Supreme Commander's direction." He added, that he was not interested "in the formation of any government or committee which presumes in any way to indicate that, until such time as the French people select a government for themselves, it will govern in France." And he stressed, that "it must be absolutely clear that in North and West Africa we have a military occupation," and that without Eisenhower's full approval "no independent civil decision can be made."[20]

This was a total rejection of the idea of a French government-in-exile on the Allied side, an idea which Churchill nourished from "the dark days of 1940" but which he was reluctant to press in view of Roosevelt's attitude. Churchill, however, now found an ally in General Eisenhower, who was most concerned with the preservation of stability and order in the occupied territories. Eisenhower was not only anxious to acquire the goodwill and cooperation of the French military and civilian officials; he also realized that his capacity to keep the French in check was limited. As Robert Murphy recalls, "by July 1943, de Gaulle's Committee had every appurtenance of a full-fledged government, and all of us in Algiers accepted the inevitable."[21] In the end, Roosevelt reluctantly conceded a point; in a formal statement of August 24, 1943, the United States government recognized the CLN as the "body administering French overseas territories."[22]

As subsequent events showed, this recognition did not represent a change of heart in Washington. Nor did it eliminate a bad aftertaste produced in the earlier stage of the occupation. De

20. *1943 Papers*, II, 156–57. By that time, most of the French colonial empire and all of the French colonies in Africa had recognized the authority of the CLN, which had made de Gaulle's political position unassailable; his real sources of strength did not depend on the Allies' goodwill.

21. Murphy, *Diplomat among Warriors*, p. 184. See also Dwight D. Eisenhower, *Crusade in Europe* (Garden City, N.Y.: Doubleday, 1948), p. 131.

22. *1943 Papers*, II, 185.

Gaulle continued to assert the distinct national interests of France, no doubt adding to the old irritations of Roosevelt (and Churchill) but moving steadily toward his goal whenever the circumstances permitted. This tense situation had consequences which went far beyond French North Africa and left its mark not only on Allied attitudes toward France, but also toward other "liberated" countries of Europe and toward one "enemy" country, Italy. At the price of this tension, however, the Allies gained substantial benefits implicit in indirect rule and, with the help of the CLN, could start tackling some problems which hitherto had defied solution.

To the U. S. Treasury Department, and to American financial experts attached to Eisenhower headquarters who for the most part were strongly anti-Vichy,[23] the creation of a French authority in North Africa had one advantage: the French could now start aiding the Allied war effort in an organized way. A legitimate local currency could be issued, thus making it possible to stop paying the American troops with dollars. The latter was considered important, for, as one American expert noted, "as long as yellow seal dollars were used, the transfer to the French authorities of all or some part of the local cash costs of the operation would be most difficult." [24]

The question of what kind of currency to use in North Africa was not, however, resolved easily. The Treasury and War Departments, as well as SHAEF, favored the Allied military franc currency which was to be printed in the United States and issued on

23. The invasion of North Africa (which meant the end of recognition of Vichy France) had as its by-product in Washington a diminution of the State Department's relative weight. Roosevelt's failure to bring Hull to Casablanca had probably less to do with his fear of Hull's "petulance" when confronted with de Gaulle than with his own desire to dramatize the end of his unpopular Vichy policy. The implied rebuff of Hull was seized upon by Hull's old antagonist, Morgenthau. A veritable purge of the French administration followed Secretary Morgenthau's visit to Algiers in the spring of 1943. One victim was Maurice Couve de Murville, a de facto Minister of Finance of the CLN, dismissed despite his strong antinazi record because of the part he played in negotiating the armistice for Vichy with the Germans. See Murphy, *Diplomat among Warriors*, pp. 147–49.

24. Southard, *The Finances of European Liberation*, pp. 18–20. SHAEF was against using yellow seal dollars even as a spearhead currency. It pointed out in a November 8, 1943, message to the War Department that it seemed "inappropriate to liberate an occupied country and immediately introduce a new currency." Coles and Weinberg, *Soldiers Become Governors*, p. 690.

the Supreme Commander's authority. The designs of the notes were approved in Washington and the printing started. But it soon had to be halted because of strong British opposition.[25] Great Britain viewed North Africa as a " liberated " territory and insisted on taking into account the French sensitivity, and on vesting the issuing authority in the CLN. Washington refused to go that far and the problem was eventually resolved by a compromise: the notes were not called " Allied military "; they were printed in the United States but by a private firm and issued by the North African banks, which operated under the supervision of the CLN. The CLN declared them legal tender and proceeded to carry out a currency conversion by calling in the notes which had circulated in North Africa prior to the Allied invasion.[26] This compromise seemed to satisfy all interested parties, including de Gaulle.

Frictions nonetheless continued. One clash took place over the rate of exchange for the franc. Prior to the invasion, it had been 176 francs to £1; immediately following it, Churchill changed it to 205 francs to £1. In order to simplify the rate of exchange, the Allied and French experts then agreed to fix it at 200 to 1, or 50 francs to $1.00. This rate somewhat overvalued the franc, but the French insisted that, given the state of their economy, the Allies should give the franc stronger backing. When the decision was brought to the attention of President Roosevelt, he ordered that the rate be fixed at 300 francs to £1 or 75 francs to $1.00.[27] The President at that time had no intention of reinforcing the economies of the " liberated " countries, least of all the French economy.

The CLN refused to yield. Since its assent was indispensable for the success of the whole scheme, the Allies were compelled to engage in prolonged and unpleasant negotiations in which no agreement was reached. Because political considerations overshadowed all others, and because the U.S. Treasury Department was willing to concede this point to the French, the Allied leaders,

25. Hilldring to McCloy, December 5, 1943, and Hilldring to CG, ETOUSA, December 17, 1943, Coles and Weinberg, *Soldiers Become Governors*, pp. 690–91.

26. *Secretary of the Treasury Annual Report: 1944–1945*, p. 391.

27. There is no record of this decision. The only witness to it was Harry Hopkins, who passed the order along. See Murphy, *Diplomat among Warriors*, p. 169.

during the Casablanca Conference, decided to abandon the 75 to 1 rate and to accept instead the old 50 to 1 rate of exchange.[28]

The next problem was to establish some order in the economic relations between the Allies and the French authorities. The negotiations with the CLN were carried on at a " low " level of the Allied Forces Headquarters, thus again avoiding the issue of recognizing the CLN as a French government. In these negotiations, a line of Allied policy developed which became the pattern for financial relations with all of the " liberated " countries of Europe. This policy found its first expression in the Reciprocal Aid Agreement, which was signed in Algiers by the American and French representatives on September 25, 1943.[29] Under this agreement, the CLN was to pay in dollars for all civilian supplies imported from the United States. Lend-lease was extended to the French army, while the CLN undertook the obligation to deliver supplies and services to the American forces free of charge. The CLN also established a special account in the name of the United States in local currency, to which it was to contribute the sums requested by the American authorities. This money was to be used for local procurement and other official purposes, as well as for administrative expenses of United States agencies, for troop pay and allowances, and for wages of American civilians. However, for the sums spent on troop pay and civilian wages, and on the Americans' administrative needs, the CLN was to be reimbursed by the United States in dollars. The rest was to be French " reciprocal aid " without reimbursement.

The Allies apparently felt that they were being generous in agreeing not to force upon the CLN (and other governments of the " liberated " countries) an obligation to pay the British and American troops, and some American officials consoled themselves that dollar credits given to France and other countries would reduce the need for assistance to them under the lend-lease and mutual aid programs already enacted by Congress. In fact, how-

28. The army post offices began using the 50 to 1 rate on February 2, 1943, but at banks and at army finance offices military personnel could exchange yellow seal dollars at the 75 to 1 rate through February 15. This peculiar arrangement offered the troops a unique opportunity to exchange dollars for francs at a finance office at the 75 to 1 rate and then go straight to an army post office and purchase money orders at the 50 to 1 rate. See Rundell, *Black Market Money*, p. 25.

29. *U.S. Statutes at Large*, Vol. 59, Part 2, pp. 1666–68. A similar agreement was signed with the British.

ever, the extent of their generosity was rather limited. Economic conditions in these countries were universally bad. To force them to contribute to the costs of occupation was an unreasonable and, especially in light of the future need for lavish American aid, shortsighted policy. As was shown in Chapter II, the German financial policy in " friendly " countries—Slovakia, Hungary, Rumania, Bulgaria—was much more considerate of their economic interests. From the financial standpoint, Allied policies in the " liberated " countries approximated those adopted by the Reich in the " occupied " countries of Western Europe. In the end, one can only guess whether the United States would have taken a more benevolent attitude toward " liberated " countries had its policy developed in a different atmosphere. The combination of the Treasury's strong dislike for " Vichyites " and Roosevelt's antipathy toward the Free French of de Gaulle certainly poisoned the atmosphere and affected financial policy decisions.

FRANCE

Friction between the French and the Americans continued through the rest of the war. One controversy centered around the so-called " supplemental francs " printed by the United States in anticipation of the invasion of France. President Roosevelt wanted to make sure that there would not be any misunderstanding, and that the compromise solution which had been effected in North Africa would not be extended to France. In this, he overruled the British who suggested using the North African francs as invasion currency for France.[30] Accordingly, around February 15, 1944, the Treasury commenced printing the Allied military franc notes which were " similar to the Allied military lire except for the change in the name of the country, the name of the currency, and the designation, ' Emis en France.' " [31] When the American representative to the CLN reported the French reaction that " it would

30. Gaston to Feis, October 22, 1943, *1943 Papers*, I, 1045–46.

31. White to Feis, October 7, 1943, and Feis to White, October 15, 1943, *ibid.*, I, 1044–45. The notes were apparently the same which the United States wanted to introduce in North Africa earlier. After some debates in the Combined Civil Affairs Committee of the Combined Chiefs of Staff, the word " military " was dropped. The British in the end concurred, and even the French mission in Washington approved the final design. See CCAC to SHAEF, January 29, 1944, Coles and Weinberg, *Soldiers Become Governors*, p. 691.

be a serious mistake from a psychological point of view to use Allied military currency [in France] as had been done in Italy, an enemy country," and that he himself felt that it would be "a great mistake for us to use a form of Allied military currency in France," [32] Secretary Hull replied: "In dealing with currency for military operation, War Department, with concurrence of State Department, has taken the position that as there is no governmental authority in existence for issuance of French currency, an Allied military currency is the only form which can be legally used. That is the way the matter now stands." [33]

Over 40 billion supplemental francs were printed in the United States and delivered to SHAEF. In addition, the Bank of England contributed 5.56 billion Metropolitan French francs. This was an equivalent of over $900 million.[34] The question of which authority was going to declare supplemental francs legal tender in France immediately became an issue. Under American pressure the Combined Chiefs of Staff (CCS) instructed General Eisenhower to issue them under his own authority. However, early in May, 1944, following extensive discussions with the French military mission in London, SHAEF suggested that all economic and financial affairs in France be entrusted to French authorities. Since the CLN proposed to extend to France the reciprocal aid arrangement which had been in effect in North Africa, SHAEF felt that the CLN should also assume responsibility for declaring supplemental francs legal tender and should continue to supply the Allied forces with all the currency they needed.[35]

General Hilldring, on behalf of the Combined Civil Affairs Committee of the CCS, approved the extension of the reciprocal aid agreement to France but instructed that "the basis of authority for the issue of supplemental francs is vested in SHAEF, and not the FCLN." [36] SHAEF replied, on May 24, that this would involve "an unnecessary assumption of sovereignty" on the part of the Supreme Commander. It pointed out that "unless the supple-

32. Wilson to Hull, December 9, 1943, *1943 Papers*, I, 1047–48.

33. Hull to Wilson, December 11, 1943, *ibid.*, I, 1048–49.

34. Coles and Weinberg, *Soldiers Become Governors*, p. 691. See also F. S. V. Donnison, *Civil Affairs and Military Government, North-West Europe: 1944–1946* (London: H.M. Stationery Office, 1961), pp. 63, 437, 443.

35. SHAEF to CCAC, May 4, 1944, Coles and Weinberg, *Soldiers Become Governors*, p. 693.

36. *Ibid.*, p. 693.

mental franc is declared legal tender there is the danger that it will not receive universal acceptance" and urged an "immediate decision."[37]

The question had become especially complicated because on May 15, 1944, the CLN had transformed itself into the Provisional Government of the French Republic, with no apparent opposition from any French quarters. This development made SHAEF conclude that General Eisenhower "had *no* real legal authority to declare this currency legal tender in liberated Metropolitan France or in the area of any other Allied Nation, and that the situation which will confront us on the Continent is entirely different from that existing in North Africa." Eisenhower's chief of staff justifiably suspected that the Provisional Government "will be particularly resentful of a declaration of legal tender by the Supreme Commander as this will be considered a flagrant violation of French sovereignty."[38]

On D-Day the question was still unresolved, and the landing troops put supplemental francs into circulation in France without any official proclamation. De Gaulle, who was then in London, informed the Provisional Government in Algiers about this development and referred to the American-printed notes as "counterfeit money." The government immediately reacted with this formal protest to the Allies:

> It has astonished the Government that this initiative should have been taken by the Allied Command as it is an initiative which no friendly army has ever undertaken before. . . . Throughout the whole of the French territories overseas military authorities have always received at once and without limit any funds they have asked for, and the same system should and could have been established in French Metropolitan territories at a time when full sovereignty is about to be acquired by the latter. . . . The Provisional Government cannot grant any legal value to the stamped paper (vignettes) which has been circulated without its consent, since traditionally the right of issuing currency has belonged to the national authority in France alone. Therefore the Govern-

37. *Ibid.*, p. 694.
38. Smith to McCloy, May 25, 1944, *ibid.*, p. 694.

ment makes reservations as to the moral, financial, and political consequences which this action may bring about.[39]

While the Allied armies were still engaged in bitter fighting in Normandy, the French currency question was moving to the forefront, with far-reaching political implications. The managers of the civil affairs problems in the U. S. War Department were alarmed, and on June 10, 1944, Assistant Secretary of War John J. McCloy telephoned General Holmes at SHAEF complaining that SHAEF seemed " to be rather hysterical about this currency " and that Churchill was, " at perhaps the price of getting de Gaulle to approve this currency, coming pretty close to recognizing the [French] provisional government." McCloy thought that " the President is adamant against taking any steps which would be tantamount to recognition of the committee or of the government." McCloy admitted that there was grave concern in Washington that de Gaulle should not denounce the invasion currency. Holmes replied that he had been told that de Gaulle was equally adamant, saying that " nobody had any right to issue French currency but Frenchmen." In answer to McCloy's question as to the further plans at SHAEF, Holmes said that " we are going to put up our own proclamation and go right ahead with this thing." [40]

Churchill, who was upset by Roosevelt's obstinacy and was convinced that to continue snubbing de Gaulle was political folly, did indeed try to use the currency question in order to prod the United States to recognize the French government. In his message to Roosevelt he complained that de Gaulle " fights at every point," and that if he did not endorse this currency, " the notes will not have any backing behind them." Churchill also warned " that the proclamation of General Eisenhower will make the governments of Great Britain and the United States separately or jointly responsible to redeem them." He did not think that de Gaulle

39. Chapin to Hull, June 8, 1944, *ibid.*, p. 707. Two days later Murphy informed Hull about two new cables which were received in Algiers from de Gaulle: " De Gaulle insists that he was deceived and forced to come to London to find a *fait accompli.* The invasion was already prepared. He was even told by the British, very impertinently, that he was expected to speak over the radio on D-Day after Eisenhower's speech. . . . The question of what De Gaulle calls 'fake money' . . . is making him furious." *Ibid.*, p. 707.

40. *Ibid.*, pp. 707–8.

"will dare" to denounce the issue, and expressed the opinion that "the notes will be accepted by the French people whether de Gaulle endorsed them, or not."[41]

In reply, Roosevelt complained that the question of currency was being used "as the method of rushing us into recognizing the Committee." He thought that the situation was not too serious, that Eisenhower was empowered to declare supplemental francs legal tender, and that it was not necessary for de Gaulle "to publish his supporting statement concerning this currency." The President proposed to be firm. He pointed out that Eisenhower was "authorized to use BMA notes or yellow seal dollars if it should develop that the French people will not accept the supplemental franc currency." Therefore, he continued, "should the French public be incited by de Gaulle not to accept supplementary currency, the Committee will be held responsible for any ill effects caused by using BMA notes and yellow seal dollars in France. One sure result will be that the French franc will depreciate on a sterling and dollar basis on a black market. This will bring to light and stress the weak spots in the monetary system of France. . . . Additional adverse results would obtain which would be evident to General de Gaulle as well as his advisors." Roosevelt reasoned that since the Allies held the upper hand, there was no need to press de Gaulle to issue his supporting proclamation. On the contrary, the General must be made to appreciate that he was menacing France's economic interests, not those of the Allies. Then, "with a clear understanding that he is acting with no concurrence from us and entirely on his individual accountability, de Gaulle can put his signature on any currency statement in any capacity that he desires."[42]

There is no evidence that de Gaulle was impressed by Roosevelt's threats or even that he had learned about them. At any rate, these threats were not serious: no infusion of dollars and pounds into France could possibly undermine the French monetary system more than the avalanche of the cheap-looking American-printed notes.[43] For the time being nothing happened. De Gaulle

41. Churchill to Roosevelt, June 9, 1944, *ibid.*, p. 708.

42. Roosevelt to Churchill, June 13, 1944, *ibid.*, p. 709.

43. In his message to Roosevelt of June 9, Churchill wrote: "I saw the specimens of the notes in question and they do not appear to us very reassuring. Forging them looks very easy. Not a thing is mentioned regarding who is responsible for issuing and redeeming them. . . . Ought we to allow de Gaulle to obtain new status as his fee for backing them, or should we assume the burden for the time

did not denounce (and did not threaten to denounce) the supplemental francs; they were accepted widely by the population of Normandy, which, as Churchill predicted, cared little about the legal aspects involved.[44] Nevertheless, in a very short time the Allies were made to realize that in a country which was considered "liberated" and in which their political authority was not recognized, their ability to manipulate local finances was limited.

This realization came as a result of a seemingly minor development. The Frenchmen, who readily accepted supplemental francs from the spendthrift Allied soldiers, had limited confidence in this imported money. In order to be on the safe side, they suddenly "showed great zeal in paying their taxes in advance with it,"[45] forming long lines in front of the tax collectors' offices.

Since de Gaulle's government was universally recognized in France, the officials appointed by the General immediately utilized this sudden zeal to pay taxes to expose the dubious legitimacy of the American-printed currency. Following his instructions, Colonel François Coulet, French civil commissioner in the Bayeux region, ordered the tax collectors not to accept supplemental francs in settlement of taxes. This greatly alarmed Allied civil affairs officers in the region who came to Coulet pleading him not to discriminate against this currency. After protracted negotiations, Coulet consented to halt the discrimination pending further instructions from *his* government. In the written agreement, he stressed the temporary nature of this acceptance, stipulated "com-

---

being, improve the issue later on, and make the settlement at the peace table . . . ?" On June 13 Roosevelt replied: "I have seen the franc notes the second time and consider their general appearance satisfactory. Due to the intricate combinations of colors, the experts on counterfeit money at the Bureau of Printing and Engraving tell me they will be very difficult to copy." *Ibid.*, pp. 708–9. Whatever the experts told the President, mass-scale forgery of the supplemental franc notes was recorded in France as early as September, 1944; according to a U.S. army finance officer, who prefers to remain unnamed, this counterfeiting continued unabated for two years, until supplemental francs were finally withdrawn from circulation.

44. Coles and Weinberg, *Soldiers Become Governors*, p. 714. Supplemental francs were also brought to France by the U.S. Seventh Army which landed, together with the French forces, at Provence in August. In a letter to me of May 21, 1962, Frank A. Southard, Jr., says that these francs were not used because stocks of French franc currency were found in abundance in local banks. This, however, was apparently only partially correct. Although supplemental francs were not issued officially, they nonetheless went into circulation because of the widespread misappropriation and theft on the part of both the Americans and the French.

45. Robert Aron, *France Reborn: The History of the Liberation, June 1944–May 1945* (New York: Scribner's 1964), p. 58.

plete secrecy in transaction," and warned that under no conditions was this consent "to be taken as any admission on our part that the special currency is now acceptable legal tender."[46]

This agreement reached SHAEF shortly and was approved there, although some dismayed officials menacingly talked about various "means of persuasion" which they thought were open to them, such as issuing dollars and pounds in France at two-and-a-half times their established value.[47] On a higher level, however, it became obvious that there simply was no way of imposing external will on a country determined to preserve its independence. The British government opened broad discussions with the French representatives on the general subject of the civil administration in occupied France. Simultaneously, Churchill kept prodding Roosevelt to modify his stand: "Under the mutual aid arrangement which we are making with the other European Allies, they will bear the cost of civil administration and of services and supplies to our soldiers in their respective countries. However the French would contribute no mutual aid to the American and British armies of liberation if we should become responsible for the whole of the military notes issued in France."[48]

Roosevelt now seemingly began to appreciate the seriousness of the situation and to suspect that eliminating de Gaulle was beyond his power. He also saw Churchill's point. He had no desire to bear the costs of civil administration in France, or of the supplies and services to the Allied armies which were borne in North Africa by the CLN. That appeared too high a price for the luxury of ignoring the French government. Through Generals Marshall (who was then in London) and Smith, Roosevelt invited de Gaulle to come to Washington and grudgingly consented to the French-British discussions.[49] He warned Churchill, however, that these discussions should involve no recognition of de Gaulle's government and that he should not be faced with a fait accompli when de Gaulle arrived at the White House.[50]

46. Coles and Weinberg, *Soldiers Become Governors*, pp. 710–11.
47. *Ibid.*, p. 711.
48. Churchill to Roosevelt, June 21, 1944, *ibid.*, p. 712.
49. According to de Gaulle, Walter Bedell Smith "literally beseeched" him to agree to a meeting with the President, "so eager was the military command to know where to turn for administrative cooperation in France." De Gaulle, *Unity*, p. 266.
50. Coles and Weinberg, *Soldiers Become Governors*, p. 713.

The visit took place in July and was not marked by great cordiality. But although the talks between the two leaders were rather general in character, some practical matters were taken up, including civil affairs in France. Roosevelt instructed the War and Treasury Departments to draw up an agreement recognizing the CLN as the de facto authority for civil government in France, with a specific provision for it to issue currency.[51] This agreement was negotiated further with the British and French a month later, and in its British version the Provisional Government of the French Republic was designated by name.

This still did not mean diplomatic recognition. Churchill abided by Roosevelt's wishes, and the United States appeared as determined as ever to follow the old course. As the War Department explained to its representatives in London while the talks were still in progress, " This has got to be on a military level. We don't want any government-to-government business on this thing. We don't want to tell, we must not tell the French that Eisenhower is signing for the United States Government. He is signing by direction of the Joint Chiefs of Staff. . . . Explain again that there were solid governmental reasons why he couldn't sign as the agent of the United States. It made it look like a treaty and we didn't want to go through the treaty procedure." [52]

Although to many in London Roosevelt's attitude was beginning to look silly, de Gaulle did not protest; he merely assigned *his* military representatives to carry out the negotiations and to sign the agreement. According to the final text, the French government alone could issue currency in France, including supplemental francs not yet distributed to the armed forces. The agreement was signed in London by General Eisenhower and General Koenig on August 25, 1944, and was supplemented by two memorandums. The first stipulated that the Allied forces in France should abide by the French regulations concerning the exchange of currency. The second stated that " francs advanced by the French Government to the United States military forces and used for net pay of troops

51. Aron, *France Reborn*, p. 219.

52. Hilldring to Holmes, August 16, 1944, *ibid.*, p. 715. A month later, Roosevelt appointed Jefferson Caffery as his envoy to France, with the peculiar title of " Representative of the United States, with the personal rank of ambassador, to the *de facto* French authority now established in Paris." On British views, see Winston S. Churchill, *The Second World War, Triumph and Tragedy* (Boston: Houghton Mifflin, 1953), pp. 244–49.

and procurement of goods and services, and other expenditures not eligible for reciprocal aid [are] to be paid for by the United States Government in dollars." [53]

The Eisenhower-Koenig agreement remained in force after the United States—under the growing pressure from most of its Allies and from its own military leaders in Europe—finally recognized de Gaulle's government on October 23, 1944. Its implementation, however, was accompanied by considerable frictions between the Allies on the one hand, and the French authorities on the other. One issue in dispute was troop spending. Even before D-Day the CLN pointed out "that it was important, both on psychological and economic grounds, that the troops should not make full and indiscriminate use of the very high purchasing power which the conversion of their pay into francs gave them in a country where most goods were in short supply." In order to limit as much as possible a rise in prices and an increase of black market operations, the CLN suggested that

> 1. The daily allowances convertible into francs should, during the first months of liberation and until such time as supplies may then become available, be limited to as low a figure as possible;
> 2. Appropriate instructions should be given by the Commander in Chief to prevent individual buying of food by the troops;
> 3. The American troops should not be allowed to bring American currency into France or exchange it for their own private purchases.[54]

The financial experts at SHAEF seemingly appreciated the dangers of troop spending, and the United States Army issued a number of orders and appeals to the troops to curtail such spending. The War Department, however, refused to limit the amount of pay given to troops "not only because it would adversely affect the morale of troops, but also because it would be unlawful: compulsory withholding of soldiers' pay would be in violation of federal law." [55]

53. *U.S. Statutes at Large*, LXI, Part 4, 4206–07.
54. Monnet to McCloy, May 12, 1944, Coles and Weinberg, *Soldiers Become Governors*, pp. 745–46.
55. Hilldring to Holmes, June 25, 1944, *ibid.*, p. 747.

In the months following D-Day army civil affairs officers routinely assured the War Department that troop spending was relatively small, that the black market was under control, and that the impact of the Allied invasion on the French economy was insignificant. At the same time they complained that at the existing rate of exchange soldiers on leave to Paris and other " leave centers " could not enjoy themselves and were often " victims of extreme financial injustice " because their pay did not go far.[56] These assurances and complaints had some foundation in fact—but not for long. As shortages of all basic commodities became increasingly acute, the inflation and black market operations increased rapidly. At the same time the American soldiers discovered that they could sell their rations, personal possessions, and even army property to the blackmarketeers at enomous profits. Whether they justified their operations by the unreasonably inflated prices in France or some other way, the effect was the same. They lived better than anyone else, they saved much of their pay, and many made small fortunes which they transferred to the United States.[57] The unfavorable rate of exchange hurt only the scrupulous few; the rest did not need to convert any part of their pay into francs either at the official, or the black market, rate of exchange.[58]

Somewhat to the surprise of both the French and the American financial authorities, the reliance of the American soldiers on the black market for their supply of local currency badly hurt France's financial interests. When the reciprocal aid settlement was finally negotiated in the spring of 1946, the French discovered that out of almost 21 billion francs officially advanced by them since D-Day

56. *Ibid.*, pp. 746–47.

57. From June, 1944, through April, 1945, the troops in the European Theater drew only 14.5 per cent of their pay, saving the rest. The Army's first efforts, in the spring of 1945, to institute controls over the conversion of black market profits into dollars were ineffective. Officers of field grade and higher were officially excluded from all restrictions although they were known to participate in the black market no less than enlisted men. Rundell, *Black Market Money*, pp. 11, 29.

58. The 50 to 1 rate lasted three years, long after it had become completely unrealistic. The Mendes-France-Morgenthau agreement of May 29, 1944, recognized this fact. But whereas the Americans demanded the introduction of the 120 to 1 rate of exchange, the French insisted that the supplies and services delivered to the Allied forces reflected fixed prices, corresponding more nearly to the 75 to 1 rate. In the reciprocal aid settlement, signed in Washington on May 28, 1946, the rate of 120 francs to $1.00 was adopted. *U.S. Statutes at Large*, LXI, Part 4, 4204.

for troop pay and procurement, only about 1.5 billion, or $29 million, represented " net " troop pay for which the United States was obligated to reimburse the French government in dollar credits. In a statement " On the Major Reasons for the Modest Level of Net Troop Pay," the War Department somewhat defensively explained that the troops had spent most of their francs in the Army Post Exchange stores and commissaries, on purchasing money orders and War and Savings Bonds, and on other transfers home. It also argued that at the 50 to 1 rate of exchange the soldiers' spending was discouraged, and the American troops and civilians preferred to acquire various luxury items in exchange for cigarettes, candy, soap, etc., as well as to indulge in " extra-legal activities." As seen by the War Department, " the very understandable desire of French citizens for a few of life's material comforts provided a great temptation to all Allied personnel having access to Post Exchanges and Quartermaster stores." [59]

The War Department avoided applying the term " black market " to business transactions of the American troops and civilians in occupied Europe. It was reluctant to admit the dimensions and significance of this problem which existed in every country where the American troops were stationed. From the point of view of the governments of the " liberated " countries, the American black market operations affected local economies in two ways: they forced the price levels up and disrupted the system of organized distribution of basic supplies to the civilian population; and by artificially reducing the amount of " net " troop pay, they denied the governments involved much needed dollar credits. As seen by the French government:

> One of the main reasons for the low amount of the net troop pay is to be found in the fact that a very important quantity of United States Army supplies was sold for francs to the French population through various channels, and specially through sales by individual members at black-market prices. Therefore the needs of the United States Armed Forces for French currency were covered to a large extent by francs obtained under conditions other than those foreseen at the time of the conclusion of the Agreement of August 25, 1944. France thereby lost an important source of dollars, amounting

59. *Ibid.*, pp. 4200–3.

> possibly to several hundred million dollars, which both American and French authorities had expected her to receive. This loss has been but slightly balanced by the advantages which resulted from the sale to the French population of various products, as these products were seldom essentials and were as a rule sold at abnormally high prices and distributed under conditions which have further upset the French economy.[60]

In the end, rather than receiving a substantial dollar credit as a result of the settlement, the French government had to acknowledge a debt to the United States of $720 million.[61] Although in later years, after the announcement of the Marshall Plan, the United States contributed greatly to the restoration of France's economy, this first experience in economic and financial relations between the two countries had lasting and unhappy political repercussions which few observers foresaw at the time.

60. *Ibid.*, pp. 4203–4.
61. *Ibid.*, p. 4175. At the new rate of exchange, 120 francs to $1.00 this was equivalent to 86.4 billion francs.

CHAPTER IV

ALLIES IN ITALY

The occupation of Italy took place against an unusual background. Italy attempted to change sides in the war and to fight its former ally on the side of its former enemies. Italy's fascist regime was overthrown on the initiative of King Victor Emmanuel III and his monarchist supporters who, for the most part, had been associated with, and therefore compromised by, the twenty years of Mussolini's rule. The July 25, 1943, coup in Rome had a tremendous political impact on the whole course of the war. But while it offered the Anglo-American coalition great new opportunities for the successful prosecution of the war, it also confronted the Allies, who had fought Italy *and* fascism at the same time, with a dilemma which they found themselves unable to resolve. This dilemma was posed by the emergence of the new government which was both legitimate and antifascist. This government wanted to join the Allies to prevent a German occupation of the peninsula and to secure better peace terms, but at the same time it refused to effect the kind of internal change which, in the eyes of antifascists everywhere, would signify a clean break with the past. The Allies could not take advantage of the fall of fascism without giving the King's government a degree of recognition; in the process they involved themselves in an extremely complex and unhappy situation.

The Casablanca Conference in January, 1943, produced two major decisions: one military, one political. The military decision was to expand the operations in the Mediterranean by invading Sicily. The political decision (which soon provoked great controversy) was to accept from the Axis powers nothing short of unconditional surrender. Its corollary was an agreement on a "tough" policy for the forthcoming occupation of Italy.[1]

1. Robert J. Quinlin, "The Italian Armistice" *American Civil-Military Decisions*, ed. Harold Stein (University, Ala.: University of Alabama Press, 1963),

The Allies landed in Sicily on July 10, 1943, and quickly occupied the island. A week later in their joint appeal to the Italian people, Roosevelt and Churchill promised them " a respected place in the family of nations," as well as " a restoration of national dignity, security and peace." [2] On July 25, Mussolini was arrested, the Fascist Party dissolved, and the government of Marshal Badoglio was established in Rome on Victor Emmanuel III's authority. The news of this event stunned the world and made headlines in the United States. But the event itself failed to change the prevailing public attitude toward Italy, and since the King was strongly asociated with the fascist regime, his act evoked little enthusiasm. President Roosevelt's first reaction indicated his determination to remain " tough ": he declared that " our terms to Italy are still the same as our terms to Germany and Japan—Unconditional Surrender.' " [3] In displaying this firmness Roosevelt was doubtless stimulated by the recent domestic controversy over the alleged softness the Allies had displayed in regard to the " Vichyites " in North Africa. And although some officials privately expressed a desire to see the policy toward Italy modified, Roosevelt and his closest advisers clung to their initial stand.[4]

Churchill, on the other hand, quickly realized the opportunities

---

pp. 211–14. For an understanding of the events which led to the armistice, it is also important to read Norman Kogan's *Italy and the Allies* (Cambridge: Harvard University Press, 1956), based largely on Italian sources.

2. U.S. Department of State, *Foreign Relations of the United States, 1943* (Washington: U.S. Government Printing Office, 1964), II, 330–31. Hereinafter referred to as *1943 Papers.* Such promises, however, were strictly for propaganda purposes. General Eisenhower was informed that in the event of a capitulation, Italy should not be offered an honorable peace and that " the terms would be unconditional surrender." Laux to Hilldring, May 31, 1943, Harry L. Coles and Albert K. Weinberg, *Civil Affairs: Soldiers Become Governors* (Washington: Department of the Army, 1964), p. 222. See also Eisenhower to the Combined Chiefs of Staff, July 19, 1943, and Marshall to Eisenhower, July 25, 1943, *ibid.*, pp. 223–24.

3. Radio Broadcast July 28, 1943. U.S. Department of State, *United States and Italy, 1936–1946* (Washington: U.S. Government Printing Office, 1946), p. 45.

4. Robert Murphy, *Diplomat among Warriors* (Garden City, N.Y.: Doubleday, 1964), p. 194. It should be noted, that the State Department—which had wholeheartedly supported Roosevelt's Vichy policy—had a much more benevolent attitude toward Italy, taking a position that " our whole approach to the Italian problem [be] based on the assumption that the Italian people and their fundamental goodwill toward [the British and the Americans] can and should be used in the prosecution of our common war effort." Hull to Winant, February 9, 1943, *1943 Papers*, II, 323.

presented by the turn of events and cabled Roosevelt that the Allies should " deal with any non-Fascist Government which can deliver the goods ";[5] the " goods " being the surrender of the Italian and perhaps German forces in mainland Italy. The same view prevailed in the Allied headquarters in Algiers. Eisenhower was anxious to eliminate Italy as a military factor in the war and, if possible, to bring it over to the Allied side in the struggle against Germany.

Once the Allied forces acquired a foothold in Italy, the Supreme Commander and the governments in Washington and London inevitably became involved in political developments in the occupied part of the country. The first problem to be solved was that of Italy's new status. Eisenhower's position, set out in a memorandum of September 18–20, 1943, was based on strictly military considerations. The Supreme Commander urged that Italy declare war on Germany; that the Italian government and the people be regarded as co-belligerents (" with their military activity subject to my direction under the terms of [the] armistice "); and that the Allies " accept and strengthen the legal government of Italy under the King and Badoglio " so as to minimize the need for the military to become involved in civil affairs.[6]

Eisenhower's view was fully shared by Churchill, who was convinced that constitutional monarchy was essential for the creation of a democratic government in the country and believed that it could serve as a rallying point for all antifascist forces.[7] Perhaps overestimating Italy's military potential, he also urged a full participation of Italy in the war against Germany, even if it meant a departure from unconditional surrender and recognition of the King's government. This idea was abhorrent to Roosevelt and most of his friends. Arguing against recognizing Italy as a co-belligerent, in a memorandum of September 20, Harry Hopkins protested: " I cannot see that a declaration of war by Badoglio gets us anywhere except a precipitated recognition of two men who have worked with the Fascists in the past. I think we should get

5. Winston S. Churchill, *The Second World War, Closing the Ring* (Boston: Houghton Mifflin, 1951), pp. 55–56.

6. *1943 Papers*, II, 370.

7. Churchill, *Closing the Ring*, pp. 188ff. Also, Robert E. Sherwood, *Roosevelt and Hopkins: An Intimate History* (New York: Harper, 1948), pp. 743–44, and Quinlin, pp. 270–73.

every possible advantage out of them but I don't think we are under any obligation to them."[8]

Another Anglo-American compromise was reached. Italy was to be given the nebulous status of co-belligerent, but its government was to function under the direction of the Allied Control Commission (ACC).[9] The King strongly objected. He insisted on the status of an ally, on building up a new Italian army before sending the demoralized and disorganized units against the Germans, on more say in ruling the "liberated" areas of Italy, and on some guarantees for his dynasty. The Allies brushed off these conditions, and since Italy was in no position to bargain, Badoglio was forced, on September 29, to signs the humiliating "long terms" of the armistice. On October 13, under continuing Allied pressure, Badoglio announced the King's declaration of war against Germany.[10]

The King's government resented the role assigned to it by the Allies. Although it remained virtually powerless, it steadfastly maintained that the status of co-belligerency superseded the terms of the armistice. This argument was greatly to aggravate the problems of administering occupied Italy.

The Anglo-American compromise on the new status for Italy did not bridge the differences in their attitudes toward the country. The British position, which London adhered to until the spring of 1946, remained the same: the authority of the King's government must be strengthened and a constitutional monarchy preserved. But, at the same time, the British were determined that Italy should be kept permanently weak and were, therefore, opposed to any move which could enhance her international standing.

The American government remained antagonistic toward the King and Badoglio. It attached little value to the importance of

8. Sherwood, *Roosevelt and Hopkins*, p. 752.

9. The ACC was a civilian arm of the Supreme Allied Commander, Mediterranean Theater (SACMED), with jurisdiction over those areas in Italy which were not under direct military control. The latter were ruled by the Allied Military Government (AMG). Both the ACC and AMG were headed by the same person and, in January, 1944, they merged into one administrative body which, for convenience' sake, will be referred to as the AMG unless otherwise specified.

10. The so-called "short terms" armistice was signed by Badoglio's representatives on September 3, 1943, and only these terms were made public. The British insisted on the publication of "long terms" as well, but were overruled by Eisenhower, who, at first, was afraid that these harsh terms would provoke such resentment in the country as to make a successful prosecution of war difficult.

political stability in Italy, favoring instead a rapid restructuring of the Italian society by *all* antifascist forces. At the same time, the United States was not averse to the improvement of Italy's international position.

The Soviet Union was not directly involved in the occupation of Italy. Although the Soviet government approved the terms of the surrender, it was greatly displeased with the whole Italian campaign, which it considered a diversion from the overriding task of the creation of the second front in France. It is difficult to establish what the Soviet expectations were with regard to Italy. In August, Stalin wrote to Roosevelt and Churchill expressing his approval of the armistice terms but demanding the participation of a Soviet representative in the negotiations with the Italians.[11] Later he advanced a proposal to create a three-power " Military-Political Commission " which would be empowered to issue orders to the Badoglio government on political, administrative, and military matters. The British and the American governments, however, reserved this function for the Allied Control Commission, which operated directly under the Commander in Chief. The Military-Political Commission was eventually given the name of the Advisory Council for Italy but its authority was restricted.

As it turned out, participation on the Advisory Council presented the Soviets with considerable opportunity to influence Italy's political life, mostly by facilitating the rise of the Italian Communist Party. It lent the communists a prestige and respectability which otherwise would not have been forthcoming and assured them a permanent role in Italy's fortunes.[12]

11. *1943 Papers*, I, 783–84.

12. Kogan, *Italy and the Allies*, pp. 18–21, 56–67, 171–75. See also *The Memoirs of Cordell Hull* (New York: Macmillan, 1948), II, 1548–69; Quinlin, *American Civil-Military Decisions*, pp. 276–77; Murphy, *Diplomat among Warriors*, pp. 209–16. One can only guess whether Soviet policies in Italy, as reflected in the tactics of the Communist Party, would have been different had the Anglo-Americans accorded their Soviet partner full recognition as a co-ruler of the occupied country. Herbert Feis, in his *Churchill, Roosevelt, Stalin: The War They Waged and the Peace They Sought* (Princeton: Princeton University Press, 1957), pp. 182–87, points out that later the Soviet government " was to maintain that the Italian setup was a good and fair model to use in countries liberated by the Red Army," i.e., to exclude the Western powers from effective participation in the affairs of Eastern Europe. This supposed connection between the two situations has often been asserted by those Western writers who have been inclined to blame the United States and Great Britain for the deterioration of the East-West relations. The fact is that the Soviets did not use this argument until after their armies

The communists contributed sizably to the difficulties in administering Italy. But there were other factors of equal importance. Besides the already noted divergencies between the American and British attitudes, there was the insufficient liaison between the AMG and the Supreme Allied Commander in the Mediterranean on the one hand and between Washington and London on the other; the inability of cumbersome Allied bureaucratic machinery to act with sufficient flexibility both on the policymaking and administrative levels; and the social and political convulsions caused by the disintegration of the old regime. These factors produced a state of affairs which was disappointing from almost any point of view.[13]

POLITICAL AND ADMINISTRATIVE PROBLEMS OF OCCUPATION

A major difficulty which the Allied Military Government had to face in Italy derived from the inability of the United States and Great Britain to arrive at a clear-cut decision on the issue of direct or indirect rule. In specific discussions of the occupation policy for Italy, the United States favored direct military rule. Roosevelt's intention was "to remove any Italians from [important] positions as they are all prominent Fascists and replace them with Army officers . . . thus avoiding stirring up factions on the ground and repercussions at home." [14]

Great Britain was opposed to this course: as Churchill put it, "it would be a mistake to flood all these places with hundreds of British and American gauleiters"; he recommended a maximum utilization of the Italians in governing the country.[15]

These divergent views were reflected in the Combined Chiefs of Staff (CCS) directive for the occupation of Sicily (which was issued in June, 1943, and remained valid for the rest of Italy)

---

occupied Rumania in the summer of 1944. Nor did they demand, after 1943, a greater say in the direction and administration of Italian affairs. In other words the question of "exclusion" simply did not arise at the time and it can be doubted that the Soviets had ever seriously counted on a full partnership in Italy or, indeed, intended to accord the same to the United States and Great Britain in Eastern Europe.

13. George C. S. Benson and Maurice Neufeld, "American Military Government in Italy," *American Experiences in Military Government in World War II*, ed. Carl J. Friedrich (New York: Rinehart, 1948), pp. 111–12. Hereinafter to be referred to as *American Experiences.*

14. Roosevelt to Churchill, June 10, 1943, Coles and Weinberg, *Soldiers Become Governors*, p. 173,

15. Churchill to Roosevelt, June 10, 1943, *ibid.*, p. 173.

which specified that " the administration shall be benevolent with respect to the civilian population . . . [which was] tired of war, resentful of German overlordship, and demoralized by the fascist regime, and will therefore be responsible to a just and efficient administration." The directive further emphasized that " the first objective must be to get and keep a local government working smoothly so as to relieve the Commander in Chief of all trouble and anxiety as regards civil population."

This was clear enough, except that the directive also prescribed a far-reaching " defascistisation," a policy which was strongly endorsed by the Moscow Conference of the Foreign Ministers in October, 1943, and which considerably curtailed the discretion granted to the military commanders by the CCS directive. It called for " the total elimination of Fascism from Italian life and the removal of Fascists from positions of economic influence and power and from all levels of the government." [16]

Not unexpectedly, " defascistisation " proved to be incompatible with the preservation of the government structure. The purges caused the quick decomposition of the administrative machinery and saddled the AMG with the formidable task of governing the occupied country at all levels of the government. Reflecting the military point of view, the army historians relate.

> " defascistisation " conflicted with military expediency in attainment of the Army's most vital goal—the continuation of Italian administration so that military operations would not be disturbed by disorder in civilian life. By its directive to liberate the people from its fascist regime, and other provisions whether mandatory or contingent upon military discretion, the CCS authorized a broad defascistisation. . . . Thus AMG had to find some formula which promised the dismissal of enough to show its political sincerity, but not so many as to threaten administrative breakdown. One formula after another was tried and abandoned because it dismissed either too few or too many.[17]

The Allies could find no replacement for the officials they removed from office. After twenty years of Mussolini's rule,

16. Kogan, *Italy and the Allies*, pp. 90–96. Cf. Benson and Neufeld, *American Experiences*, p. 122.

17. Coles and Weinberg, *Soldiers Become Governors*, pp. 373–74.

practically everybody with administrative experience was compromised by fascism. The United States government saw a solution in the " democratization " of Italian politics, largely through the encouragement of the Italian left, both in the occupied South and in the growing partisan movement in the North, and through the return to Italy of the antifascist emigres who had escaped from Mussolini. The British, by and large, opposed this line on the grounds that avowed antifascists were almost invariably antimonarchists who agitated against the King's government, thus undermining the only element of stability in Italian political life. The British opposition, however, soon began to crumble.[18]

The *Comitato di Liberazione Nazionale* (CLN) was founded in Bari in January, 1944.[19] It consisted of a bloc of six antifascist parties of unequal and still-to-be-tested strength: Communist, Socialist, Action, Democracy of Labor, Christian Democrat, and Liberal. These parties acquired their own uncensored press and their activities were not controlled by AMG officials, who were ordered to maintain a strictly neutral attitude toward Italian internal problems. At the same time all of these parties received encouragement from the Allied Control Commission, which was now committed to a quick " democratization " of Italy.

This commitment created a difficult situation for the AMG: the encouragement of the antifascist groups, which were also in opposition to the King and Badoglio's government, threatened the " liberated " part of Italy with precisely the kind of political turmoil which the military had been so anxious to prevent. It induced the AMG to retain full military control (despite its ineffectiveness), even over provinces far removed from the front line. At the same time the pressures from the left accounted for the recurrent American effort to force the King to abdicate.[20]

18. See the State Department memorandum of November 10, 1943, *1943 Papers*, II, 423–25. In practice, the differences between the British and American views resulted in confusing and contradictory measures which the more ardent partisans of either approach effected in occupied Italy wherever they felt they could get away with it.

19. On the CLN origins and developments, see Kogan, *Italy and the Allies*, pp. 14–18, 52–65, 92–111; Adlai E. Stevenson, " Report of FEA Survey Mission to Italy " (unpublished MS, 1943), p. 33; H. Stuart Hughes, *The United States and Italy* (Cambridge: Harvard University Press, 1953), pp. 139–47; and particularly Coles and Weinberg, *Soldiers Become Governors*, Chapter XV.

20. See Roosevelt-Churchill exchange of messages in March 1944, *ibid.*, pp. 444–45.

The so-called Institutional Question plagued Italian politics throughout the first three years of the occupation. In the spring of 1944, the King survived one particularly severe crisis not so much because of the British support (which was already waning) as because of a sudden Soviet move: on March 13, the Soviets extended diplomatic recognition to Badoglio's government. This announcement caused consternation in London and Washington, who still dealt with the Italian government through the Political Section of the Allied Control Commission and had no intention of granting full sovereignty to Italy.[21] Although under sharp protest from Roosevelt and Churchill (who maintained that under the terms of the armistice Italy had no right to establish diplomatic relations with foreign powers), Stalin changed de jure and de facto recognition. The long-range effects of this episode were of great significance. The Soviet Union suddenly appeared as Italy's friend, and the Italian Communist Party gained in prestige among the more nationalistic-minded groups.

Badoglio never had an opportunity to re-establish a centralized administration. His government controlled regional administration in several impoverished provinces of the South. Until the fall of Rome in June, 1944, it was kept in Brindisi and later in Salerno, "completely out of touch with Allied headquarters and also with the population it was presumably governing."[22] With the capture of Rome, King Victor Emmanuel III turned all the powers of the Crown to his son,[23] Badoglio resigned, and the first clearly "antifascist" government, based on the CLN, was formed under the premiership of Bonomi. The Allies quickly passed the task of further "defascistisation" to the new government. The purge gained even greater dimensions after the "liberation" of the North and the formation of the Parri government, which was the most radical of all postwar Italian regimes. The purge in-

21. The Soviets explained that they recognized Badoglio because the existing political conditions in Italy were detrimental to a successful prosecution of the war, and that by enhancing the King's status they hoped to facilitate the unity of all antifascist forces. Moscow also complained that, as the matters stood, it had "no direct contact with the Italian government [and therefore] was in an unequal position as compared to its Allies." Soviet Embassy to the State Department, March 19, 1944, *ibid.*, pp. 446–47.

22. Murphy, *Diplomat among Warriors*, p. 212.

23. In the referendum of June, 1946, the Italians voted for a republic by a majority of 2 million votes (or 8.5 per cent). The South—where the Allied occupation was the longest—voted heavily for the preservation of the monarchy.

volved few individual excesses: with the exception of those fascists and " reactionaries " in northern Italy who were summarily executed by the partisans, relatively few persons were sent to prison or deprived of property. Nevertheless, the destruction of the administrative machinery of the country continued, to the satisfaction of those Americans who favored an even more radical change in Italian politics.[24]

PLANNING OF OCCUPATION AND OCCUPATION CURRENCY

The first official statement of American policy on military government and occupation was contained in the War Department's *Basic Field Manual on Military Government* (FM 27–5), released in the summer of 1940. It reflected the American occupation experience in the Rhineland after the Armistice of 1918 and the liberal spirit of the Hague Rules. This spirit was subsequently subjected to severe criticism in the War Department's School of Military Government. The future administrators of occupation were told that the only legitimate objective of military government was to win the war; that " military government [was] not a missionary enterprise " and that it would be " utterly misleading to put the welfare of the governed on a par with military necessity." [25]

Although FM 27–5 was not officially revised until December, 1943, the directive of the Combined Chiefs of Staff issued in June already incorporated these new ideas and the spirit of unconditional surrender. Since the revised FM 27–5 was designed for the combat phase of occupation, military necessities were held paramount. The manual explained that " while the welfare of the inhabitants should be considered . . . such a policy should not

24. The American's first favorite was Count Carlo Sforza, the leader of Italian antifascists in exile. He was brought to Italy in spite of Churchill's objections and took the lead of the noncommunist left. His chances of replacing Badoglio were scuttled when Churchill, on February 29, 1944, violently—and publicly—denounced American efforts to expedite the change. See Hull, *Memoirs*, II, 1551–56; *1943 Papers*, II, 402–40, *passim*; Coles and Weinberg, *Soldiers Become Governors*, Chapter XV, Part 7. Immediately after the reunification of the country, many Americans tended to favor Ferrucio Parri, a radical northern " actionist," and even Luigi Longo, the leader of northern communists and partisans. See Hughes, *The United States and Italy*, pp. 144–51; Kogan, *Italy and the Allies*, pp. 121–28, 178–83, 193–200.

25. Merle Fainsod, " The Development of American Military Government Policy during World War II," in *American Experiences*, p. 32.

affect the imposition of such restrictive or punitive measures as may be necessary to accomplish the objectives of military government." Yet despite various restrictions, FM 27–5, as well as the CCS directive, retained the principle of economy of effort and indirect rule. The manual's main characteristic was its general vagueness, which allowed diverse interpretations and afforded occupation administrators considerable flexibility. But this vagueness was absent in the economic and financial sections, which were much more specific—and more negative—than most other features of both documents. Not only did the manual put the needs of the military operations first, but it provided guidelines which clearly reflected departure from the meaning of the Hague Rules. It stated, for example, that if the minimum needs of enemy populations were to be supplied at all, this was "to be done not primarily for altruistic or humanitarian reasons, but to protect the health of the occupation forces." The same nonaltruistic spirit permeated the sections dealing with the monetary arrangements in which a special military currency, proposed by the U.S. Treasury Department, was expected to play a crucial role.

The idea of issuing Allied military lire was first presented by Assistant Secretary of the Treasury Harry Dexter White, in February, 1943, to the *Ad Hoc* Committee on Monetary and Fiscal Planning of the Combined Civil Affairs Committee, which was a part of the Combined Chiefs of Staff establishment. In prolonged deliberations, as White fought for a hard economic policy toward Italy, he had to overcome the objection that a massive infusion of paper money would weaken the country's economy, thus putting an additional burden on the Allied war effort. White's arguments, however, were convincing. In the light of the North African experience, the issue of Allied military (AM) lire as a supplemental currency appeared justifiable. Unlike BMA currency it would be limited to one country, and although issued on the authority of the Allied Military Government, it would be legal tender at par with the lire issued by the Bank of Italy. It could be utilized by the troops of all the Allied forces in Italy. And since AM lire would be the responsibility of some future government of the country, its introduction offered a seemingly simple way to make Italy pay for the Allied occupation costs.[26]

26. Testimony of Assistant Secretary of State John H. Hilldring, *Hearings before the Committees on Appropriations, Armed Services and Banking and Currency,*

The policy directive of the Combined Chiefs of Staff embraced the Treasury proposals to a large extent: it was "based on the proposition that the AM lire was an Italian currency, that the expenditures necessarily made by the Allied forces were for Italian government account, and that there would be no reimbursement." [27]

The nature of the AM lire was further revealed in the *Ad Hoc* Committee's decision in regard to its rates of exchange. It has been noted that the British had overvalued the pound sterling vis-à-vis the lira in Tripolitania, and that they considered the overvaluation "a good piece of political and economic warfare." Some British experts still held to this view, while others suggested a rate of 50 lire to $1.00 as less damaging to the local economy.[28] One American, pointing out that the President had taken a reasonably benevolent attitude toward the Italian people, recommended a rate of 60 lire to $1.00. White rejected these suggestions on the grounds that such a rate would be too favorable to "Italian fascists" and that the Allied soldiers deserved a better break. The Committee settled on the rate of exchange of 100 lire to $1.00, and 400 to £1. Everybody was aware that the purchasing power of one lira was much higher than one cent, but no one was interested in establishing its precise value. As it turned out, this rate of exchange overvalued the dollar by more than 200 per cent, many times more than the overvaluation of the reichsmark by the Germans anywhere.[29]

The Treasury Department announced the birth of the new lira currency on August 2, 1943, and on August 17, followed the announcement with a more detailed press release explaining the reasons for introducing occupation currency in Italy and the ways

80th Congress, 1st Session, June 17–18, 1947, pp. 115ff. Paul Y. Hammond, in his "Directives for the Occupation of Germany: The Washington Controversy," in Stein's *American Civil-Military Decisions*, pp. 348–49, points out that "the Treasury approached the fiscal and monetary problems of the Italian liberation with a far greater emphasis on punitive objectives than did the State or War Departments."

27. Frank A. Southard, Jr., *The Finances of European Liberation, with Special Reference to Italy* (New York: King's Crown, 1946), p. 30.

28. They were supported by the argument that the black market rate for £1 in North Africa fluctuated between 500 and 800 lire, and that a better rate for the "enemy" currency would offend the friendly Arab population.

29. Bruno Foa, *Monetary Reconstruction of Italy* (New York: King's Crown, 1949), p. 17. Also, C. H. S. Harris, *Allied Military Administration of Italy, 1943–1945* (London: H.M. Stationery Office, 1957), p. 382.

in which it differed from the "spearhead" yellow seal dollars. The Treasury Department also stated that AM lire spent by the Army for troop pay, supplies, and other expenditures would be charged against the relevant War Department appropriations for the dollar equivalent of such expenditure, so that "no change in the customary control by Congress over the size and nature of Army appropriations" would incur. It promised that in all cases complete records would be kept and that a detailed accounting procedure would facilitate "the adjustment of financial matters growing out of the military operations of the Allied Forces in the occupied areas."

The Treasury Department did not enlarge on the question of this "adjustment" and did not state that these expenditures, in full or in part, would eventually be charged to the Italian government. It did say, however, that Allied Military Government expenditures of the occupation currency for local civilian needs would not be subject to the same accounting procedure because they had nothing to do with the War Department's appropriations. No limits to these expenditures were set or implied.

The Treasury Department's announcement immediately provoked objections in the United States. Some were on legal grounds. Since the issue of new currency needed congressional authorization, it was argued that the Treasury Department had acted in violation of the Constitution.[30] It was held that charging a part of the expenditures made in Allied military currency to the War Department's appropriations did not alter the fact that the total mass of money in circulation for which the United States was responsible was increased without the consent of Congress. The Treasury Department tried to skirt the issue of responsibility by asserting that the Allied Military Government had the right under international law to issue currency for occupied areas.[31] The critics still maintained that insofar as this currency was redeemable in dollars to the American troops, it was the responsibility of the United States.

30. See Walter E. Spahr, *Allied Military Currency* (New York: Economists' National Committee on Monetary Policy, 1943), *passim.* On the legality of occupation currencies from the point of view of international law, see Ernst H. Feilchenfeld, *The International Economic Law of Belligerent Occupation* (Washington: Carnegie Endowment for International Peace, 1942), pp. 70–83, 90.

31. See the Statement of the Treasury Department, March 14, 1945, in *The Secretary of the Treasury Annual Report, 1944–1945*, p. 391.

Other critics pointed out the danger of overissue of occupation currency. With no legal restraints placed on the Allied Military Government, such overissue was likely, with the prospect of a chaotic monetary situation in Italy. Unrestricted redemption was thought to present another danger. As experience in North Africa had already indicated, the troops did not hesitate to make black market profits. Two economists, having visited Italy early in 1944, reported on the growth of transactions of this nature and on the inadequacy of controls over redemption procedures. Almost anyone could send home practically unlimited amounts of money, for "Who [was] to say that a G.I. turning up with a wad of bills did not win them at a crap game?"[32]

These criticisms were ignored. Congress made no attempt to challenge "the first truly Allied venture into the field of military monetary expedients," as the first Treasury announcement put it. The public—and most of the officials concerned—did not see anything wrong with having the soldiers make some money while fighting the enemy. The question of inflation in Italy was understood by very few, and since the Treasury Department was bent on a punitive policy toward Italy anyway, it was not interested in measures that could prevent inflation, apparently feeling that inflation in Italy would in no way impair the economic interests of the United States. This attitude prevailed for a long time, even after Italy had joined the Allies in the war against Germany.

ECONOMIC AND FINANCIAL PROBLEMS OF OCCUPATION

For a considerable time after Italy's withdrawal from the Axis, the majority of Italians were so preoccupied with the task of physical survival that they had little time to concern themselves with such matters as Italy's new status in the world, the future of the monarchy, or the direction of internal politics. For almost two

32. Donald L. Kemmerer and T. Eugene Beattie, *Allied Military Currency in Italy* (New York: Economists' National Committee on Monetary Policy, 1944), p. 3. The fierceness with which the War Department defended the soldiers' right to gamble and do whatever they pleased with their gaming profits was truly remarkable, even if these profits, due to the accounting techniques, were to come out of the American taxpayers' pocket. See Walter Rundell, Jr., *Black Market Money: The Collapse of U.S. Currency in World War II* (Baton Rouge: Louisiana State University Press, 1964), pp. 37–38.

years their country remained a battleground; Allied armies were advancing slowly up the peninsula, subjecting the cities, roads, and railways to systematic bombardment. As a historian relates, "In the devastation inflicted by the war, Italy suffered more heavily than any Western nation except Germany. And in Italy the hardships endured by the civilian population were even more severe than those undergone by the Germans. From 1943 to 1946, the Italian people passed through the hardest trial of their history as a united nation." [33]

For those in the South, "liberated" (or "occupied") by the Allies, the war was over. They were anxious to return to normalcy; they believed that the worst was over, that an improvement in their living conditions was imminent. In this, they were bitterly disappointed. The decline in the standard of living in the Allied-occupied areas was sharp and rapid:

> To most Italians, Allied, and in particular American, liberation meant a definite expectation that food, clothing, and other necessities would become available promptly and on a large scale. The man in the street could hardly understand or appreciate the gigantic problems of supply and transportation brought about by the war. . . . Hence, it came as a surprise to most people that economic conditions deteriorated sharply after the liberation, rather than improved. Envious comparisons were made between the wealth of food and resources available to the American forces and the meager diet of the civilian population.[34]

The aggravation of the economic conditions in the South was inevitable, particularly in view of its separation from the food-producing and manufacturing areas of the North, which were still held by the Germans. But this fact alone is insufficient to account

33. Hughes, *The United States and Italy*, p. 183. This is not to suggest that the Italians had been affluent before the fall of Mussolini. Even before Allied bombings greatly intensified beginning in the spring of 1943, the Italian economy had been under severe strain. The war had clearly been beyond Italy's means. Yet although there had been signs of discontent and labor unrest, shortages of foodstuffs had at no time been significant enough to cause starvation; the system of rationed distribution had worked sufficiently well to assure an adequate, if somewhat meager, diet.

34. Foa, *Monetary Reconstruction of Italy*, p. 16. Also see Coles and Weinberg, *Soldiers Become Governors*, p. 346.

for the very grave inflation which developed under the Allied occupation. To it must be added two features of the occupation itself: the almost complete failure to maintain effective controls over the economy, and the massive and almost totally uncontrolled troop spending.[35] It is very difficult to measure the relative weight of these factors among many others, such as the fall of productivity due to the destruction of industries and railroads, the haphazard requisition and procurement practices, the disintegration of traditional commercial channels, and the system of distribution of supplies to the civilians. Most observers agree, however, that inflation in the occupied territories would have taken a considerably milder form, and the corresponding economic and social dislocations would have been much less drastic, had the Allies made a greater effort to control prices and wages and the spending of their troops.[36]

Economic Controls and Troop Spending

Economic controls played a major role in war-torn countries. Even if sometimes inadequately enforced, they assured a subsistence level for the people and prevented runaway inflation. These controls were a practical necessity; they had become an integral part of the whole economic structure of Italy. The Combined Chiefs of Staff directive, however, omitted any reference to the necessity to preserve and enforce the existing control regulations. It was not simply due to the lack of concern for the well-being of the population. More than anything, this omission reflected an official repudiation of the old rules for waging war. As a British historian

35. Years later, some Americans who participated in the execution of the Allied economic policies in Italy took a different view. For example, Bruno Foa wrote to me on June 15, 1962, that "no one was in a position to anticipate fully the impact of large injections of military currency in a context of physical disruption and extreme shortages of fuels and all other commodities." Frank A. Southard, Jr., in a letter to me on May 16, 1962, maintains that "the price level did not skyrocket [and] the impact of Allied procurement practices was not unduly bad." But Southard's contention—as well as some of his statements in his book—have been hotly contested by Italian economists who support their position with convincing figures. Foa perhaps is right insofar as the military government officials in Italy were concerned. But it is difficult to believe that the Treasury economists who set the Allied financial policy in Italy were unaware of the consequences of "large injections of military currency" into Italian economy.

36. The reasons why the Allies did not make such effort in the ex-enemy countries will be discussed in Chapter VII.

noted, the CCS directive "transgressed the letter of the Hague Rules which, in Article 43, require the military authority occupying hostile territory to do all in his power to restore public order and safety 'respecting at the same time, unless absolutely prevented, the laws in force in the country.'"[37]

It is true that World War II generated bitterness which made the Hague Rules look obsolete; and perhaps few Allied occupation planners felt constrained by this international agreement, which still appears in the Statutes at Large of the United States of America and thus still is the law of the land. And although some may argue ex post facto that the Allied occupation authorities were "absolutely prevented" from enforcing the laws of the defunct regimes,[38] it is also true that the thought of upholding these laws did not enter their minds.

The recurrent argument that price and wage controls could not be maintained because of the lack of administrative and enforcement machinery is hardly valid. By giving priority to a thorough "defascistisation" of the existing administration, the Allies were doubtless responsible for the destruction of whatever governmental structure survived the fall of the old regime. The conclusion seems inescapable that economic chaos and inflation were part and parcel of the Allied policy. As was shown earlier, the occupation of Italy was intended to be "hard." The question is whether the policymakers, as well as AMG officials, realized that the economic situation might get entirely out of hand.

Perhaps the greatest inflationary factor throughout the years of occupation was the spending of the Allied troops, combined as it was with certain facets of the Allied finance policy—the existing salary scale and the rates of exchange between the dollar (and the pound) and the lira.

The occupying soldiers, especially the Americans, were paid at a level unknown to Italians. With the rate of exchange of 100 lire to $1.00, an American private could draw and spend in

37. Harris, *Administration of Italy, 1943–1945*, p. 14.

38. One authority states that "the term 'absolutely prevented' has never been interpreted literally, but it means at least that new laws can only be supplements to old laws, that they must be sufficiently justified, and that the benefit of doubt belongs to the old, not to the new, laws." Feilchenfeld, *Belligerent Occupation*, p. 89. In Italy, however, the Allies did not engage in law-making as such: they issued decrees which simply ignored the existing laws and failed to enforce either the old laws or the new decrees.

Italy as much money as a top Italian government official. While the British and Canadian armies withheld sizable portions of their troops' pay, the American army made no effort to restrict the spending power of its troops.[39] An American private looked like a millionaire to an average Italian. Guido Jung, Italian Minister of Finance, illustrated the point in the following way: "During July and August 1943 a daily newspaper in Sicily cost 60 centimes of a lira. The American soldiers casually handed over a 10-lire note and never demanded the change. . . . All occupation troops paid correspondingly for their purchases: for wines, liquors, foods, and souvenirs of every variety to be sent to their wives and girl friends in the home country . . . and always new impulses were given to the inflation machine."[40]

Shopkeepers—those who still had goods to sell—immediately quadrupled their prices, realizing that the lira was now at one-fourth its former value. The Italians, who remembered that before the war the rate of exchange was 20–25 lire to $1.00, bitterly resented the new rate, which accounted for the first big jump in their cost of living.[41]

39. Frank A. Southard, Jr., told me in a letter of April 25, 1962, that he had strongly recommended, in the summer of 1944, to Colonel Bernard Bernstein, then chief finance officer of the U.S. forces in Europe, that similar restrictions be imposed on the American troops, and that special military scrip, rather than local currency, be used for troop pay. Bernstein rejected these recommendations on the grounds that withholding a part of the pay was contrary to any feasible United States policy and that "all hell would break loose in the U.S. Congress if any effort were made to limit the pay." Bernstein had "no cogent objections" to the use of military scrip except that it "had not been planned." A year later, under different circumstances—and for different reasons—Bernstein himself became an advocate of military scrip in Germany.

40. Giulio Pietranera, "Considerations on the Dynamics of the Italian Inflation," *Banca Nazionale del Lavoro Quarterly Review*, Vol. 1 (Rome, 1947–48), p. 26. In order to keep transportation costs down, the economy-minded Treasury Department insisted on shipping to Italy a larger proportion of notes of the largest denomination. According to observations on the spot, this discouraged soldiers' frugality—and kept stakes in crap games unusually high. See Kemmerer and Beattie, *Allied Military Currency in Italy*, p. 2.

41. As an FEA mission to Italy noted, "to the country at large, the rate of 100 lire to a dollar came as a surprise and a shock . . . and reduced the lira to about ¼ of its assumed value." Stevenson, "Report of FEA Survey Mission to Italy," p. 27. The psychological effects of inflation are stressed by Professor Epicarmo Corbino in his "Currency and Exchange Policy in the Post-War Years," *Ten Years of Italian Economy: 1947–1956* (Rome: Italian Government, 1956), pp. 207–08. Corbino further points out that with the end of the air raids, the

The Italian government was aware of the inflationary pressures of troop spending and several times asked that the rate of exchange be changed to 50 lire to $1.00. These requests were turned down by both Washington and London, not without the concurrence of the military leaders, who were bent on giving the troops every possible advantage; the threat of inflation in "enemy" countries was of no concern to the Allied governments.

The cost of living index, which stood at 600 at the time of the landing in Sicily (1938 = 100) reached 3,500 by April, 1944, and 4,000 a year later.[42] This development could not be ignored by those Allied officials who became aware that governing occupied Italy entailed responsibilities to the governed. This awareness first appeared on the lower levels of the AMG; it took months to reach the higher levels and much longer to reach policymakers in Washington and London. But once conditions became chaotic, it was impossible to reverse the trend. During the winter of 1943–44, the AMG issued a number of proclamations aimed at checking the rapid increase in prices, but there was no effective way of enforcing these proclamations, either directly or through whatever local government existed. The people, who quickly realized the impotence of the authorities, ignored all regulations with impunity. Moreover, while fixing price ceilings, the AMG approved the raising of wages under the economically naïve theory that they were thus raising the standard of living of Italian workers.[43] Wages went up from 70 to 400 per cent despite a general decline of productivity. When, belatedly, the AMG attempted to freeze wages, no one paid much attention, least of all Allied military units, who made it their practice to break down prices and wage controls. With the troops doing whatever they pleased, and with the black market already in full swing, it was impossible to hold the line even when Allied officials realized the need to do so. A British historian of the occupation relates that the impact of the Allied occupation was "immediately and intensely inflationary, and the attempt to hold prices at the existing level broke down

people stopped hoarding money. Aware of the soaring prices, having no confidence in the lira, and seeing no end to inflation, the Italians developed an inflationary mentality which had an immense influence on the price situation.

42. Paolo Baffi, "Monetary Developments in Italy," *Banca Nazionale del Lavoro Quarterly Review*, No. 47 (Rome, December, 1958), p. 415.

43. Benson and Neufeld, *American Experiences*, p. 141.

completely, not without diminution in the prestige of AMGOT which found itself quite unable to enforce its regulations. With the official rate of exchange at 400 to £1 and a military wage-rate [for the British troops] of more than twice the existing rate for civil labour, the task was hopeless." [44]

Early in 1944, the ACC created the Allied Anti-Inflation Committee, composed of high-level American and British economic experts. The economists did not come up with any specific recommendations, mainly because they could not agree with each other as to whether Italy needed more controls or less. Most agreed, however, that the importation of more food was necessary if the rise in prices was to be checked. These conclusions coincided with those of Badoglio, who appealed to the Allies for more supplies. The Italian Prime Minister pointed out that the actual food ration ranged "from 500 to 540 calories per person, compared to the 3000–3200 necessary for the average person for light work, and 4000–5000 necessary for heavy work." Stating that all food reserves "have been exhausted for some time," Badoglio said that the population was totally dependent on what the Allies were importing." [45] But the importation of more food was ruled out: the CCS warned the ACC that "the greatest possible effort should be directed towards agricultural rehabilitation [of Italy], the purpose being to hold the demand for foodstuffs made upon U.S. and U.K. to the absolute minimum." [46]

Economic Conditions in the North

Economic conditions during 1943–45 in the North when it was occupied by the Germans and ruled by Mussolini's government were considerably better than in the South during the same period. This was partly due to the more enlightened policies of the Ger-

44. Harris, *Administration of Italy, 1943–1945*, p. 91. The FEA Mission concluded that the fixing of maximum prices was "next to impossible." Stevenson, "Report of the FEA Survey Mission to Italy," p. 30.

45. Badoglio to Mason-MacFarlane, March 24, 1944, Coles and Weinberg, *Soldiers Become Governors*, p. 358. Mason-MacFarlane, in his reply, suggested to rely on "supplementary food such as vegetables and nuts which are very high in calorific property." He blamed food shortages on the Italian producers' failure to deliver the required quotas to food collection points and maintained it would be difficult to persuade the Allied governments to "help a population which in this respect had failed collectively to help itself." *Ibid.*, p. 359.

46. Hilldring to Holmes, March 21, 1944, Coles and Weinberg, *Soldiers Become Governors*, p. 358.

mans and partly the result of factors beyond Allied control, such as the greater agricultural and industrial potential of the North vis-à-vis the South. A major difference, of course, was that the Germans controlled the rich Po Valley with its agricultural resources and developed transportation facilities. This made possible the relatively efficient movement of supplies. The Anglo-American forces fighting their way across the narrow peninsula, through areas which had always depended on supplies from outside, were denied this advantage.

On the other hand, the North was continuously and heavily bombed by the Allies. The Germans, abandoning their earlier inhibitions, lived increasingly off the land. During the 19½ months of their occupation, they exacted 184 billion lire in various occupation costs, including goods and services as well as cash for military expenditures. Mussolini's regime spent another 170 billion, of which only 50 billion was drawn from taxation; the rest was supplied by the printing press.[47] Public resentment against foreign occupation was strong and partisan resistance was increasingly active. Yet it was noted that the large occupation levy did not create surprise or excitement among the people; the Germans were expected, after all, to behave like enemies. In addition, they relied on indirect rule. The existing administrative machinery of the fascist regime cushioned the effects of the occupation, diverting some of the public indignation from the Germans to the fascists. On the whole, life continued to go on as usual almost until the end of the hostilities. The cost of living rose very slowly: by April, 1944, the index reached about 850 (1938 = 100) in Milan, as against 4,000 in the South, food conditions remained tolerable, and ration cards continued to be honored.

Deficit government financing was inevitable. The printing press of the Bank of Italy turned out great quantities of paper currency. Between August, 1943, and April, 1945, the note issue increased by 159 billion lire, doubling the amount which was in circulation at the time of the Allied invasion. Public confidence in money—of the familiar Italian design—was not, however, undermined; savings in banks, as well as the hoarding of notes by the peasants, continued at such a high rate that there were not enough notes in active circulation and commercial banks began issuing bearer

47. Baffi, *Banca Nazionale del Lavoro Quarterly Review*, No. 47, pp. 407–8.

checks in fixed denominations which were accepted at par with money.[48] The shortage of currency was so acute that the Bank of Italy could not pay the Germans the balance of about 13 billion lire which still stood on the books at the time of the German surrender. As a result, in March and April, 1944, the German troops received only a part of their pay.

The situation in the North helps to illustrate that inflation in occupied areas could be kept in check if there were adequate food supplies, rigidly enforced controls over wages and prices, and a stable administration capable of maintaining law and order. Monetary inflation, by itself, was not a decisive factor so long as the issue of currency remained within bounds and, particularly, so long as public confidence in money was retained. As they did elsewhere, the Germans in Italy, even on the eve of their surrender, did not allow monetary inflation to get out of hand; the lira's purchasing power diminished only slightly.

Procurement Policy

Following the practice they had developed elsewhere, the Germans relied on Italian authorities for supplying their troops, avoiding direct requisitions as much as possible. This technique paid off. It put limits on arbitrary seizure, and it offered some protection to civilians. In a sense, it eliminated most features of the specific economics of occupation such as developed in the South.

The Allied armies, particularly the Americans, were lavishly supplied from home and did not depend on Italian resources for most of their needs. Nevertheless, the troops took advantage of the meager supplies which the economy could still produce. The effect was a further reduction in the amount of food available to starving civilians, and a corresponding increase in free market prices. This effect was not offset by Allied deliveries of foodstuffs (mostly wheat), which began only in 1944, in line with the CCS directive of June, 1943, instructing maintenance of subsistence levels in occupied areas.

AMG officials soon became aware of the problem, but they had no control over the army units. About all the AMG could do was

48. *Ibid.*, p. 415. The total amount of various bearer checks in Italy by the end of 1945 was 61 billion lire, UNRRA, Italian Mission, *Survey of Italy's Economy* (Rome, 1947), p. 11. Hereinafter referred to as UNRRA.

to place Italian restaurants off limits to military personnel and appeal to military commanders to avoid local procurement of foodstuffs. These appeals were rarely heeded; military units continued to draw food from the market. Full statistics are not available but conservative estimates are that by August, 1944, the Allied armies had purchased approximately 150,000 tons of food, not counting 110,000 sheep and an uncounted number of eggs.[49] This practice continued unabated until the end of the occupation.

The procurement was conducted in three ways. Some food was requisitioned outright, some was bought on the black market, and the rest was purchased at what was supposed to be fixed prices in a presumably orderly manner. The question arose as to who should pay for it. The first directive, issued by Allied headquarters in December, 1943, was based on the assumption that Allied requisitions would be promptly paid for by the Italian government. The latter, however, had no efficient system for dealing with these matters, and in any case was in no hurry to take responsibility for such an unpopular function: fixed prices were considerably below those of the black market. As a result, Allied procurement officers, unfamiliar with local prices and conditions in general and reluctant to alienate the population, ended up paying for supplies and services with considerable lavishness. Since this practice led to further increases of price levels, subsequent orders prohibited cash payments for public property, communications, transportation, utilities, port works, plants and equipment, real estate and buildings, and for private movable property unless its requisition without payment "would cause hardship to an individual owner."[50] In many cases such nuances were disregarded and the payments were made.

The consequences of Allied procurement practices in the economic field were not nearly as grave as they were in the area of Italian-Allied relations. Because the Italians considered the Allies rich and because many illusions were raised by Italy's "new status," Allied requisitions and seizures created more resentment than did the German practices in Western and Northern Europe earlier in the war. There—as in the North of Italy—the cooperative and relatively efficient quisling governments paid promptly,

49. Benson and Neufeld, *American Experiences*, p. 145.
50. Southard, *The Finances of European Liberation*, pp. 164–66.

in reasonable prices, for the deliveries and services required by the Germans; in many cases they also served as a kind of lightning rod, bringing upon themselves public wrath whenever political or economic conditions deteriorated.

The Allies in Italy denied themselves the benefit of having such a quisling government. They ruled the country directly, without really governing it. Worse still, they kept the King's government, which neither ruled nor governed and which loudly and constantly disclaimed any responsibility for the chaotic situation in Italy.

Black Market

One of the major problems which plagued Italy during the occupation was a flourishing black market in which hundreds of thousands, if not millions, of Italians, actively participated. The black market was a manifestation of a breakdown in the orderly distribution to civilians of the limited supplies available. Once this breakdown occurred, the only effective way to combat the black market would have been a substantial increase of food supplies at fixed prices. This food could come only from abroad, mostly from America. It has been claimed since that such an undertaking would have been impossible in view of the shipping crisis of 1944–45. In actual fact, however, neither the United States nor Great Britain considered burdening itself with the task of feeding " fascists " beyond what was viewed as an absolute minimum required to prevent starvation.

During the first winter of the occupation, the daily bread ration was 5 oz. per person. Later it increased to 7 oz., and only in the spring of 1945, at the end of the war, was it raised to 10 oz. In addition, some vegetables could be obtained in season at occasionally reasonable prices. But for everything else the people depended on the black market, where " the acute and indeed, desperate shortage of vital commodities led buyers to bid to the limit against each other. Paper currency inflation enormously increased effective demand. Each producer, or stock of commodities, became for a while a monopolist." [51]

This great demand was exploited by local producers who diverted the commodities which would have normally been dis-

51. Foa, *Monetary Reconstruction of Italy*, p. 19.

tributed through the ration system to the black market. But the principal beneficiaries of this demand were the Allied troops, especially the Americans, the best supplied fighting force in the world. While no shipping could be spared for sending food to the Italians, the Army received more than it could consume. Before long, the markets in occupied Italy were filled with American merchandise; canned food, wheat, sugar, cigarettes, uniforms and underwear, razor blades, and army blankets were seen everywhere. The prices determined by supply and demand were very high and the profits of " wholesalers " distributing American goods, and of the Americans who sold them, were enormous. There were no restraints. The Army viewed the GI's participation in the black market with equanimity. The troops' " profits " enabled them to buy anything they wanted on the market and to save the rest by purchasing postal money orders and United States Savings Bonds at Army Post Exchanges with their AM lire. This explains why the American forces drew only a relatively small part of their pay for local expenditures. A few figures help illustrate the point. Before the black market developed—between the landing and April, 1944—the United States forces spent locally 44 per cent of what they drew in cash. By contrast, in the last quarter of 1944, they spent only 17.6 per cent.[52] Although the statistics for the next two years are not available, there is no reason to suppose that the troops' propensity for " saving " their pay decreased.

The temptation to get rich was great. Theft of army property was common. The early shipments of foodstuffs brought to the port of Naples were delivered by the American truck drivers directly to black marketeers and never reached the starving communities for which they were designated.[53] Jobs in army and UNRRA warehouses, in mess halls, and in the ports where the incoming ships unloaded were highly valued, not only by Italian laborers but also by a good many Americans. Bags of flour and sugar, cans of bacon and coffee, boxes of cigarettes, tires and many other items streamed through illicit channels to the black market,

52. Southard, *The Finances of European Liberation*, p. 169; Rundell, *Black Market Money*, pp. 11–12. The British troops, who had less to sell and whose pay was smaller, spent 69 per cent of their cash drawings during the last quarter of 1944. The figures for the Australians, Brazilians, and others were still higher.

53. Benson and Neufeld, *American Experiences*, pp. 136–37. One qualified source estimated that in 1943–45 up to sixty per cent of the total tonnage unloaded in Naples was stolen and sold on the black market.

further aggravating the already serious logistic problems of the Allies. It has been established, for instance, that the rate of loss in army trucks around Naples in 1944 was much higher than that near the front lines. And it was rumored that in January of that year a 10,000 ton liberty ship, loaded with wheat flour, vanished without a trace from the port of Bari.

While the war continued, army regulations made transmission of funds from Italy to the United States difficult. After V-E Day these restrictions were lifted and operators started transferring their profits home in large amounts. Because army finance offices were less cooperative and on occasion resorted to arbitrary seizure of illegally acquired money (and even arrests), army post offices for a while became favorite places for currency transfers. In many instances, for a sizable commission, American officers and soldiers purchased dollar money orders for Italian black market dealers who would then send them to their agents in the United States, often using the facilities of the Bank of Vatican City, which, because of its special status in occupied Italy, had unique advantages.[54]

In an effort to stop transactions in dollars, the AMG declared them illegal, but as more and more nouveaux riches appeared in Italy, the demand for dollars rose steadily and a lively smuggling traffic developed. Dollar notes came in mostly by mail, hidden in letters and parcels addressed to American military and civilian officials, and to some enterprising refugees in UNRRA camps. In spite of the growing supply, the price of the dollar rise from 104 lire in August, 1943, to 390 lire by the end of 1945, and to 635 lire by the end of 1946.[55]

The availability to the more prosperous Italians of the Post Exchanges' and other supplies sold by Americans had a mildly anti-

54. Rundell, *Black Market Money*, p. 55.

55. Pietranera, *Banca Nazionale del Lavoro Quarterly Review*, Vol. 1, p. 21. It was observed by some American officials that until the end of the war, the chief American trading on the black market was in commodities. After the shooting stopped, it began to shift to dollars, jewelry, and gold, especially after certain restrictions on the redemption of lire into dollars at the official rate of exchange were introduced by the United States Army in 1946. The trade in gold was carried out mainly by United States Air Force and RAF personnel who smuggled gold coins from such places as Cairo and Tangier. Dollar paper currency arrived in Italy mostly by American Express offices. The Soviets also benefited from the black market in Italy: gold in bullion and coin was brought in in diplomatic pouches and sold through trusted local traders.

inflationary effect on the Italian economy. But since the quantities were not large enough to make a significant difference, this effect was more than offset by troop spending, and by the disorganizing influence of the black market. From the Italian point of view, it would have made much more sense to enforce economic controls and to channel that part of the army supplies which ended up in the black market into the organized distribution to the civilian population. This, however, was contrary to the Allied, and particularly American, policy.

Allied Military Lire

The experience with occupation currency in Italy was, on balance, rather unfortunate. Its issue placed a heavy economic burden on Italy, brought limited financial benefits to Great Britain and none to the United States, and seems to have created many more problems than it solved. In retrospect, perhaps the main defect of "the first truly Allied venture into the field of military monetary expedients," as the U.S. Treasury Department's press release put it, was precisely the fact that it was an *Allied* venture: no single sovereign government felt responsible for the performance of the AM lire. To begin with, there was little concern for the appearance of the notes or the quality of paper on which they were printed. In the haste with which the notes were manufactured some incredible "slips" occurred. The first series of the AM lire did not even bear denomination in words (as well as in figures). As a result, many such notes were increased by adding an "0" to the 50 and 100 lire note. Later, "plant" counterfeiting began and complete 1,000 lire notes were forged.[56]

In time, counterfeiting developed into a major industry in occupied Italy. In all large cities counterfeit business operators were selling AM lire notes by the pound almost openly. The price depended on the quality of the merchandise but usually the discount from the face value was no more than 50 per cent. It was

56. Andrew M. Kamarck, "Allied Financial Policy in Italy" (unpublished MS., Harvard University Library), p. 27. One AMG official told me in March, 1962, that upon the landings in Salerno in September, 1943, the Allies seized two full truckloads of fake AM currency of the kind they had introduced in Sicily only two months earlier. The flood of counterfeit notes was so great that a new series (1943A), harder to alter and reproduce, was introduced in 1944, and the old notes were called in.

almost legitimate business and few counterfeiters were caught and punished.[57]

Whether or not the Italians were aware of the abundance of forged notes, they definitely tried to get rid of AM lire quickly, not hesitating to pay premium prices for goods they could not normally afford to buy; savings went entirely out of fashion. This was particularly noticeable in the early period of occupation and had the effect of increasing the rate at which currency changed hands. One reason for this phenomenon was doubtless the very poor quality and primitive design of AM lire. Another was that unlike the German *Reichskreditkassenscheine* (which were favored throughout nazi-occupied Europe and had a high hoarding value), AM lire were not a victor's currency. It was not clear who was going to be responsible for it. The King's government never went beyond the September 23, 1943, decree which declared as legal tender "the paper currency issued by the Allies," and to many Italians it remained "a distinctive occupation currency which involved the stigma of a subject status." [58]

The economic effects of the Allied attitudes toward cheap occupation currency were significant because of the tremendous purchasing power of the combined military-occupation establishment. Although troop spending directly affected a relatively narrow sector, its secondary effects were felt everywhere, hopelessly ruining whatever was left of the natural balance of the economic factors. Since the Americans had no incentive to exercise frugality the situation could have been remedied only if the soldiers were restricted in their expenditures. But the United States army (unlike the British and Canadian) rejected this course. It felt that the

57. Colonel Philip J. Corso, former chief of the American counterintelligence operations in Rome, told me that in 1944–47 in that city alone three AM lire printing plants were seized. One of these plants was operated by two Italians, former POW's in the Soviet Union, where they had been trained as printers. Upon return to Italy they found employment at Istituto Poligrafico in Rome, whose printing plant they used for forging not only AM lire notes but also those of the Banca d'Italia. The investigation established that they had been receiving the paper they needed through Tito's Yugoslavia. The operation was carried out on such a large scale that the Banco d'Italia called in the whole issue duplicated by the counterfeiters. To Corso's knowledge, the Americans who were involved in forgeries of this type (mostly in the passing of notes) were never court-martialed, although their names were reported to the FBI as income tax evaders. However, no cases were prosecuted. See also Kemmerer and Beattie, *Allied Military Currency in Italy*, p. 6.

58. Foa, *Monetary Reconstruction of Italy*, p. 16.

temporary freezing of part of the soldiers' pay would have impaired morale, and would possibly result in congressional investigations. Such restrictions, however, could have had effect only very early in the occupation. Before long, as it was shown, the soldiers had much more cash in their pockets than they received as pay from their paymasters.[59]

Loose spending was not limited to individual soldiers. Military commanders and AMG officials were equally lacking in thriftiness. In part, of course, this was a consequence of a general wartime easy attitude toward money. In part, however, this attitude resulted from the special nature of occupation currency. The Allied accounting system was simplified as much as possible to reduce the burden of finance officers. Expenditures in cash for local Italian needs were recorded only pro forma. The British, French, Brazilian, and other forces received lump sums for which they never accounted. The accountancy in the American finance offices was also simple, but the amounts of AM lire issued to the United States forces were promptly reported to the War or Navy Departments in Washington, whereupon their appropriations were charged and the Treasury credited with a special AM lire suspense account.

This account was instituted "just in case," in view of the possibility that the occupation currency might after all become a charge against the United States.[60] In theory, AM currency issued to the troops had to be regarded as regularly appropriated funds. In practice it commanded none of the respect of the "home" currencies of the occupying powers; any qualified Allied paymaster could draw bulk amounts of lire in sealed boxes from any Allied financial agency or agent on a simple receipt, with the British army paymasters ordinarily taking care also of dominions' forces, the

59. The introduction, in January, 1946, of the rate of exchange of 1 to 225 made it less profitable for the Americans to remit their black market profits home than before. Nevertheless, since the open market rate was then 1 to 382, profits continued on a fairly high level. And in the fall of that year the rate of exchange reached 1 to 1,000.

60. Because of the King's government's insistence that the status of "co-belligerency" changed Italy's position, the Treasury had to keep this account until the final settlement. Similar suspense accounts were instituted for all "liberated" countries where American troops obtained local currency from Allied governments. It was out of these accounts that these governments eventually paid the reimbursements for "net" troop pay due to them according to the "reciprocal aid" agreements they had with the United States. See *Secretary of the Treasury Annual Report: 1944–1945*, pp. 393–94.

Polish Corps, and the Greek Brigade.[61] Unlike the Americans, the British regarded the amounts of AM lire received as a net cash income; they considered it most unlikely that they would ever reimburse the Italian government for the lire spent by them in Italy.

Many officers professed genuine preoccupation with the threat of inflation, yet attempted to place no restrictions on troop spending. Moreover, the attitude toward AM currency as cheap money visibly induced the Allied command to be more generous with pay, bonuses, and allowances to the troops and to the locally employed auxiliary personnel.

No figures are available for the amounts of occupation currency, vis-à-vis indigenous currency, which circulated in the areas occupied by the Allies prior to the " liberation " of the North in the spring of 1945. Since most of the increase in Italian lire took place in the North, it is impossible to establish with accuracy the actual Allied contribution to the inflation in the South.[62] The picture for the country as a whole was as follows: [63]

CURRENCY IN CIRCULATION

(in millions of lire)

Date	*Italian Lire*	*AM Lire*	*Total* [a]	*% AM Lire*
8/31/43	113,615	2,065	115,680	1.78
12/31/43	156,632	17,855	174,487	10.23
12/31/44	248,644	63,841	312,485	20.46
12/31/45	296,021	86,028 [b]	382,042 [c]	22.51

[a] To these totals must be added the amounts of bearer checks which circulated alongside the lira. At the end of 1943, the amount was 16,597 million; 1944, 45,666 million; and at the end of 1945, 61,434 million lire. UNRRA, p. 11.

[b] 16,821 million lire more were in the safes of the Bank of Italy at the end of 1945 when the Allies discontinued issuing AM lire. Some of these notes were put into circulation after that date. The last AM lire were withdrawn from circulation in 1950. Corbino, *Ten Years of the Italian Economy: 1947–1956*, p. 214.

[c] It is interesting to note that the amount of currency in circulation at the end of 1945 deflated by the price index was only 40 per cent of that at the end of 1943—another illustration of the decline in the purchasing power of the lira, of the increased velocity of circulation, and the general flight from the currency.

61. Southard, *The Finances of European Liberation*, pp. 24–25.

62. Corbino, *Ten Years of Italian Economy: 1947–1956*, p. 207, estimates that at the end of 1943, AM lire constituted 35 per cent of the total amount of currency in circulation in the South.

63. Pietranera, *Banca Nazionale del Lavoro Quarterly Review*, Vol. 1, p. 25. *UNRRA*, p. 3, gives slightly different figures.

The question of responsibility for the issue of AM lire remained unsettled for a long time. The U.S. Treasury Department kept insisting that Article 23 of the " long terms " armistice obligated Italy to " withdraw and redeem in Italian currency " at the request of the Allies " all holdings in Italian territory of currencies issued by [them] during military operations or occupation " and " hand over the currencies withdrawn free of cost to the United Nations [i.e., the Allies]." The Italian government, however, with the full and enthusiastic support of public opinion, kept reiterating that the terms of the armistic became obsolete after Italy declared war on Germany and that the Allies should pay their own way.

The persistence displayed by the successive Italian cabinets on the question as to who should bear responsibility for AM lire illustrates the great symbolic significance which nations attach to the right to issue currency. The Italian government objected not so much to the fact that Italy's economy was made to support the Allied armies—this was common practice in all " liberated " countries of Europe—as to the way it was done: to the issue of the Italian currency by foreign powers and to the utilization of this currency as a means of transferring Allied occupation costs to Italy. The amounts involved were not questioned, and these, at any rate, were soon dwarfed by the large and growing American aid to Italy.

A New Deal for Italy

The reversal of the United States' official attitude toward Italy had taken place in the fall of 1944. It was prompted by development which had little to do with the conditions in the country or a desire to make up for the " injustices " done to a nation which had joined the Allied cause. The credit for this reversal belongs entirely to President Roosevelt, who was then running for his fourth term in office and became alarmed at the prospect of losing the Italian vote and the election. Most Americans of Italian descent came from Southern Italy; many had relatives in the mother country. As communications improved, vivid stories of misery and poverty under the Allied rule began to pour into the United States. Sympathy toward Italy—and criticism of the Administration—spread, affecting not only the Italian but also the much larger Roman Catholic electorate. The Republicans, as well as many influential Democrats, vigorously demanded that the policy toward Italy be changed, and that the Italian people be given immediate aid.

Following the Second Quebec Conference, Roosevelt and Churchill announced, on September 26, 1944, that the Italian government would be given an increasing measure of control over internal affairs and would be invited to appoint direct representatives to Washington and London. Although in private Churchill strongly objected to this modification in the Allied policy, the same Hyde Park declaration—which was immediately hailed as " the New Deal for Italy "—promised that the Italians would receive more food (from the Army and through UNRRA),[64] more tranpsort, and assistance with industrial rehabilitation.

On October 4 Roosevelt made his promises to send civilian supplies to Italy more specific, and on October 10 he issued a detailed statement about new financial arrangements for Italy. Roosevelt declared that the Italian government would receive (*a*) " the dollar equivalent to the Italian lire issued up to now and hereafter as pay to United States troops in Italy "; (*b*) " the dollar proceeds of remittances made by individuals in the United States to friends and relatives in Italy "; and (*c*) " the dollar proceeds of any products exported by Italy to the United States." This money, said Roosevelt, would enable Italy to finance the procurement of supplies in the United States.[65]

64. The Army was always anxious to get UNRRA into Italy to take over the task of supplying the civilians, and at one point an agreement was reached for UNRRA's takeover of these functions in October, 1944. But because of the resistance of the more outspokenly antifascist Washington officials, meaningful UNRRA aid did not start arriving in Italy until 1946. See Coles and Weinberg, *Soldiers Become Governors*, pp. 345, 643. See also *United States and Italy: 1932–1946*, Department of State Publication No. 2669 (Washington: U.S. Government Printing Office, 1946), pp. 121–25.

65. *United States and Italy*, pp. 91ff. See also Kogan, *Italy and the Allies*, pp. 80–86; Sherwood, *Roosevelt and Hopkins*, pp. 820ff.; Hull, *Memoirs*, pp. 1566–67. Up to that time the Italian government, contrary to international practice, had received no dollar credit for private money transfers to the Italians from America. Instead, the Italian government's occupation costs account had been credited in lire. The so-called " products exported by Italy to the United States " were goods (mostly raw materials) shipped to America under the auspices of the Economic Section of the Allied Control Commission. These were not exports in the normal sense of the word, but rather a form of spoliation, especially since the expenses involved in these exports were apparently charged against the occupation costs' account. The export policy was modified in February, 1945, but even then the Allies reserved the right of fixing the prices for exported goods. See Coles and Weinberg, *Soldiers Become Governors*, p. 517.

In a further step, on October 12, Roosevelt removed the status of "enemy alien" from Italians, and on October 26 the State Department announced the resumption of diplomatic relations with Italy. Finally, on the eve of the elections, the State Department released Assistant Secretary Acheson's letter to the Mazzini Society in which all past and present American aid to Italy was rather immodestly listed, and all Roosevelt's intentions to improve matters further were recapitulated. Simultaneosly, the news was leaked to the press that Roosevelt had ordered Allied army headquarters in Italy to provide the Italians with a bread ration of 10 oz. a day per person.[66]

By these decisions the United States extended to Italy the policy which hitherto had been adopted toward "liberated" countries of Europe. The British objected to this change of policy on the grounds that Italy would be treated even better than the countries which had been victims of Italian aggression.[67] They pointed out, for instance, that the French government of de Gaulle was still waiting to be recognized by Washington. Roosevelt disregarded Churchill's protests: the elections were too important.

In practice, the promise to reimburse in dollars the pay to American troops brought the Italian government less than it had expected, because only the "net" troop pay (that is, less soldiers' savings, remittances home, and money spent in Army Post Exchanges) was actually reimbursed.[68] Italy eventually received up

66. This order was contained in Roosevelt's letter to Stimson of October 31, 1944, and was published in full in *Il Progresso Italo-Americano* (New York) on November 19, 1944. Its contents had been publicized earlier in *The Stars and Stripes in Italy*, and in Italian newspapers.

67. Churchill wrote to Roosevelt, on November 11, 1944: ". . . you have jumped a good many fences in your directive [to Stimson] about the Italian ration of grain. . . . I hope your people will consider that it will be difficult to give more to our ex-enemies in Italy than to our Greek and Yugoslavian Allies." Coles and Weinberg, *Soldiers Become Governors*, p. 501.

68. Until 1947 the promise to reimburse Italy for the amount of lire spent in the country by the American troops remained strictly a unilateral obligation of the United States, and $100 million in credits were advanced to the Italian government on Roosevelt's orders. Hull, *Memoirs*, p. 1567. In August, 1947, a memorandum of understanding between the two governments was signed which merely stated that the United States waived claims arising out of "dollars transferred or to be transferred to Italy, equivalent to the net lira expenditures of the United States Armed Forces in Italy." In September, 1947, another agreement was signed respecting the rights and privileges of United States forces in Italy and the transfer of responsibility from the AMG to the Italian government. It provided for the retention of most of the privileges that Americans enjoyed under the occupation

to $160 million in credit from this account, instead of the over $300 million it expected to receive; the payments for Italian "exports" during the occupation brought $360 million more.[69]

While the United States could unilaterally decide to give Italy dollar credits, other decisions—including shipments of foodstuffs—required British consent and a formal CCS directive. This procedure was brought to the attention of CCS by General Wilson, SACMED: "Joint statement on Italy by the President and the Prime Minister issued to the press on 26 September, which has been given wide publicity in Italy, has naturally occasioned many inquiries from Allied as well as Italian sources. In the absence of directives from you as to the time and manner of implementation of the policies laid down, I am instructing the Chief Commissioner that specific action is to be withheld." [70] Wilson demanded instructions on how to handle the political matters raised by Roosevelt and Churchill, and asked for "an opportunity to comment" on a possible reorientation of the functions of the Allied Control Commission. This request was granted, and in December, 1944, Harold Macmillan, then acting president of the ACC, presented a detailed memorandum on the possible modification of the Allied policy in Italy.[71] Discussions at the CCS followed. The British representatives took a harder line, while the Americans favored a rapid liberalization of policy and an immediate conclusion of a Preliminary Treaty of Peace with Italy.[72] The new CCS directive,

regime, except that from then on the Italian government was to be paid a flat sum of $250,000 a year for services furnished to the troops. *U.S. Statutes at Large*, Vol. 61, Part 4, pp. 3661–66.

69. Harris, *Administration of Italy, 1943–1945*, p. 244. An Italian source gives a smaller figure—$339 million *in toto*. See *The Development of Italy's Economic System* (Rome: Italian Government, 1952), p. 89. Kamarck, "Allied Financial Policy in Italy," p. 34, sets the figure at $310 million. This interpretation as to what part of troop pay was subject to reimbursement by the United States resulted in bitter disappointments to all the governments of the European countries in which American troops were stationed at one time or another.

70. Coles and Weinberg, *Soldiers Become Governors*, p. 507.

71. *Ibid.*, pp. 508–13.

72. The British government resented "the New Deal for Italy," feeling it could not afford to imitate American generosity. Nevertheless, it was compelled to bear a small share in the program of relief by agreeing to give the Italian government sterling credit for its share in Italian "exports." The British resentment was shared by all other Allied governments which had their troops in Italy; they refused to pay anything. In the spring of 1947 Great Britain consented to reimburse Italy for the AM lire spent in the country after June 1, 1946, by the British troops whose numbers by then had been greatly reduced. At the same time, London

issued on January 30, 1945, presented a compromise in its political and administrative sections, and a virtual British victory in its economic sections.

Italy did not obtain a status of equality until the peace treaty was signed. No industrial rehabilitation was undertaken until after the war. The distribution of supplies by UNRRA did not even start until the spring of 1945. The deliveries of wheat to Italy actually suffered a setback because of the lack of shipping.[73] But in the 1944 elections, the Catholic vote in the United States went heavily for Roosevelt.

The reaction in Italy to Roosevelt's generous gesture was mixed. Although the editorials were overwhelmingly enthusiastic, the public remained skeptical. When the promised food deliveries failed to materialize, anti-American demonstrations—not all of them by the left—occurred in many cities and towns.[74] Nor was the Italian government greatly moved by the visible change in American attitudes. On January 9, 1945, it demanded, as a matter of right as well as of economic necessity, *complete* reimbursement in dollars and pounds sterling for *all* lire spent by or in behalf of the Allied forces. This was much more than the American and the British governments were granting to their Allies. The request was rejected.

The next important development took place shortly before the first postwar elections in Italy, the outcome of which was of considerable interest to the United States. By the agreement which was concluded in January, 1946, Italy was finally permitted to resume private and direct trade with foreign countries. In order to deflate prices and improve Italy's export position, the Allies

presented counterclaims, and as a result Italy ended up by paying Great Britain £8 million. Kogan, *Italy and the Allies*, pp. 119–20. Although Great Britain waived reparations in the peace settlement, British animosity toward Italy remained deep and lasting. Great Britain took the lead in stripping Italy of its colonies and backed higher demands for reparations from the ex-enemy by other countries. As late as the summer of 1947 the Attlee government insisted that Italy be excluded from the European Recovery Program.

73. *Ibid.*, pp. 86–88, 113–14. The question whether shipping was actually available cannot be answered with a certainty. Its availability was questioned by the military and used as an excuse by the politicians throughout the winter of 1944–45. But the U.S. Quartermaster General seems to have established that there were enough ships to secure 10 oz. bread rations after all. See Coles and Weinberg, *Soldiers Become Governors*, p. 495.

74. *Ibid.*, pp. 524ff.

stopped issuing AM lire and credited Italy (the United States immediately, and Great Britain under reserve of settlement) with all further cost of troop maintenance. In turn, the Italian government pledged to supply the currency requirements of the Allied troops—without prejudicing the ultimate settlement. The agreement also provided for the devaluation of the lira: the rate of exchange of 225 lire to $1.00 was established for private commercial transactions, for receipts and payments under previous clearing arrangements, and for remittances from abroad. The same rate applied to the payments made to the Allied troops, and to the Italian and foreign diplomatic and consular expenditures.[75]

All these measures stimulated Italy's exports, but they also led to another round of inflation, which, in spite of the official denials, was intensified by new rumors of the forthcoming currency reform; the price of the dollar on the open market increased from 281 lire in April to 1,000 lire in October, 1946.

The question of occupation currency flared up for the last time during the Paris Peace Conference, where the terms of peace treaties with former enemy countries were established. Resisting the Allies' reparations claims and hoping that they would give credit for the occupation costs, Italy presented counterclaims. It estimated its contribution in the war against Germany at $5.5 billion and the damages suffered by the country after the Allied invasion at over $13 billion.[76] And, as before, Italy insisted that the Allies assume responsibility for the AM lire.

In this stand, the Italian government was vigorously supported by all Italian political parties, from the communists to the monarchists. But the counterclaims were disregarded by the Allies (as were most of the other Italian remands), and Article 76, paragraph 4, of the treaty stated that "the Italian government shall resume full responsibility for all Allied military currency issued in Italy by the Allied military authorities."[77]

The Allied occupation of Italy lasted longer than anybody had expected, at least partly because the bureaucracy of the occupation establishment developed a strong vested interest in the perpetuation of its rule and resisted everything which would reduce its

75. *UNRRA*, pp. 10–14.
76. Kogan, *Italy and the Allies*, p. 151.
77. Treaties and Other International Acts Series 1648, *Treaty of Peace with Italy* (Washington: U.S. Government Printing Office, 1947), p. 158.

prerogatives. Nevertheless, this rule had to end, and on January 11, 1947, the Combined Chiefs of Staff ordered the abolition of the Allied Control Commission as of January 31. Many considered this move misguided, and two army historians later said that it "could not have come at a more unfortunately premature time." Perhaps so. As they relate, "The bad economic situation, and perhaps even more the depressing prospects at the Paris Peace Conference, had influenced the November elections, which resulted in heavy gains by the extreme left and fascist right at the expense of the pro-Allied parties." They continue that "there was a real danger that the good will which the Allies had built for themselves in Italy for five years would now be substantially lost." [78]

A certain self-deception of the American military seems to be reflected in the latter point. The weakening of the "pro-Allied parties" in the November election was much more due to the fact that they were "pro-Allied" than to the bad economic situation at that particular moment, or to the yet unknown depressing prospects of the peace settlement. The Italians had had enough of the Allied rule; and even if the governing coalition in Rome had preferred to assume full responsibility for the affairs of the country under more cheerful circumstances, there is no proof that the continuation of Allied tutelage could have changed things. There is substantial evidence that the Italians' goodwill had been declining ever since the high point in the summer of 1943, when the country switched sides in the war. This process undoubtedly was affected by the bleak economic picture, for which the Italians tended to blame the Allies. But it needs to be remembered that much as Allied policies and practices aggravated inflation, they were not the prime cause of Italy's economic collapse.

The motivations of the Allies appear fairly clear in retrospect. At the beginning, they wished to benefit from the occupation, and to hurt the country economically, though Great Britain also had an over-all goal of reducing Italy permanently to a role of a small and weak country; in this, the British were moved—at least in part—by a spirit of vengeance. The United States did not share this goal. By the end of 1944, it began to modify its punitive policy. At first reluctantly, and later willingly, it assumed the burden of rehabilitating the war-ravaged country. The Ameri-

78. Coles and Weinberg, *Soldiers Become Governors*, p. 618.

can efforts in assisting the economic resurrection of Italy were enormous. Other Allies helped, but the initiative and the overwhelming share of this aid came from the United States, as is evident in the following list.[79]

a. Food and raw materials supplied by the Allied armed forces during the war—$490 million (U.S. share—$363 million);

b. Aid by the Federal Economic Administration—$144.1 million;

c. Aid by UNRRA—$589.4 million (U.S. share—$442.5 million);

d. American " Grant in Aid " program—$116.6 million;

e. American " Interim Aid " program—$176.1 million.

Total Allied aid to Italy—*before* the Marshall Plan had started—was $1,516,200,000 (U.S. share—$1,242,300,000).[80]

Aid to a former enemy on such a gigantic scale has had no precedents in human history. It helped to restore the economy and put its future development on a solid foundation. It also helped to erase bitter memories and to establish closer political bonds between Italy and her erstwhile enemies. But quite apart from the changes caused by the downfall of the fascist regime, the economic upheaval of 1943–47 left an indelible impression on the Italian social and political fabric.

The monetary inflation continued long after the end of the military government. By the end of the 1947 the amount of lire in circulation was close to 700 billion. Financial order was eventually restored through the efforts of the Italian government. Thanks to American aid, European cooperation, and Italy's own enterprise, the economy of the country was finally rehabilitated, and the Italian currency acquired a high degree of stability.

But Italy was a very different country. Not only fascism but many established traditional forces lost ground. The social groups which were the hardest hit in the inflation—the lower middle class, the workers, the intelligentsia—formed a vast pool of " protest " voters who gave their support to the left. The leftist vote continued to grow in later years, from 31.0 per cent in 1948 to 36.9

79. *The Development of Italy's Economic System*, pp. 79–81.

80. Under the Marshall Plan, Italy received an additional $1.65 billion. See *Statistical Abstract of the United States: 1963* (Washington: U.S. Government Printing Office, 1963), p. 865.

per cent in 1958 to almost 40.0 per cent in 1963. The Communist Party of Italy became the largest communist party outside the communist bloc.[81]

One cannot of course ascribe these developments solely to the postwar inflation, for many other factors helped determine the direction of Italian politics. One of them doubtless was the aid and encouragement which the Allies gave to the communist-dominated partisan movement in the North in the hope that this would help defeat the nazis. After the country was reunited, ex-partisans (and many who merely claimed to be ex-partisans) began to play a disproportionally large role in Italian politics, with the AMG helplessly watching the growth of lawlessness and public disorder. Yet the left would not have gained as much as it did had not the occupation caused so many resentments and had not the inflation caused such momentous economic and social dislocations. The relative decline of the normally conservative forces had thrown Italy into a state of perpetual flux which has accounted for subsequent internal instability and neutralist trends in Italy's foreign policies.

It appears undeniable that the introduction of the Allied military lire, coupled with monetary policies of occupation, contributed substantially to the great postwar inflation. The almost absolute power the Allies had over the currency issue and circulation was not used either for the benefit of the United States and Great Britain or for the benefit of the Italian people. It was simply misused. The only motive behind the monetary policy which was consistently manifest throughout the occupation appears to be that of assuring the troops the maximum buying power. Many finance officers in the field made great efforts to bring the monetary situation in order. However, because such efforts had to await a change in the political climate, their results came too late to be effective, and in any case they never amounted to a uniform and systematically pursued policy.

There is one more lesson to be drawn from the experiences of the Allied occupation in Italy. The idea behind the issue of AM

81. It has been the best organized and the best financial political force in Italy. The communits kept gold and " hard " currency caches worth perhaps over $100 million, which they seized at Dongo together with Mussolini who tried to escape to Switzerland.

lire was to protect the financial interests of the Allies by forcing the enemy to pay a part of the cost of his own defeat. But in this instance, Italy's losses were not necessarily the Allies' gains. Whatever "savings" were made by the United States and Great Britain were more than offset by the destructive consequences of inflation. Italy's contribution to the Allied war effort would have probably been much greater had it not been for the economic chaos which accompanied the occupation.

While the British might have saved some of their monetary resources by issuing AM lire, for the United States this "venture into the field of military monetary expedients" resulted in a net loss of impressive dimensions. What the Treasury planners overlooked was that, once defeated, Italy could not be held down indefinitely and that a different psychology was certain to begin determining American policies, especially when so many American voters happened to be of Italian descent. In the end, the United States was compelled to spend close to $3 billion to rescue Italy from the economic morass for which the shortsightedness of American policies must take a considerable portion of the blame.

CHAPTER V

THE CASE OF THE DUPLICATE PLATES

The transfer by the United States to the Soviet Union of a duplicate set of plates for printing Allied military mark currency had extremely significant economic repercussions for occupied Germany and the United States Treasury. It was also a unique act in the history of currency manufacturing: never before had any government voluntarily relinquished its sovereign control over the issue of currency. This act can only be understood if we acquaint ourselves with the reasoning and modes of operation of some of the personalities who played crucial roles in the development of the occupation finance policies. In exploring this episode we would also be able to take a closer look at the complexities of a policymaking process which involved cooperation among the wartime Allies. First, however, it is necessary to give a summary of the political atmosphere within which this essentially economic decision was made.

In the military occupation in North Africa, Italy, and the liberated countries of Western Europe, the United States acted in accord with Great Britain. There were disagreements—sometimes quite sharp—over matters of broad policy and military strategy. But almost until the end of the war Washington and London succeeded in composing their differences, mainly because they were linked in a political, as well as a military, alliance. There was a close and continuous personal relationship between Roosevelt and Churchill, and the joint conduct of the war was institutionalized in the Combined Chiefs of Staff establishment in Washington.

In the military occupation of Germany, the situation was much different. The Soviet Union joined the anti-Axis powers not by choice but because Hitler attacked Russia in June, 1941. The military alliance of the Big Three was formed, but because of the unbridgeable differences which separated Moscow from London and Washington, it never became a political alliance. Yet the intensity of the war and the emotions it generated were such that the emergence of widespread hopes for a perpetual Big Three unity was all but inevitable.

The United States began to furnish the Soviet Union with evidence of its goodwill long before its own active entry into the war by extending lend-lease aid, which eventually totaled some $11 billion. The first lend-lease agreement was negotiated in Moscow by the Beaverbrook-Harriman mission in September, 1941. Its terms were virtually dictated by Stalin and involved no quid pro quo, political or otherwise. Anxious to ensure that the flow of aid be unhindered by officials not sympathetic to the Soviets, Roosevelt appointed Harry Hopkins, his trusted aide, to supervise this program directly.[1]

In spite of generous, if not entirely unselfish, American (and British) aid, the Allied relations continued to be marred by Soviet suspicions and unreasonable political demands. These relations reached their lowest point in the fall of 1943. Undismayed, Roosevelt displayed great perseverance in his efforts to establish friendly relations with the Soviets. He consistently ignored the frequent difficulties; he made sure that only those officials who harbored no ill-will toward the Soviets be allowed to deal with Stalin and his representatives. And he passionately strove to meet Stalin in order to establish the kind of personal rapport which he felt was much more important than any formal arrangements.

Roosevelt finally did meet Stalin at Teheran in November–December, 1943, soon after the Foreign Ministers' Conference in Moscow, where the ice in Allied relationships seemed to have been broken for the first time. Teheran unquestionably was the highest point of the Big Three collaboration, and it was there that Roosevelt's " Great Design " took its final shape. Forrest Davis, who interviewed Roosevelt at length after Teheran, wrote that the " Great Design " rested on two sweeping assumptions: (1) that the Soviet Union would become a permanent great power with

1. General P. R. Faymonville, in charge of lend-lease at the Moscow end, communicated Soviet requests directly to Hopkins, by-passing the Ambassador and the State Department. Rated as decidedly " pro-Soviet," Faymonville could not bring himself to say " no " to any Soviet demand, even if the requested items had no relation to the war effort, and he had no way of checking " whether effective use was being made of the supplies we were sending at great sacrifice to ourselves." John R. Deane, *The Strange Alliance* (New York: Viking Press, 1947), p. 91.

worldwide interests to be reckoned with, and (2) that Soviet interests could be reconciled to those of the Atlantic powers, China, and the small nations of Europe and America.[2]

According to Davis, Roosevelt was "gambling for stakes as enormous as any statesman ever played for"; his policy was based on the premise that the Soviet Union needed peace and "was willing to pay for it by collaborating with the West." Roosevelt was "by no means unaware of the risks," continued Davis, but nevertheless he declined "to acknowledge them even to close associates. . . . The alternative—a Russia excluded, aggrieved and driven in on itself to prepare for the inevitable war of the continents—was to him so much worse that he saw himself with little choice."[3]

Some observers, at the time as well as later, trying to explain the spirit of Teheran, suggested that Churchill and Roosevelt were motivated by the fear that Stalin might conclude a separate peace treaty with Hitler, and by a desire to secure Soviet cooperation in the war against Japan. All the documents which have been published since the war indicate that such was not the case, and that the explanation of the Western leaders' desire to win Stalin's trust and friendship can be found solely in their conviction that this was the only way to secure postwar peace. Churchill, who had Europe and the British Empire to think about, embarked on this course with reservations. Roosevelt, much more detached whenever Europe's and, especially, British Empire's fortunes were involved, appeared to be willing to go all the way to meet Stalin's wishes.[4]

2. Forrest Davis, "What Really Happened in Teheran," *The Saturday Evening Post* (May 13, 1944), p. 37.

3. *Ibid.*, p. 37.

4. On the question of separate peace, see George F. Kennan, *Russia and the West under Lenin and Stalin* (Boston: Little, Brown, 1960), pp. 362–64. U.S. Department of State, *Foreign Relations of the United States, 1943* (Washington: U.S. Government Printing Office, 1963), I, 484–512. Hereinafter referred to as *1943 Papers.* Some rumors about the possibility of a separate peace undoubtedly originated with Soviet officials. See September 16 and 24 entries in the diary of Joseph E. Davies, Library of Congress, Washington, D.C. Hereinafter referred to as *Davies Papers.* On Stalin's determination to fight until victory, see Foreign Relations of the United States. *The Conferences at Cairo and Teheran: 1943* (Washington: U.S. Government Printing Office, 1961), pp. 513–14, 532, 600ff. Hereinafter referred to as *Teheran Papers.* On Stalin's desire to join in the war against Japan, see Hull, *Memoirs*, 1309–11; *Teheran Papers*, pp. 147, 489, 499. See also Robert E. Sherwood, *Roosevelt and Hopkins: An Intimate History* (New

Most of the President's closest advisers shared—and, indeed, helped develop—his views and supported his Russian policy. So did many important officials in various government agencies, particularly in the Treasury Department. The dissenters were mostly concentrated at nonpolicymaking levels in the State Department; they could also be found in the War Department. Having been more involved in day-to-day dealings with the Soviets, professional diplomats and soldiers seriously doubted whether the "Great Design" would work with the communists. Some of them were aware of the tremendous price which the United States and other Western nations would have to pay if the "Great Design" failed to materialize. None, however, dared to challenge the President's position; public criticism was limited for the most part to conservative periodicals and the hard-core Republican opposition.

The Teheran Conference was looked upon in the Allied capitals as an unqualified success. Although some skeptics were disturbed by the attitude of the President who thought "of winning Stalin's affections as the one and only way of winning the war and securing the peace,"[5] others believed that the Conference marked the high point of Roosevelt's career. According to Sherwood, the President came out of Teheran feeling sure that "Stalin was 'getatable,'" and that "when Russia could be convinced that her legitimate claims and requirements—such as the right of access to warm water ports—were to be given full recognition, she would prove tractable and cooperative in maintaining the peace of the postwar world."[6]

This conviction and the spirit it generated carried over into 1944 and helped to avert attention from the clouds which were gathering on the horizon. Few specific issues dealing with the postwar organization of Europe were resolved, or even extensively discussed, at Teheran. But in Washington and London (and perhaps even in Moscow), the feeling persisted that the spirit of

---

York: Harper, 1948), pp. 779–86. It is worth noting that Anglo-American military plans for the defeat of Japan "were not contingent on the active participation of the Soviet Union in the Pacific war," although this participation was taken for granted. See Herbert Feis, *Churchill, Roosevelt, Stalin: The War They Waged and the Peace They Sought* (Princeton: Princeton University Press, 1957), pp. 400–2.

5. Deane, *The Strange Alliance*, p. 43.

6. Sherwood, *Roosevelt and Hopkins*, pp. 798–99.

Allied unity would somehow translate itself into concrete decision, satisfying all those concerned on the basis of compromise and mutual give-and-take. Early in 1944, however, there seemed to be no need for the Western leaders to decide which Soviet claims were "legitimate" and which were not. Even an issue as important as the future of Germany did not appear to be pressing. Since it looked as if most of the critical decisions could be postponed, it was easy to be optimistic; the spirit of cooperation dominated the Washington scene.[7]

Nevertheless, there were technical questions which had to be dealt with at once. One such question was that of introducing military currency into Germany. There seemed to be plenty of time to work out and coordinate the financial policies of occupation, but there was an urgent need to have a sufficient amount of notes manufactured which would be put at the disposal of the Allied armies the moment they crossed Germany's borders. This looked like a relatively minor technical problem compared to the other preparations necessary for the major assault on "fortress Europe." But before long it developed unexpectedly into a problem of considerable proportions.

There was one similarity and two differences between the issue of the Allied military lire and the issue of the Allied military mark. The similarity was that in neither case was the issue of the currency the responsibility of a single sovereign government; both were strictly military currencies to be used by the victors for their convenience and benefit.

The first difference was with regard to the control over the printing of the currencies. In Italy the United States retained full control over the printing of the military currency. The Treasury Department knew at all times how much currency had been printed and how much of it had been issued to each of the allies or to the Italian government. As we have seen, the Allies with military forces in Italy could have on request any amount of AM lire, for which they were not required to account. There was, however, an agreement on the rates of exchange; and since there was a single Allied Military Government, all the Allies followed a uniform financial policy. The only important difference was the disparity in the pay of the troops of different nationalities.

7. On Roosevelt's tendency to postpone decisions, see Sumner Welles, *Seven Decisions that Shaped History* (New York: Harper, 1951), pp. 124–39.

In Germany the United States did not regain control of either the printing or the issue of the Allied military mark currency. Germany, unlike Italy, was divided into four separate zones of occupation, each governed by a major ally, with its own economic polices; and there was no agreement on the rates of exchange.

The second difference was more important. Although American and British attitudes toward occupied Italy were not the same, and although from time to time their policy preferences were in sharp conflict, nevertheless, in the end, these differences were usually ironed out, and, what was more significant, these differences had relatively little effect on the military government in Italy which was administered for the most part under a single set of instructions. In other words, this was truly a *joint* occupation.

No such arrangements existed, or were even envisaged, for the occupation of Germany. The differences in Allied objectives with regard to Germany were so great that any attempt to reconcile them was doomed. Even the United States and Great Britain failed to work out a common policy for Germany. The Soviet Union, which had waged what for all practical purposes had been a separate war against Germany, had never considered a joint occupation of that country; nor had it been approached by its Western Allies with any proposals to that effect. Nevertheless, the American and British officials who early in 1944 were responsible for planning the occupation of Germany were guided in their labors by a rather vague notion of Allied unity. They sincerely hoped that this unity, born of war, would continue in peace and make possible an agreed and lasting settlement in Europe.

Encouraged by what looked like a successful experiment with Allied military currency in Italy, Supreme Headquarters Allied Expeditionary Forces (SHAEF) requested that a certain quantity of the Allied military mark currency be printed for use in Germany. Since the British had undertaken the task of printing currency for "liberated" countries of Western Europe (except for France), the two Treasuries decided that the currency for Germany would be printed in the United States. By the middle of January, 1944, the Bureau of Engraving and Printing of the Treasury Department produced the designs for all denominations, with the inscriptions in German, and the plates from which the currency was to be printed. Time was short and the task was big. Therefore, the Treasury Department decided to use the same simple and inexpensive method of offset printing which had been used in the production of AM lire. Because the Bureau of Engraving and Printing was unequipped for printing such quantities of currency on short notice, it entered into a contract with the Forbes Company in Boston, an old reputable firm of banknote printers.

Production was slow to start. The difficulty was that in this case, for the first time during the war, the British and the Americans were to undertake a truly joint project with the Soviets. Their ability to collaborate—not merely to cooperate—was subjected to its first test. The plans for issuing common Allied currency for Germany were conveyed to Moscow as early as November, 1943, By then enough information on the experience with the Allied military lire in Italy had accumulated to convince American and British financial experts that the undertaking was a success and that for the occupation of Germany a similar currency should be introduced. The United States and British ambassadors submitted their Treasuries' proposals to the appropriate Soviet officials in Moscow, hoping that such a seemingly simple question would be resolved quickly. However, for awhile there was no reaction from the Soviet government. This caused a certain uneasiness in Washington because before the AM marks could be produced, it was important to find out whether the Soviet government was going to accept the very idea of common currency. If it did, all parties concerned would have to agree on the design of the notes and the approximate quantity to be produced. Another question was that of the mark-ruble exchange rate. It was felt that a connection between the domestic currencies of the occupying powers in their relation to the mark should be determined in advance.

The desirability of a common currency in Germany seemed unquestionable to many Western officials. If carried through, this plan would facilitate a common economic policy in occupied Germany; it was also in line with the strong desire of the United States government to harmonize the interests of the Allies in the postwar world. This feeling was shared by the British. On January 29, 1944, the United States ambassador in Moscow, W. Averell Harriman, cabled to Cordell Hull: "The British government feels it most desirable that all occupation forces use the same currency so far as possible. . . . Great importance is attached by the British government to the Russian government's participation in this arrangement." [8]

But the Soviet government was in no hurry. Before committing itself, it had to establish whether the proposed scheme would offer it a clear advantage. After several attempts to clarify the Soviet position regarding the AM marks, Cordell Hull cabled to Harriman: "We shall have to begin printing starting February 14 at the latest. . . . We are very desirous of ascertaining whether Soviet expects to use this kind of currency and if not, what type of currency they contemplate using." [9]

The reply came on February 15. Harriman reported the contents of a letter he had received the previous day from V. M. Molotov, Commissar for Foreign Affairs. In this letter Molotov expressed the readiness of the Soviet government to cooperate with the British and American governments in the issuance of military currency. The end of the letter, however, contained an unexpected request. Molotov suggested that part of the currency should be printed in the Soviet Union "in order that a constant supply would be guaranteed to the Red Army." Thus, the United States would have to furnish the Soviet government "with plates of all denominations, a list of serial numbers, and model of paper and colors for printing M-marks." [10] Molotov's suggestions were put in categorical terms, leaving no room for interpretation or misunderstanding.

Washington reacted slowly. James C. Dunn, Director of European Affairs of the State Department, forwarded Harriman's cable to Major General John H. Hilldring, Director of the Civil Affairs Division of the War Department, without comment, but suggested that Hilldring get in touch with the Treasury.[11] It was not before March 1 that the *Ad Hoc* Committee on Monetary and Fiscal Planning discussed the contents of the cable. During the

8. U.S. Congress, Senate, Harriman to Hull, January 29, 1944, *Hearings before the Committees on Appropriations, Armed Services and Banking and Currency*, 80th Congress, 1st Session, June 17–18, 1947, p. 147. Hereinafter referred to as *S-47*. The published volume with these hearings contains the texts of several hundred authentic documents which were submitted to the Senate by the War, State, and Treasury Departments. The citations in this chapter are from this collection.

9. Hull to Harriman, February 8, 1944, *S-47*, p. 147.

10. Harriman to Hull, February 15, 1944, *S-47*, p. 148.

11. Dunn to Hilldring, February 23, 1944, *S-47*, p. 149.

discussion, a Treasury representative, William H. Taylor, Assistant Director of the Division of Monetary Research, said that the Treasury had never before allowed the use of their plates by others. He also reported that the matter was already under consideration at the Treasury.[12] Since the Forbes Company was already producing the AM marks, the Treasury decided not to bother to clear with the Soviets the designs of the banknotes; the photostatic copies of the notes were sent to the Soviet Embassy only "for information." [13]

The controversial matter of furnishing the Soviets with the duplicate plates quickly reached the highest levels of the Treasury. On the morning of March 3, 1944, it was discussed by Under Secretary Daniel Bell and Director of the Bureau of Engraving and Printing, Alvin W. Hall. Hall could not believe his ears. To furnish another government with a set of duplicate plates? Out of the question. In the first place, no banknote manufacturer would ever agree to the duplication of printing; it would be against all the security rules which traditionally safeguard the production of currency. An unauthorized use of the plates might result in a national, or possibly international, scandal. "I do not believe that under any circumstances would the contractor agree to the manufacture of duplicate plates to be used by an agency outside his plant, and it is doubtful that the Treasury Department could force him to do so," insisted Hall. "To remove from the country complete designs in the form of plates would be extremely unwise." [14]

At the request of Under Secretary Bell, Hall put his objections

12. Minutes of the meeting, March 1, 1944, *S-47*, pp. 227–28.

13. White to Gromyko, February 9, 1944, *S-47*, pp. 173–74. The British were shown the designs and approved them immediately.

14. U.S. Congress, Senate, Exhibit No. 2. *The Hearing before the Subcommittee on Investigations on Government Operations Abroad of the Permanent Subcommittee on Investigations of the Committee on Government Operations*, 83d Congress, 1st Session, October 20–21, 1953, pp. 45–46. Hereinafter this source will be referred to as *S-53*. The text of this hearing is supplemented by a number of authentic documents, labeled "exhibits" by the Subcommittee. Hall's position is corroborated by another source: "Mr. Hall took very violent exception primarily on the grounds that a man who prints currency plates does not make that plate available to anyone else; that if he makes it available, there is no telling what other people will do with it; that you lose complete control." U.S. Congress, Senate, The Permanent Committee on Investigation of the Committee on Government Operations, *Testimony of William Henry Taylor*, 84th Congress, 2d Session, October 19, 1953, p. 77. Hereinafter referred to as *Taylor's Testimony*.

in writing; subsequently Bell, a career Treasury official, fully agreed with Hall.[15] Nevertheless, to turn down the request of a major American ally was not simple. Besides, since the question concerned another government, the person to consult with was Assistant Secretary Harry Dexter White, who was in charge of international monetary matters and who had a great deal of influence with Secretary Morgenthau.[16]

Bell forwarded Hall's memorandum to White and on March 7 a meeting took place in Bell's office at which White was present with two aides, Taylor and Aarons. White said that he had read Hall's memorandum with considerable interest, but that he was somewhat troubled with the views expressed therein.[17] He added that a negative answer to the Soviet request would be construed by the Russians as an expression of lack of confidence. Naturally, such an outcome had to be avoided.

Bell, who was not concerned with the wider issues of international politics, argued that the Treasury had never made plates available to anybody and that private companies printing the currency would probably prove very adamant on this point. White repeated that he was loath to turn down the Russian request. He said that in this instance American currency was not being printed and that Russia must be trusted to the same degree and to the same extent as the other Allies. Bell failed to note that no other ally had in fact demanded the privilege of printing the currency. White recommended that they not settle the question immediately but that they keep talking to the Soviet ambassador and in the meantime review the whole matter with Secretary Morgenthau. If the decision nonetheless remained negative, the Treasury should clear the matter with the State and War Departments; otherwise it might be charged that the Treasury had rejected this proposal on a narrow accountancy basis without considering the political implications of its action.[18]

15. Testimony by Under Secretary Daniel W. Bell, *S-53*, p. 15.

16. See Treasury Department Order No. 43 of December 14, 1941, and the communication of Morgenthau to White of February 25, 1943, *S-53*, pp. 58–59.

17. White had been informed of developments in the affair from the beginning but did not participate in any formal discussions until Hall's memorandum reached his desk. See Exhibits 10-a, 10-b and 5, *S-53*, pp. 50, 51, and 47. Also John L. Snell, *Wartime Origins of the East-West Dilemma over Germany* (New Orleans: Houser, 1959), p. 66.

18. Memorandum for the files by William H. Taylor, March 7, 1944, *S-47*, pp. 179–80.

Of all the top-ranking officials who in the course of events became involved in the case, White was the one in a position to see a much wider basis for rejecting the Soviet demand. He was a very able man and had at his disposal the whole Division of Monetary Research, where some of the best economic brains were employed. He was aware of certain negative aspects of the military currency experiences in Italy: finance officers in the field maintained close liaison with the Treasury. As an economist, he was fully conscious of the necessity of preserving a measure of control over the currency circulation. As a monetary expert, he knew the paramount importance of preserving the identity of currency. He should have envisaged that the means to print the AM marks in the hands of another government, especially if it chose to be uncooperative, could easily lead to a chaotic monetary situation in Germany.

In order to appreciate White's position, it is important to remember that at this time the United States, Great Britain, and the Soviet Union still favored the dismemberment of Germany and that President Roosevelt felt that the zones of occupation should approximate the future boundaries of the separate states to be carved out of Germany. Nobody had yet advanced the idea of economic unity for occupied Germany; in fact, such unity would have involved a contradiction of all the arguments in favor of dismemberment. The Anglo-American offer to the Soviets to establish a common currency in occupied Germany was inconsistent with the expressed Allied policy which implied the breaking up of Germany; and the Soviet acceptance of this offer would have implied a similar contradiction. Only a *joint Allied rule* in Germany could have justified a common currency, but even joint rule would not have warranted handing over the plates to the Soviets; all that would have been needed was joint control of the *issue*, not *printing*, of the common currency.

Moscow's request for the duplicate set of plates had nothing to do with either the plans for dismemberment or with the yet unborn idea of the economic unity of occupied Germany or even with military expediency. Harry Dexter White was an ardent promoter of the dismemberment of Germany and consequently the concept of economic unity of the occupied country was totally alien to him. Therefore, he would normally have been expected to recommend the rejection of Moscow's request either on broad political grounds or on the perfectly valid technical grounds such as those elaborated for him by Hall and Bell. He did neither. To White, Soviet feelings on the matter were overriding; the Ally had to be accommodated regardless of the consequences.

Hall's objections, however, proved to be difficult to overcome. Two days later, on March 9, 1944, the matter was given further consideration at a meeting which Bell and White held with Secretary Morgenthau. The details of this conference are not known, but a memorandum drafted as a result of it indicates that the views of Hall prevailed over those of White. It was decided that the Secretary should meet the Soviet ambassador and try to talk him out of demanding the plates.[19] Meanwhile the Soviet Embassy was informed about complications arising from the Soviet request.

The Gromyko-Morgenthau meeting took place on the afternoon of March 18 at Morgenthau's home; White was present. Gromyko stated that he had already explained to his government the difficulties involved in producing the duplicate plates, but that his government would like to get the plates and necessary materials anyway. Morgenthau replied that he was sorry that the Soviet government still wanted the plates after his explanation of the difficulties and that he had not expected that they would. He said that the Forbes Company had refused to produce the currency if a duplicate set of plates were given out. The Soviet government could have any amount of the American-printed currency it desired. The Soviet ambassador retorted that all these considerations would not alter the request of his government, upon which Morgenthau promised to review the situation again and inform Gromyko within forty-eight hours.[20]

The review produced nothing new. The objections of Bell and Hall remained the same. Although by now the issue had become sufficiently clear, Secretary Morgenthau appeared reluctant to decide the matter one way or the other on his own responsibility. At his request, on March 21 Hall prepared yet another memorandum where he restated his main objections:

—that unavoidable differences in appearance of the notes produced from the duplicate plates would facilitate counterfeiting;

—that if the plates were to be given to the Soviets and if the

19. Taylor to Bell, March 8, 1944, *S-47*, pp. 177–78.

20. Memorandum for the files by H. D. White, March 18, 1944, *S-47*, pp. 179–80.

Forbes Company, as a result, stopped production, six to eight months delay in fulfilling the SHAEF order would ensue;

—that there was no real need to furnish the Soviet Union with the plates since it could get an unlimited amount of AM marks from the United States supply, and at a much earlier date than if it were to undertake the printing in Moscow.

Hall concluded his memorandum by saying: "The Russian request to print their own currency might be met by a suggestion to them that they print a mark currency of their own design. In this connection, the Treasury would be glad to assist the Soviet government in the development of new designs. . . . The Bureau will, if desired, manufacture negatives and positives from which the actual printing can be made in the U.S.S.R."

Up to this point we see that the memorandum—which eventually went into the Treasury files unsigned—was dealing exclusively with the technical matters of security in printing the currency, the only matters Hall ever raised. As the Director of the Bureau of Engraving and Printing for two decades, he would hardly have been concerned with anything else. The whole meaning of the document was the reiteration of an emphatic "no" to the Soviet request. But at the very end of the memorandum we find one more paragraph completely contradicting Hall's position and, in effect, canceling his objections. It read (italics added): "The use of a separately designed mark currency by the U.S.S.R. need not raise any economic or financial difficulties. *However, it may be politically undesirable at this time to give the appearance of lack of financial uniformity among the three powers.*" [21]

The first sentence in this paragraph, whatever the merits of the idea expressed in it, was characteristic of Hall, who was not versed in either finance or economics. The second sentence, the effect of which was to support the argument Hall had fought against from the very start, was a repetition of what White had insisted on at the meeting in Bell's office on March 9. Its meaning was to justify the surrender of the plates to the Soviets. And it seems reasonable to assume that this last sentence was added to the Hall memorandum through the influence of White himself.

The memorandum was taken by White to Secretary Morgenthau the next morning, but the Secretary refused to undertake the

21. Memorandum for the Secretary of the Treasury, March 21, 1944, *S-47*, pp. 180–82.

responsibility for the decision. Accordingly, a letter was sent to Admiral Leahy, the President's Chief of Staff, stating the case and asking him to place it before the Combined Chiefs of Staff, and to advise the Treasury whether it should give the plates to the Soviet government. In this letter, Morgenthau appeared to play down Hall's objections. He did not suggest that the duplications of printing might lead to a monetary disorder in occupied Germany. "The chief difficulty," according to the Secretary, was that "if, as a result of the transfer of the plates the Forbes Company would stop production of the AM marks, the desire of General Eisenhower to have a half of the initial order for the currency would not be fulfilled and that a delay of six to eight months would be likely to ensue." [22] To this letter Morgenthau attached the Hall memorandum. Copies of both were sent to Cordell Hull, who immediately cabled Harriman, summing up the situation and adding that "it is not expected that the Combined Chiefs of Staff will favor the delivery of plates to the Russians." [23]

At a conference on the morning of March 22, the Secretary instructed White to visit Gromyko and explain Hall's objections again—possible delays in production, etc. He apparently also permitted White to take the memorandum which he was sending to Leahy to the Soviet Embassy so that he could prove to the Russians that the Treasury was doing its best to cooperate.

That same night White appeared at the Soviet Embassy and was ushered into Gromyko's office. Listening to White's explanation, Gromyko showed his annoyance. Why should the Forbes Company object to giving a duplicate set of plates to his government? After all, the Soviet government was not a private corporation or an irresponsible government. White tried, apologetically, to explain the feelings of the Forbes Company on the matter, but Gromyko "remained unimpressed." Then White informed Gromyko that Secretary Morgenthau was sending a letter to the Combined Chiefs of Staff, together with this memorandum. Gromyko started reading it. All these arguments he had heard many times before; there was nothing new in it. Or perhaps there was? Gromyko looked at his visitor and read the end of the memorandum carefully once again. "He wanted to know," relates White, "whether our government was ready to suggest

22. Morgenthau to Leahy, March 22, 1944, *S-47*, pp. 182–83.
23. Hull to Harriman, March 23, 1944, *S-47*, p. 150.

to his government that it could print its own designed mark currency. I told him that such was not necessarily the view of our government but was merely an expression of the possibility in the memorandum and that it would have to be cleared through other departments and doubtless with the British before it could be regarded as an official specific proposal. He seemed interested in the possibility of printing their own currency." [24]

Now we arrive at the crucial point of the episode. If the Soviet government wanted to have a separate currency for its zone of occupation, it could have had it by a simple unilateral action and the Allies would have been powerless to prevent it. But as we saw, the Soviets were very anxious to get hold of the plates. If one is to consider the general disposition of the Soviets toward independence of action and their extreme reluctance to be tied down by agreements with the Allies, such a desire could indicate only one thing: that the tremendous economic advantages of having a common currency for the whole of Germany had been duly appreciated in Moscow—provided, of course, that the Soviet government could produce it without any control from the West.

Gromyko had undoubtedly been instructed to make every effort to get the plates. So far he had made no headway. And now, talking to one of the most influential officials of the U.S. Treasury, a man who—as Gromyko probably knew—had been a proven friend of the Soviet Union, he suddenly saw an opening.[25]

The Soviets had, of course, been aware of the general preoccupation in London and Washington with the preservation of the appearance of unity between the Allies and had exploited it many times before. It seems very plausible that all Gromyko needed at this point was a hint that this preoccupation, if once again exploited, would bring about the surrender of the plates.

24. Memorandum for the files by H. D. White, March 22, 1944, *S-47*, pp. 183–84.

25. Much of the Chambers-Bentley story about White's involvement with the Soviet espionage operations in Washington is by now widely accepted, if only because a great many of their allegations proved to be correct and their data on White sufficiently corroborated. See Whittaker Chambers' *Witness* (New York: Random House, 1952) and Elizabeth T. Bentley's *Out of Bondage* (New York: Devin-Adair, 1951). Also, Herbert L. Packer, *Ex-Communist Witnesses* (Stanford: Stanford University Press, 1962), pp. 103–4. White's defense, although pointing out certain discrepancies in the Chambers-Bentley story, does not disprove the charge. See Nathan I. White, *Harry Dexter White, Loyal American* (Waban, Mass., 1950): see footnote on page 30 for one apparent discrepancy in Miss Bentley's testimony.

On April 8, 1944, two-and-a-half weeks after Harry Dexter White paid his visit to Gromyko (sufficient time for a thorough study of Gromyko's report in Moscow), Harriman cabled to Hull a note he had received from Molotov on the same day. Having reviewed the matter of plates—and we notice here an almost verbatim repetition of what Gromyko had reportedly said to White—Molotov declared:

> It appears that the private concern engaged in printing of M-marks interposes objections to making available to the People's Commissariat of Finance the plates, samples, and colors and the lists of numbers, and that in the opinion of the Treasury Department of the United States there is no possibility of overcoming these obstacles. The Soviet government cannot consider as sound the objections set forth on this point. . . . It would be appreciated if you would let me know whether a favorable decision can be reached. . . . In the event that the reply is in the negative, I must point out that the Soviet government will be forced to proceed with the independent preparation of military marks for Germany of its own pattern.[26]

This constituted a Soviet threat "to go it alone" in postwar Germany—exactly what the Western Allies feared most and could not bring themselves to face. Such action could destroy the hopes still nurtured by American leaders for postwar Allied unity and upset the whole psychological foundation of United States policy toward the Soviet Union.

Even before the Soviet gambit became known in Washington a certain change had taken place in Treasury thinking. Some of White's colleagues who had been doubtful about the affair began to come around to his point of view. The arguments White used were, first, that if the United States was ready—and it had already made it clear that it was—to supply the Soviets with an unlimited amount of currency, it would make little difference if the Soviets were to print such currency themselves; second, that if the Soviets were to introduce their own currency in Germany, the United States would be forced to recognize it as legal tender anyway; third, that, in any case, the United States had not been doing

26. Harriman to Hull, April 8, 1944, *S-47*, p. 151.

enough for the Soviet Union all along and that if the Soviets profited as a result of this transaction we should be happy to give them this token of our appreciation of their efforts.[27] These arguments, at least in retrospect, were hardly sound. "Unlimited" seldom really means unlimited, especially where money is involved; sooner or later a limit to Soviet request would have been stipulated. Had the Soviets introduced their own currency in Germany, it would probably have been recognized by the Allies, but in any case, if Soviet financial policies had clashed with those of the Western powers, this recognition could have been withdrawn.

The change of attitude, however, was limited to the Treasury. In other places, the case of the duplicate plates was moving slowly from one desk to another. On April 1, a meeting of the Combined Civil Affairs Committee took place at the Pentagon at which comments on Morgenthau's memorandum of March 21 were exchanged. Lt. General G. N. Macready, a British representative, pointed out that the British government was against the production of two sets of notes of the same design lest they should discredit the whole issue. James C. Dunn of the State Department said that the Soviet government had already been informed of the problems but nevertheless continued to insist on getting the plates. It was generally agreed that more discussion with the Treasury was necessary before any final decision could be made.[28]

Another meeting took place in McCloy's office a few days later. William H. Taylor, a Treasury representative, pointed out that the Soviet views regarding the rate of exchange of the AM marks remained unknown and that the matter of supplying the plates to the Soviets was still being considered by the Combined Chiefs of Staff.[29]

The atmosphere was quite different at a meeting in the same office on April 12; by then the Soviet threat had become known to some of the participants. Maj. General Hilldring reported that the Morgenthau communication to Admiral Leahy had been turned

27. This information is based on a private interview in January, 1960, with one of the former aides of White who prefers to remain unnamed. White's eagerness to push through the decision on the plates' transfer apparently increased after he failed to secure for the Soviet Union an interest-free $10 billion loan which was a subject of low-level negotiations in Washington in the spring of 1944.

28. Minutes of the Combined Civil Affairs Committee meeting, April 3, 1944, *S-47*, p. 151.

29. Minutes of the meeting in McCloy's office, April 8, 1944, *S-47*, pp. 229–30.

over to the Combined Chiefs of Staff, which turned it over to the Combined Civil Affairs Committee, which had also received London's views on the matter which were then being studied within the Civil Affairs Division of the War Department.[30] Hilldring said the issue was " too hot " for the Combined Chiefs of Staff.[31] He reported that the Combined Civil Affairs Committee had decided after long consideration to recommend that the question of the transfer of the plates to the Russians should not be settled on military grounds.

The General stressed that the decision on the whole matter was a political one, a point that caused Dunn to raise objections, since the State Department did not want to take responsibility for it either. Dunn argued that there were political implications in this matter, but that it also had to be settled on technical grounds; it should, therefore, be the responsibility of the Combined Chiefs of Staff, since all technical matters involved in the conduct of the war were really up to the military to resolve. Dunn's position was supported by two representatives of the Treasury who pointed out that the technical aspects of the problem had been clearly set forth in the Secretary's letter to Admiral Leahy. It was at this point that Dunn put his cards on the table. He informed his colleagues that according to the latest cable from Harriman, the Russians would not accept American explanations and were only asking whether the plates would or would not be given to them. Dunn pointed out that " in the event the plates were not made available, they were prepared to proceed with the printing of their own variety of mark currency."

Everyone was impressed. General Hilldring hastened to express the hope—based on " military considerations "—that all the Allies

30. By " London's views " the General probably meant those of the British War Office or the Cabinet Committee on Post-war Germany. It is to be noted that the State Department experts held an extremely low opinion of the activities of the Civil Affairs Division headed by General Hilldring and of the competence of his staff. See Philip E. Mosely, " The Occupation of Germany," *Foreign Affairs*, XXVIII, No. 4 (July, 1950).

31. Three years later General Hilldring (then Assistant Secretary of State) testified that " a very plausible and reasonable case was made by the Russians. . . . It would have been an exceedingly difficult thing, in the light of conditions existing in the spring of 1944 . . . to have decided that we would have two Germanys instead of one " by turning down the Soviet request (see *S-47*, p. 119). The logic of this statement seems rather questionable. Had the Soviets wanted one Germany instead of two, an American refusal to surrender the plates wouldn't have made much difference; they still could have used American-printed AM marks.

would use identical currency. This shift to "military considerations" was important. Hilldring spoke for both the War Department (as Chief of the Civil Affairs Division) and the powerful Combined Chiefs of Staff (as a ranking member of the Combined Civil Affairs Committee). Dunn immediately added that "it would have a very nice effect upon the German people if we all used the same type of currency." Taylor pointed out that if the U.S. failed to furnish the plates, the Russians would not only embark upon a currency of their own but they also might establish monetary and financial programs of their own, and in such an event the likelihood of developing a uniform and coordinated Allied pattern of action toward Germany would be jeopardized.[32]

The moment the officials were confronted with the prospect of a conflict with a major ally, the picture began to change. Dunn and Taylor still remained hopeful that the responsibility for the decision would be assumed by the higher authority—the Combined Chiefs of Staff—if only because, as Hilldring put it, "military considerations" were involved. But the Combined Chiefs of Staff would not accept responsibility either. At the Combined Civil Affairs Committee meeting the next day, General Macready said that in their reply the Combined Chiefs of Staff had merely brought the matter to the attention of the Secretary of the Treasury; in his view, their letter (which will be examined presently) took the matter out of military hands and returned it to the State Department, the British Foreign Office, and the two Treasuries.[33]

Thus, as far as we know, despite some change of attitude following the arrival in Washington of the Soviet threat to print their own marks, there was no significant change in the official position by the evening of April 13, 1944. Although one occupation currency for Germany was considered desirable, no one was willing to take responsibility for the transfer of the plates.[34] The available record of those days has many gaps; it does not reveal all that went on behind the scenes. Three years later, testifying

32. Memorandum for the files by Taylor and Aarons, April 13, 1944, *S-47*, pp. 184–85.

33. Minutes of the Combined Civil Affairs Committee meeting, April 13, 1944, *S-47*, pp. 46–47.

34. General Hilldring and his former aide, Colonel Hilliard, interviewed in February, 1960, were very positive that "to the very last, everybody in the Combined Civil Affairs Committee was against giving the plates to the Russians."

before the Senate hearings, John J. McCloy stated that he " had an impression " that Roosevelt was consulted on the matter, and that " it was a matter of such importance that either the Secretary of State or the Secretary of the Treasury did go to the President about it." [35] William H. Taylor, who was involved in the affair from the very start, seemed to have been more positive. In a 1946 memorandum he wrote that " to the best of my knowledge the decision to make the AM mark currency plates available to the U.S.S.R. had been reviewed at the highest levels of the Government including the President." [36] Still, among the hundreds of contemporary documents submitted by the Departments of State, War, and Treasury to the Senate in 1947 and in 1953, there is no conclusive evidence of such a high-level review. Even more remarkable is the fact that at the Senate hearings of 1947 all the distinguished witnesses insisted that the authority for the Morgenthau decision to give the plates to the Soviets was amply provided for in the letter from the Combined Chiefs of Staff signed by General George C. Marshall.

This letter—mentioned by General Macready at the Combined Civil Affairs Committee meeting the day before—was delivered to Harry Dexter White early in the morning on April 14. The letter said that the present commitments of furnishing SHAEF with the AM marks should be met, and that it was understood that they would be fulfilled by May 1. After that, said General Marshall, " if the United States Treasury and the State Department, in conjunction with the Foreign Office and British Treasury, decide to furnish duplicate plates to the Soviet government, it appears that this action could be taken any time after May 1, 1944, without interference with General Eisenhower's requirements for Allied military mark currency." If the Soviet government needs the currency urgently, added General Marshal, about 2 billion marks could be made available to them immediately.[37]

It was clear that this letter returned the matter to the Treasury and State Departments; the Combined Chiefs of Staff were making no decision. It was then that Harry Dexter White decided to cut through this red tape. At about 9:30 A.M. he called up Alvin W. Hall and asked him to come to his office immediately. Upon his

35. Testimony by John J. McCloy, *S-47*, p. 132.
36. Exhibit 19-a, *S-53*, p. 57.
37. Marshall to Morgenthau, April 13, 1944, *S-47*, pp. 45–46.

arrival Hall found Taylor and Luxford also there. White informed him that "the Combined Chiefs of Staff had directed that the glass positives [of the plates] be turned over to the Russian government." Luxford said that the Forbes Company might stop printing the currency, and for this contingency he prepared a draft of a presidential order authorizing the Army to operate the printing plant or have it taken over by the Treasury. Hall begged them not to do it, for he felt he could convince the Company that they should accede to the decision made by the Combined Chiefs of Staff; Marshall's letter was not shown to him and he had to take White's word for it.

After that everybody went to Morgenthau. There, after some discussion, the Secretary irritably announced that the plates would be turned over to the Russians. Hall recorded the next day that "the session in the Secretary's office was rather hectic as he [the Secretary] had implied that he had not been fully informed in the matter; he said that if he had known all the facts, a decision would have been made at a much earlier date." [38]

At this meeting Morgenthau did not refer to Marshall's letter; we do not even know whether he had read it. We know, however, that at the end of the meeting he made two telephone calls. One was to James C. Dunn. He told Dunn that he was informing the Soviet ambassador that the duplicate plates would be furnished to the Soviet government and asked whether the State Department was willing to share the responsibility for this action. Somewhat evasively Dunn replied that from the political point of view, "it is highly advisable" to have the plates furnished lest the Soviets proceed to produce a separate currency. In the opinion of the State Department, "it would be a pity to lose the great advantage of having one currency used by the three Armies, which itself would indicate a degree of solidarity which was so much desired." Again, neither one mentioned Marshall's letter.

Having recorded this conversation, Dunn justified the transaction as follows: "It has become perfectly clear to us that the Soviet government is not ready to join in the common use of the same currency unless it receives the duplicate plates from us. In order to convince the Soviet government of our sincerity in the desire to have the closest collaboration it becomes essential that

38. Hall's memorandum for the files, Exhibits 3 and 12, *S-53*, pp. 46–52.

we make every effort within our possibility to furnish the plates to that government." [39]

The second call was made to Gromyko. Morgenthau asked him to come to his office at 3:30 in the afternoon, for he had a decision to announce regarding the plates. Before the meeting broke up, Hall pointed out to the Secretary that " it would only be fair to inform the Forbes Company what we are about to do." In answer to this " the Secretary emphatically stated that under no circumstances should the Forbes Company be informed that duplicate positives would be dispatched to Moscow . . . that the military and political status of affairs were such as to require complete cooperation with the Russian government, and that the transaction should be considered a military secret." [40]

The same afternoon, at a conference in his office, Morgenthau announced to Gromyko that the United States government, anxious to cooperate with the Soviet government, had decided to supply the Soviet government with a set of duplicate plates for printing Allied military mark currency for Germany and all the data and materials necessary for that purpose. In reply to a question from Mr. Gromyko, Hall said that the plates, the formulas, and specimens of inks and paper would be ready for shipment the following Monday. Morgenthau added that he would be glad to dispatch representatives of the Bureau of Engraving and Printing to Moscow to assist in getting the Soviet printing plant into production. Gromyko said that they could easily produce the currency in Moscow and that no further help would be needed. The Secretary then handed the Ambassador a memorandum of the United States' decision.[41]

Next morning in his office Hall prepared another memorandum —for his own files—describing the conference in the Secretary's office. At the end of it he wrote, " From the first time the Russian request came to my notice I have strenuously objected, in oral argument and in writing, to furnishing duplicate glass positives of the mark currency to the Russian government. There may be

39. Memorandum of telephone conversation by James C. Dunn, April 14, 1944, *S-47*, pp. 152–53.

40. Memorandum for the files by Alvin W. Hall, April 15, 1944, *S-53*, pp. 46–47.

41. Memorandum to the Soviet Ambassador from Secretary Morgenthau, April 14, 1944, *S-47*, p. 186.

serious repercussions when this transaction becomes public information." [42]

Hall's forebodings did not materialize. The transaction remained a closely guarded secret for over three years until June, 1947, when the Senate Committees on Appropriations, Armed Services, and Banking and Currency looked into it. The hearings had no consequences. The affair came to public notice again in 1953 when Senator Joseph McCarthy decided to investigate the supposedly subversive aspect of it, but by that time most of the participants had left the official scene.[43]

Morgenthau has never explained how he reached the decision to turn the plates over to the Soviets. The question remains—did he, or did he not, go to the President with this matter? He was never noted for his resoluteness. Would he not therefore have been inclined to get a "green light" from someone of higher authority? The Marshall letter obviously did not relieve him of the responsibility for the transaction. A visit to the President would have been the logical thing. On the other hand, this episode might have coincided with one of those periods of coolness in relations between the two men; perhaps this was an occasion when Roosevelt simply would not talk to Morgenthau. It also could have been that Morgenthau, who had been a staunch believer in Soviet-American friendship ever since the United States extended recognition to the Soviet Union,[44] did not want to risk a possible though unlikely presidential veto. Finally, it is possible that whatever doubts Morgenthau had at that point were dispelled by the persuasiveness of Harry Dexter White.

42. Exhibits 3 and 12, *S-53*, pp. 46–52.

43. G. R. Jordan, *From Major Jordan's Diaries* (New York: Devin-Adair, 1952), pp. 227–29. The author describes a super-secret atmosphere surrounding the shipment of the plates and other materials to Russia.

44. In the 1933 negotiations which led to recognition of the Soviet government, Morgenthau acted as a personal representative of President Roosevelt. Throughout his public life, and particularly since the beginning of the Japanese and German aggressions, Morgenthau firmly believed that the Soviet Union represented a force for peace; this belief apparently was not shaken even by the Stalin-Ribbentrop Pact. See Robert Paul Browder, *The Origins of Soviet-American Diplomacy* (Princeton: Princeton University Press, 1953), pp. 99–102, 128, 131. Cf. John Morton Blum, *From the Morgenthau Diaries: Years of Crisis, 1928–1938* (Boston: Houghton-Mifflin, 1959), p. 467; his *From the Morgenthau Diaries: Years of Urgency, 1938–1941* (Boston: Houghton-Mifflin, 1965), pp. 256ff., and Julius W. Pratt, *Cordell Hull* (New York: Cooper Square, 1964), p. 594.

Morgenthau cleared the matter with Dunn but did not bother to wait for the consent of the British—which he received one day *after* he committed himself to Gromyko.[45] That the decision was Morgenthau's and his alone is stated clearly in a letter which Bell wrote to Hall two weeks later.[46] But it is equally clear that the initiative throughout came from White, his closest adviser and the man in charge of international monetary matters in the Treasury.

Whether White, in his campaign for the surrender of the plates acted under direct Soviet " orders " (as was alleged later by Miss Bentley) is of secondary importance and, indeed, is open to question.[47] The important fact is that by virtue of his economic training and his position in the Treasury he should have appreciated the

45. Crow to Taylor, April 15, 1944, *S-47*, p. 187. It is plausible, however, that Morgenthau was taking the British consent for granted. In those days it happened very rarely that the British government would not go along with Washington, especially in financial matters.

46. Bell to Hall, April 27, 1944, *S-47*, pp. 192–93.

47. In her testimony before the McCarthy Committee, Elizabeth T. Bentley alleged that she personally transmitted such " orders " to White from a Soviet espionage agent in New York. She repeated this allegation in her book, *Out of Bondage*, p. 241. Also *S-53*, p. 27. Of course, it is conceivable that the Soviet espionage operators in the United States were not aware that the affair was proceeding smoothly. Actually, until April 14, 1944, nobody, including the officials involved in the case, had any inkling that a favorable decision was forthcoming. Besides, the underground " channels " were not necessarily coordinating their efforts with those of Gromyko and could have duplicated them. What weakens, if not altogether destroys, Miss Bentley's case is the timetable. According to her testimony, at least two weeks passed between the time when White, through his friend Ullman, supplied her with the samples of the AM marks, and the time when she returned them to Ullman with the word that White should strive for the official transfer of the plates. The record shows that White himself received the first specimens of the AM marks only on March 27. So, even under the most ideal circumstances Miss Bentley could have returned from New York with her " orders " only by the time the duplicate plates were already in the Soviet Embassy.

What is more, on March 15 while ordering fifty specimens of the AM marks White indicated that eighteen of them would be sent to Gromyko—which was a normal and logical procedure. It hardly made sense for White to take extra risks by simultaneously sending a set of the mark specimens to the Soviet spies through Miss Bentley. Finally, testifying before the McCarthy Committee on October 21, 1953, Miss Bentley said that the specimens were returned to her by the Russians with the comment that " they were unable to photograph them so that they would be useful " (*S-53*, p. 30), i.e., that they could not counterfeit the AM marks. Why should they have wanted to counterfeit the currency they could receive in an unlimited quantity in any case? And, if they wanted to, they certainly could have done it, so relatively simple were the techniques of producing the notes. Many private entrepreneurs have done it since, and quite successfully.

significance of this transaction better than anyone else on a comparable level in the government. President Roosevelt could have decided to give the plates to the Soviets as yet another proof of American goodwill, but it was the function of the Treasury to inform the President of the possible economic costs of such an act. The decision to transfer the plates deliberately ignored the possible or even probable economic consequences of an uncontrolled currency deluge in occupied Germany. It amounted to giving the Soviet Union an outright gift of yet unknown dimensions by denying the United States an opportunity to control, or even participate in controlling, the monetary situation in Germany. It appears immaterial that this decision might have been made in the spirit of accommodation held by the President toward the Soviet ally. Any accommodation must be subject to limitations, and the President himself had turned down a number of Soviet demands which appeared to him unreasonable or impossible to fulfill. In this instance, a far-reaching decision was made by lower-level policymakers.

CHAPTER VI

THE GREAT POWERS' DIFFERENCES OVER GERMANY

The end of World War II marked the end of one period of international relations and the emergence of a new international situation. The occupation of Germany was an extension of the old period, but it developed in a very different international climate. Germany, even in total defeat, was of enormous strategic importance to each of the occupying powers, although the Americans and the British at first were not sure of this. The occupation was intended to be a joint undertaking, but even before it began, cooperation between the occupying powers proved to be difficult, and in the end their disagreements led to a division of the country. The fate of the German nation thus became involved in the struggle for the allegiance of postwar Europe and the consolidation of the two major power blocs. Peculiarly, many of the policies and practices followed in the occupation zones seemed to ignore the realities of the new setting; they mirrored wartime international politics in a postwar international situation which was passing through a period of a rapid and radical transition.

The complexities involved in the occupation of Germany came to be primarily, if not exclusively, determined by the policies and the interrelationships among the victors. Unlike Italy, where the Italian government and Italian politics played a part in various convolutions of the occupation, the Germans were merely an object of occupation. The absence of a German government and German politics does not seem to have made the Allied administration any more efficient by comparison. Nor did the political void in Germany and the reaffirmation of the victors' right to settle the German future by a unilateral action make the final settlement any more feasible. Their differences, which had emerged long before the end of the Third Reich, continued to intensify, and the seemingly warm personal relations between Churchill, Roosevelt, and Stalin deteriorated to the point where no meaningful agreement on Germany could be negotiated.

Churchill, shortly after his meeting with Stalin in October, 1944, concluded that it was unrealistic to expect Soviet cooperation in the postwar world. He realized that in their efforts to communize East Europe, the Soviets were prepared to crush those pro-Western democratic elements who had survived the years of the Axis domination, and he began to fear that Great Britain and her traditional allies in Europe would emerge as the principal losers in the postwar settlement.

Churchill's growing opposition to Soviet expansion annoyed President Roosevelt, perhaps the more so because his own hopes for friendship with Stalin were fading under the impact of Soviet aggressiveness. Nonetheless, Roosevelt was determined to remain neutral in what he visualized as a Soviet-British rivalry, if necessary by denying support to Great Britain. By 1944 many important people in the United States were inclined to blame the "imperialistic-minded" British Prime Minister for the disintegration of the Grand Alliance and the dissipation of hopes for a perpetual peace.

Of the Big Three, it was only Stalin who never lost sight of the future. As the tide turned and the Red Army started moving westward, scoring one victory after another, Stalin's vistas expanded. He appreciated the recognition accorded to him by Churchill and Roosevelt and their acceptance of him as an equal. But he never committed himself to any scheme which would have restricted his freedom of action or made Soviet fortunes permanently dependent on the goodwill of his allies. Knowing his own aspirations, he also knew that this goodwill would one day be exhausted and that the Soviet interests would clash with those of the West.

There were many indications of the impending clash in the second part of 1944, but it was probably at Yalta that Stalin made up his mind to pursue a fully independent course. At that conference Stalin was opposed by Churchill, and even by Roosevelt, not only on such matters as the future of Poland and France's role in the occupation of Germany—matters in which he felt he could depart somewhat from his rigid position—but he was also opposed on two major issues which he felt should be settled on terms dictated by the Soviet Union, namely, the dismemberment of Germany and the size of reparations to be paid to the Soviet Union by the Germans.

Partition of Germany and Zones of Occupation

At the Teheran Conference the treatment of Germany was the one European issue on which Roosevelt, Churchill, and Stalin reached an easy agreement. All expressed the conviction that Germany should be partitioned and that effective measures would be taken to prevent German reunification. Both Stalin and Roosevelt favored very harsh treatment of the Germans, and even Churchill said the Big Three should assure safety for the world for at least fifty years "by preventing rearmament, by supervision of German factories, by forbidding all aviation, and by territorial changes of a far-reaching character."[1] Churchill's proposals for the partition of Germany differed from those of Roosevelt; Stalin presented no partition proposals except insofar as he put forward a claim to Koenigsberg. Everybody agreed that they had only a "very preliminary" survey of a vast political problem, and no decisions were made.

In retrospect, it appears remarkable that in the months following Teheran none of the Big Three suggested a more specific inter-Allied discussion of the partition of Germany.[2] There were some discussions on the subject in Washington, but apparently none in London or Moscow. Roosevelt and Churchill tackled it briefly and

1. Winston S. Churchill, *The Second World War, Closing the Ring* (Boston: Houghton Mifflin, 1951), p. 360. On other relevant Teheran discussions, see also pages 358–61, 373–74, 400–6. Also U.S. Department of State, *Foreign Relations of the United States. The Conferences at Cairo and Teheran: 1943* (Washington: U.S. Government Printing Office, 1961), pp. 184–85, 253–54, 513–14, 600–3, 845–47. Hereinafter cited as *Teheran Papers.*

2. The schemes for the dismemberment of Germany are a subject in themselves. See, for instance, Sir Llewellyn Woodward, *British Foreign Policy in the Second World War* (London: H.M. Stationery Office, 1962), pp. 488–92, 524–27; Sumner Welles, *The Time for Decision* (New York: Harper, 1944), pp. 439–52; Paul Y. Hammond, "Directives for the Occupation of Germany: The Washington Controversy." *American Civil-Military Decisions*, ed. Harold Stein (University, Ala.: University of Alabama Press, 1963), pp. 314–17. Also articles by Philip E. Mosely, "Dismemberment of Germany: The Allied Negotiations from Yalta to Potsdam," *Foreign Affairs*, XXVIII, No. 3 (April, 1950), and "The Occupation of Germany: New Light on How the Zones Were Drawn," *Foreign Affairs*, XXVIII, No. 4 (July, 1950). Particularly, see William M. Franklin, "Zonal Boundaries and Access to Berlin," *World Politics*, XVI, No. 1 (October, 1963).

unsuccessfully at the Second Quebec Conference in September, 1944, Churchill mentioned it in his talks with Stalin in Moscow in October, but until the Yalta Conference the Allies seemed to be rather studiously avoiding any formal moves which might predetermine a solution of this enormous problem.

It is no less remarkable that the Anglo-American plans for the occupation of Germany were produced without any consultation with the Soviet government. They were developed on the " technical " level of the Combined Chiefs of Staff; neither the State Department nor the British Foreign Office participated in the formulation of these plans. This could be explained on the grounds that the occupation was viewed as a temporary undertaking, in no way related to the dismemberment of Germany. But this does not explain the failure to consult the Soviet military, which is all the more strange since everybody in Washington and London knew that the Soviets would also occupy a sizable part of Germany.

Originally, there was no talk about national zones. The British and American Chiefs of Staff had sketched on a map the " spheres of responsibility " in Germany, within the context of RANKIN, a contingency plan which was to be activated in case of a sudden weakening or even collapse of German resistance. In its earlier version, as it originated with Lt. General Sir Frederic Morgan, Chief of Staff to the (then nonexistent) Supreme Allied Commander, RANKIN envisaged only a limited occupation of Germany. A later British scheme was based on the idea of total occupation and—except in Berlin—of zones under a national rather than joint administration. When this scheme was presented to Roosevelt (who was then on his way to the Teheran Conference), the President immediately appreciated this aspect of RANKIN and its possible long-range implications. He remarked that " whatever territorial dispositions were made should conform to geographic subdivisions of Germany." Since he was sure that the Soviets " will offer no objections to breaking up Germany after the war," he felt that the United States should " take " a certain section of the country while the Soviet Union and Great Britain would occupy the rest, thus creating " a logical basis for splitting up Germany." [3] The linking of RANKIN and the " breaking

3. *Teheran Papers*, pp. 253–54.

up " of Germany was peculiar to Roosevelt alone. He apparently did not bring this point up at Teheran, and it is doubtful that the British shared his views either before or after the conference. Along with the military, Churchill believed that the principle of national, rather than joint, administration should be adopted strictly for technical reasons. He would have never agreed with Roosevelt that " the zones of occupation ought to conform to . . . projected lines of dismemberment," [4] partly because his ideas for the partition of Germany differed greatly from Roosevelt's, and partly because to him these were two entirely separate problems.

In addition, an Anglo-American agreement to relate the occupation to the partition of Germany was ruled out by a sharp conflict over the allocation of the " spheres of responsibility." Roosevelt wanted a very large zone of northwestern Germany for the United States because he did not want the American communication lines to go through France, fearing great instability there after the war and disliking General de Gaulle. The British, because the plans for the invasion of Germany provided that they operate in the north, insisted that the United States should take the southern zone. This conflict was not settled, in principle, until September, 1944, and formally in January, 1945, when the agreement on the access to the Bremerhaven enclave through the British zone was signed in Washington.[5]

Throughout this period the State Department had been kept in the dark on orders from Roosevelt, who resented the diplomats' attempts to work out long-range solutions for Germany. He knew that such solutions had to await an agreement of the Big Three. By placing the matter in the hands of the military, he thought he could circumvent this obstacle while retaining full flexibility in the forthcoming discussions with his partners. The American military, led by Marshall, understood him well and successfully repelled the attempts of the State Department (after January, 1944) to have more say in the arrangements for the occupation, on the grounds that " the whole problem of German surrender, in-

4. Franklin, *World Politics*, XVI, No. 1, p. 10.

5. See U.S. Department of State, *Foreign Relations of the United States. The Conferences at Malta and Yalta: 1945* (Washington: U.S. Government Printing Office, 1955), pp. 198–201. Hereinafter referred to as *Yalta Papers.* No effort was made to negotiate Anglo-French-American access to Berlin. Cf. Robert Murphy, *Diplomat among Warriors* (Garden City, N.Y.: Doubleday, 1964), pp. 231–33; also his Chapter XIX.

cluding zones of occupation, was a military matter to be decided in due course by the appropriate military authorities." [6]

Long before London and Washington settled their differences over the northwestern zone, they had decided on the western border for the Soviet zone. Their decision was not communicated to Moscow directly but passed—in January, 1944—to the American and British representatives on the European Advisory Commission (EAC), a body which had been set up in London by the Moscow Conference of Foreign Ministers to coordinate Allied planning for the postwar Europe.[7] The Soviet representative on the EAC was duly notified; he routinely relayed the news to Moscow and, on February 18, 1944, announced that the Soviet government accepted the Anglo-American proposal. There were no arguments and no bargaining. The matter was closed insofar as the configuration of the Soviet zone was concerned.

It is difficult to say whether Stalin at that time viewed the emergence of the concept of national zones as a part of the program for the dismemberment of Germany. But it is reasonable to suppose that a formal allocation of a sizable part of Germany to the Soviet jurisdiction was taken in Moscow as an important and welcome political decision. Now the Soviet Union had a *right* to occupy Eastern Germany with the consent of the Allies, not simply by the virtue of military conquest. This arrangement enabled the Soviets to occupy greater territory than they actually conquered, and to keep Anglo-American troops out of strategic Berlin and Czechoslovakia. Stalin could now wait, knowing that anything temporary could be made permanent: for him, the question of Germany's partition had obviously lost its initial urgency.

In the spring of 1944, Eisenhower proposed that there be one Anglo-American zone, chiefly because he wanted to preserve the established machinery of SHAEF. He was overruled. At the Second Quebec Conference, Roosevelt accepted for the United States the southern zone, and on September 12, 1944, the EAC

6. Franklin, *World Politics*, XVI, No. 1, 15. See also Hammond, *American Civil-Military Decisions*, pp. 334–35.

7. For more on the discussion of the zonal arrngement in the European Advisory Commission, see the articles by Mosely. For the British report on the EAC, see Lord William Strang, *Home and Abroad* (London: Deutsch, 1956), pp. 199–225. For the documentation on the establishment of the EAC, see U.S. Department of State, *Foreign Relations of the United States: 1943* (Washington: U.S. Government Printing Office, 1963), I, 801–19. Hereinafter cited as *1943 Papers*.

approved the delineation of the zones. Despite the apparent finality of this act, the available record shows that Roosevelt and Churchill regarded, or at least pretended to regard, the formation of the zones of occupation as having nothing to do with the territorial settlement with Germany.

Partition of Germany: From Yalta to Potsdam

The agreement on the zones of occupation had one significant consequence. Since it provided each of the Great Powers with sovereign rights within their respective zones, the question of a general agreement on the treatment of the German nation became largely academic; they could now treat the Germans as they wished, without any interference from their partners and without having to seek compromise solutions. Because of this—and because their attitudes toward the Germans remained largely similar—the Big Three, in their discussions at Yalta in February, 1945, found themselves in accord on most issues. They formally approved the EAC agreement on the zones of occupation—and modified it so as to carve out a zone for France and to admit the French to the Allied Control Council for Germany. Stalin, who resisted this modification the most, finally gave in since the French zone was to be carved out of the British and American zones, and perhaps, also, because he felt that the presence of de Gaulle's representatives on the Council would not necessarily be to the advantage of the British and Americans.

The three leaders failed to agree at Yalta on two major issues related to Germany; these were precisely the issues which could not be solved within the framework of the zonal arrangement as it then stood: the formal dismemberment of Germany, and the size of reparations to be paid to the Soviet Union by the defeated nation. Referring to various Teheran discussions, and to his talks with Churchill the previous October, Stalin demanded that the partition of Germany be decided upon immediately. He agreed with Roosevelt's proposal to charge a Commission of the Foreign Ministers to work out the details, but insisted that a specific dismemberment clause be incorporated in the instrument of surrender. Churchill, who had come to Yalta determined to prevent any binding decision on this far-reaching issue,[8] categorically opposed Stalin. Roosevelt was for a postponement of

8. See his January 4, 1945 letter to Eden in Winston Churchill, *The Second*

such a decision, pointing out that the surrender was going to be "unconditional," which implied that the Big Three reserved the right to split up Germany whenever they chose. Stalin backed down, and subsequently the "Declaration Regarding Defeat of Germany and Assumption of Supreme Authority by Allied Powers" of June 5, 1945, simply stated that the United States, Great Britain, the Soviet Union, and France "will hereafter determine the boundaries of Germany or any part thereof and the status of Germany or of any area at present being part of German territory."[9] This nonbinding declaration was admittedly a far cry from the professed intentions of the Big Three. Yet Stalin's defeat at Yalta might not have been as great as it appeared, for having lost on the issue of dismemberment, he quickly switched to the issue of the territorial compensation of Poland at the expense of Germany. Here he fought hard and successfully because Roosevelt and Churchill were committed to compensating Poland ever since they proposed at Teheran that the Curzon Line should be established as a new Soviet-Polish frontier.

Stalin's defeat was much more obvious on the issue of reparations, an issue of crucial importance to the Soviet Union. Firmly backed by Roosevelt, Churchill rejected Soviet demands that the reparations to the Soviet Union be fixed at $20 billion, or at any other specific amount. After some heated discussions, the issue was relegated to a committee.[10]

The relative ease with which Stalin abandoned his position on the dismemberment of Germany suggests that he considered the arrangement on the zones of occupation as a de facto partition of the country. Soviet tactics between Yalta and Potsdam also indicate Stalin's desire to assure that this arrangement be put into effect without further modifications; his refusal to let Anglo-American troops into Berlin until Saxony and Thuringia, conquered by the Americans, had been transferred to the Soviet authorities, can be explained in this light.[11] Stalin's bitter com-

---

World War, Triumph and Tragedy (Boston: Houghton Mifflin, 1953), pp. 350–51. Cf. his position in March, *ibid.*, p. 443.

9. See U.S. Congress, Senate, The Committee on Foreign Relations *Documents on Germany: 1944–1959*, 86th Congress, 2nd session, pp. 13–24.

10. On the discussions of the dismemberment of Germany at Yalta, see *Yalta Papers*, pp. 611–33.

11. See Murphy, *Diplomat among Warriors*, pp. 258–60. On the other hand, there is some extremely intriguing evidence that Stalin did not expect the United

plaint to Harry Hopkins on May 28, 1945, that Great Britain, with tacit American support, had backed out of the Yalta understanding, was clearly intended to put Hopkins on the defensive and make him state that " President Truman was inclined toward dismemberment and in any event was for the detachment of the Saar, Ruhr and west bank of the Rhine under international control." [12] But, again, Stalin made no specific proposals for the dismemberment and probably had none to make. He spoke in favor of having a unified policy toward Germany for the Allied Control Council to work on, but it was intended mainly to prevent the Germans from attempting to play one ally off against the other.[13]

At the Potsdam Conference, which opened on July 16, 1945, the dismemberment of Germany was not even discussed.[14] When at one of the sessions Stalin remarked that " the views of all seemed to have turned against dismemberment," neither Churchill nor Truman contradicted him, and the matter was dropped.[15] But by pursuing the line established at Yalta, that is by fighting for the best territorial settlement regarding Poland, Stalin virtually reached his goal. The Big Three agreed that " pending the final determination of Poland's western frontier," the territories east of the Oder-Neisse line, including that portion of East Prussia not placed under the Soviet administration " shall be under the administration of the Polish State and for such purposes should not be considered as part of the Soviet zone of occupation in

---

States to live up to the zonal agreement and to withdraw from Thuringia and Saxony, which had been occupied by the American forces; the Soviets were at first incredulous when it happened. If this is so, Churchill appears to have understood his Soviet partner much better than Truman or Eisenhower. See Murphy, p. 273. Some Soviet officers thought that the entry of the Allied troops into Berlin was delayed simply because the Soviet authorities needed time to remove from the city all usable equipment and materials without accounting for it in the forthcoming bargaining over the reparations.

12. U.S. Department of State, *Foreign Relations of the United States. The Conference of Berlin: 1943* (Washington: U.S. Government Printing Office, 1960), I, 50. Hereinafter cited as *Potsdam Papers*.

13. *Ibid.*, I. 51.

14. France was not represented at Potsdam. Even Churchill, then upset over recent frictions with de Gaulle over French aggressiveness in Val d'Aosta and over the conflict in Syria and Lebanon, did not insist on French participation in the conference. Herbert Feis, *Between War and Peace: The Potsdam Conference* (Princeton: Princeton University Press, 1960), pp. 128ff.

15. *Ibid.*, p. 239.

Germany." [16] The reservation about the need to wait for a final settlement was perfunctory; for all practical purposes, about 23 per cent of German territory (in terms of the Versailles boundaries) was given to Poland and the Soviet Union, and since almost all the Germans either fled or were expelled from this territory, there were no illusions about the finality of the settlement.

However strange it may appear, these decisions—as well as the separation of Austria and the territorial awards to Czechoslovakia—apparently were not regarded as dismemberment. Churchill and Truman seemed to agree with Stalin, who had referred to this process as "merely the slicing off of portions of Germany." [17]

But how about the zones of occupation in which each of the victors had sovereign powers with the freedom of action guaranteed by the veto power in the Allied Control Council? Did the participants in the Potsdam Conference realize that this arrangement, at least potentially, amounted to the partition of the defeated country? As it has been pointed out, there can be little doubt that Stalin was aware of it. The fact that he did not bring this up at the conference only confirms this assumption; it was in Stalin's interest not to arouse any suspicions in his partners that they had in fact lost any subsequent opportunity to influence the course of events east of the Elbe. At that point, Stalin still needed the cooperation of the United States and Great Britain (*a*) to legalize the Soviet and Polish acquisitions at the expense of Germany, (*b*) to have them consent to the future Soviet acquisitions at the expense of China and Japan, (*c*) to assure the flow of reparations to Russia from the western zones of Germany, (*d*) to obtain as much aid—credits, lend-lease, and through UNRRA—as possible, and (*e*) to preserve the appearance of Allied unity which, to him, was of high political value.[18] Stalin was not going to jeopardize the prospect for all these benefits by stressing a likelihood that the Soviet zone would never be reunified with the rest

16. *Potsdam Papers*, II, 1509.

17. *Potsdam Papers*, I, 51.

18. During their talks in Moscow in May–June, 1945, Harriman and Hopkins seriously negotiated a $10 billion loan to the Soviet Union. The deal would have probably gone through if not for the disagreement over a relatively minor issue of interest rates, which again indicates the high hopes of the Soviet government and confidence in its ability to obtain concessions from the United States. This informaton was supplied to this author by Francis B. Stevens, who was at that time an aide to Ambassador Harriman.

of Germany and that the Soviet power had now reached the heart of Europe. He confidently signed the Potsdam protocol, with all its provisions for various joint policies in the economic and political fields, knowing all along that these provisions were unenforceable and that the Soviet zone would be ruled the way he saw fit.

If any member of the American or British delegations understood Stalin's strategy or the over-all imperatives of the situation, there is no record of it in the available documents. On the contrary, everything points out that the Western expectation was that there was going to be *one* occupied Germany, administered jointly by the victors through the Allied Control Council. Insofar as I could ascertain in later interviews with members of the American delegation, no one at Potsdam seemed to have any apprehensions that the absolute sovereignty of each power in its zone of occupation, combined with the veto power in the Allied Control Council, might make the concept of joint rule unworkable. Such lack of foresight may sound incredible today, but if the statesmen's intentions and sincerity are to be regarded as a measure of their responsibility for the decisions they made, the Western Powers should be absolved of the blame for the subsequent division of Germany.[19]

The Victors' Divergent Objectives in Germany

The creation of national zones was a tacit admission of the inability of the Allies to act in accord. Although none of the victorious governments admitted it at the time, it did violence to the concept of joint rule. In retrospect, the falling out among the wartime allies appears natural, for now it is realized that the Alliance had been held together exclusively by the need to defeat the common enemy. Hence, once the war was over, the policies which each victor pursued in his zone came to be determined not by any uniform scheme but by his attitudes toward the German nation, and by his own designs for the future of Germany. Here the objectives of the victors differed so much that any agreement based on a reasonable compromise was virtually impossible. More-

19. Soviet historians have consistently maintained that the Potsdam Conference represented a great victory for the forces of "peace and democracy," meaning, of course, the Soviet Union. See, for example, Verner Rosenberg, "Kollokvium, posviashchennyi 20-letiiu Potsdamskogo soglasheniia," in *Voprosy istorii*, No. 11, Moscow, 1965.

over, before long Germany became a testing ground where the latent differences between the former Allies were brought out into the open, and where their new relationships and policies developed, shaped not so much by ideas and vague plans determined by the four governments but by the demands imposed upon them by political and economic realities.

The United States came to Germany intending to stay there only for a short time. Its prime concern was to punish the Germans by destroying German society as it had formed under the Third Reich, and to make a future resurrection of the German nationalistic and militaristic spirit impossible by a combination of punitive and educational measures. It wanted to make Germany as weak as possible and, in order to do so, was prepared to accept the prospect of having the Soviet Union fill the power vacuum created in Europe by the defeat of the Third Reich.

The Soviet objectives were manifold. With half of Germany east of the Elbe firmly in its hands, the Soviet government was not immediately concerned with additional guarantees of security. The Soviet leaders became, in fact, so self-confident that, keeping their eye on the future, they were the first to advocate a unified German state. They officially rejected the notion that the German nation was responsible for the crimes of the Hitler era, hoping to make clear in German minds the distinction between their forgiveness and the vengefulness of the Western Powers. They alone came to Germany bringing with them a German government which they had taken care to create in Moscow while the war was still on. The Soviet plan was to start a trend for a Soviet-German rapprochement which would result in a Soviet-oriented Germany.

This was a long-range political objective. The more immediate and urgent objective, however, was economic. The Soviet government wanted to extract everything of value out of Germany, both East and West, and to use German (and East European) resources to rebuild and strengthen the Soviet economy, which had been damaged during the war. The Soviets were not unaware that this economic policy, as well as the territorial annexations in the East, was bound to create resentment among the Germans, and thus defeat some of their political objectives, but they had no alternative.

The British government, unlike the American, was not interested in punishing the German nation, or in a peace settlement which would be so punitive that it would create a breeding ground for another outburst of German nationalism. Under the Labor Government (which came to power during the Potsdam Conference), Britain became inner-directed, preoccupied with the task of economic recovery and the creation of a welfare state much more than with world affairs. It wanted a firmly controlled and disarmed Germany. Unlike the United States, Britain also believed in an economically solvent Germany which would be no burden to the victors and which would eventually evolve into a moderate and liberal state. But, dependent on substantial American aid, the British took little initiative in Germany, often falling into line with the United States against their better judgment.

The French came into Germany exacerbated by their inferior status; they were assigned a zone of occupation and a seat on the Allied Council only because of the unrelenting pressure of Churchill at Yalta, who finally succeeded in overcoming Stalin's and Roosevelt's objections. They were not invited to participate in the Potsdam Conference and hastened to declare that they were not bound by its decisions.

The French attitude toward the Germans was less bitter than after World War I.[20] The French government was not concerned with either the punishment or re-education of the Germans. It believed that Germany should pay for the damages of the war. But the most important French objective was security. This security was envisaged in the creation of an independent German state under international control in the Rhineland, in a loose federation of other German lands, and in the internationalization of the Ruhr.

These divergent policy objectives had existed in the Allied capitals before the victory. They underlay all the negotiations between the Big Three from Teheran to Potsdam. Although not formulated openly, they were so pronounced that they made a peace settlement with (or rather, on) Germany all but impossible. Having failed to reach accord on the substance of the problem, the Big Three implicitly recognized their failure by leaving unresolved questions for the future. In this they had no choice. With public emotion and optimism what they were, it was all but mandatory for the leaders and officials alike to preserve for the time being, or at least appear to be preserving, a façade of unity.

20. Dorothy Pickles, *French Politics: The First Years of the Fourth Republic* (London: Royal Institute of International Affairs, 1953), pp. 184ff.

To work out a few vaguely worded declarations and agreements in an international conference turned out to be easier than to implement them on a day-by-day basis in constant contact at the Allied Control Council. In the effort to solve a multitude of problems of mutual concern—reparations, repatriation of refugees, denazification, interzonal trade, currency controls, the government of Berlin, and many others—the Allies discovered the extent of their differences. Before long, the irreconcilability of the Soviet and the Western outlooks became evident, causing a fundamental reappraisal, in the light of reality, of policies in the West.

The experience with occupation currency in Germany reflected this process. Along with the Nuremberg Military Tribunal, the Allied Control Council, the Berlin Kommandatura, and the Spandau Prison, this currency was a concrete expression of Allied unity and of the optimistic idea that, pending the peace settlement, Germany would be ruled jointly by the victorious powers. The currency was one and the same for the whole of Germany west of the Oder-Neisse line. At the same time, in the absence of a joint Allied financial and economic policy, it was subject to regulations which vastly differed from zone to zone, corresponding to the individual victor's interests and objectives. When the clash of these interests and objectives could no longer be kept from bursting into the open, the common currency collapsed, bringing down with it the remaining symbols of Allied unity.

Chapter VII

THE ORIGINS AND DEVELOPMENT OF UNITED STATES ECONOMIC POLICY TOWARD POSTWAR GERMANY

At the Casablanca Conference in January, 1943, Roosevelt and Churchill announced a doctrine of unconditional surrender. At Teheran in November of the same year, the Big Three agreed on some geographic alterations in Europe and on the generally punitive treatment of postwar Germany. They assigned the actual planning of policy to the European Advisory Commission (EAC). The EAC never had a chance to fulfill its task. Although the problems of ruling postwar Germany were studied by its American and British members, the participating governments limited the Commission's activities from the outset. President Roosevelt felt that the Commission ranked " on a tertiary and not even a secondary level " [1] in its task of coordinating Allied policies. Churchill, also a believer in personal diplomacy, paid little attention to the Commission. The Soviet government restricted its representatives to the promotion of Soviet views on such relatively minor matters as the distribution of UNRRA aid in liberated areas. The few policy recommendations which the Commission succeeded in working out were never ratified by the three governments. Outside the Commission, there were no contacts between the Soviet and the Anglo-American policy planners.

The Anglo-American war effort was effectively coordinated through the Combined Chiefs of Staff (CCS). In June, 1943, the CCS created the Combined Civil Affairs Committee (CCAC) to deal with the task of preparing policies for areas where the Soviets

1. Roosevelt to Hull, September, 1944, in U.S. Department of State, *Foreign Relations of the United States. The Conferences at Malta and Yalta: 1945* (Washington: U.S. Government Printing Office, 1961), p. 155. Hereinafter referred to as *Yalta Papers.*

would join the Western Allies in occupation. However, after a year of heated discussion, no distinct policy for Germany emerged from the CCAC or any other Allied agency in Washington.[2]

For a while this did not appear to be a problem of great urgency. The end of the war was not yet in sight. It was expected that the Allies would have to occupy a considerable part of Germany before the Reich would surrender, but it was felt that the pre-surrender occupation was essentially a military problem. In order to prepare for an orderly military government in the liberated and conquered countries, special " country units " were established by SHAEF in Great Britain.[3] Along with the training of personnel, the German Country Unit worked out temporary policy guidelines for the Allied officers who were to operate the military government in Germany until the end of the war. These guidelines were formulated in the *Basic Handbook for Military Government of Germany.* It incorporated the views of British and American officials in SHAEF and was approved by General Eisenhower. The British

2. At General Eisenhower's request, the CCS approved " informally " on April 28, 1944, the so-called pre-surrender directive known as CCS-551, which instructed the Allied military administration in Germany to be firm, just, and humane, and prescribed measures intended for the restoration of normal conditions among the civilian population. CCS-551 served as an initial basis for occupation planning at SHAEF but was never implemented in Germany except, with modifications, in the British zone. Paul Y. Hammond, " Directives for the Occupation of Germany: The Washington Controversy," *American Civil-Military Decisions*, ed. Harold Stein (University, Ala.: University of Alabama Press, 1963), pp. 328–29. Hammond gives what probably is the best account of the fruitless efforts to work out a policy toward Germany. Other descriptions of interdepartmental bickering in Washington, and of the frustrations of the American representatives on the EAC can be found in Mosely's articles in *Foreign Affairs*, in the books by E. F. Penrose, *Economic Planning for the Peace* (Princeton: Princeton University Press, 1953), *passim*; by Merle Fainsod and Dale Clark, *American Experiences in Military Government in World War II*, ed. Carl J. Friedrich (New York: Rinehart, 1948), hereinafter referred to as *American Experiences*; and in B. U. Ratchford and William D. Ross, *Berlin Reparations Assignment: Round One of the German Peace Settlement* (Chapel Hill: The University of North Carolina Press, 1947). The Department of State's publication, *Postwar Foreign Policy Preparations: 1939–1945*, ed. Harley A. Notter (Washington: U.S. Government Printing Office, 1949), is an official account useful for technical references. *The Memoirs of Cordell Hull* (New York: Macmillan, 1948), Chapters 116–22, provide a good guide to the State Department's efforts in the field of policyplanning.

3. One of the instructors who participated in training of the future administrators in occupied Europe, Sir Denis W. Brogan of Cambridge University, recalls that this program was ironically referred to as " The School for Gauleiters " and considers his own part in it " the silliest job I had in the last war." See " Below the Surface, Passions Are Still Volcanic," in the *New York Times Book Review*, July 12, 1964.

government's approval was taken for granted. It was hoped that similar approval would be forthcoming from the White House.

In the United States the question of what to do about Germany after an Allied victory had been a subject of a lively public debate since early in the war.[4] The postwar policy toward Germany was studied and discussed in the State Department and in a multitude of interdepartmental committees. The State Department's planning was the most advanced and in its direction paralleled the views prevailing in SHAEF and among United States representatives on the EAC: defeated Germany was to be dealt with sternly but its nonmilitary economy was to be re-established. It was expected that the victors would claim reparations; it was also recognized that Germany's economy represented an important part of the European economy. Many State Department officials also felt that without economic rehabilitation Germany would become a great burden to the Allies, especially if the country were to be dismembered.

The main feature of the State Department's approach to the problem was its insistence on close coordination of Allied policies in Germany. The EAC in London produced an agreement on the Allied Control Council machinery for military government in the occupied country. But along with the State Department, the EAC felt strongly that this machinery could not be made to function unless the Big Three provided their representatives on the Council with uniform, specific, and detailed policy directives to be enforced throughout Germany. The British government shared this feeling, and its representatives easily found common language with the Americans on the EAC. But, because of Roosevelt's and Stalin's attitudes, their detailed draft directives remained mere scraps of paper.

Stalin's position was understandable. His reluctance to delegate authority was notorious. Roosevelt's attitude was more complex. The President was keenly aware that he alone could speak for the United States, and he treasured this privilege. He also had a strong

4. See a bibliographical article by Donald F. Lach, "What *They* Would Do about Germany," *The Journal of Modern History*, VII, No. 4 (November, 1945). Of the books on the German problem, Sumner Welles' *Time for Decision* (New York: Harper, 1944) and L. Nizer's *What To Do with Germany* (Chicago: Ziff-Davis, 1944) were probably the most widely read. See Hajo Holborn, *American Military Government* (Washington: Infantry Journal Press, 1947), p. 42.

preference for handling important inter-Allied matters personally, particularly those which involved Soviet interests. Constantly fearful of alienating Stalin, he also had little regard for the opinion of State Department officials, who, in the view of his more liberal friends, were insensitive in their approach to the Soviets to the point of hostility. The State Department's attention to the problem of creating an equilibrium in postwar Europe was widely interpreted as a manifestation of " pro-German " leanings. As in the case with the zonal arrangements, the State Department's attempts to take part in the planning of policies for Germany were definitely unwelcome in the White House.[5]

A major consequence of this situation was an increase in the influence of the military. Because of Roosevelt's preference for dealing directly with the Joint Chiefs of Staff (JCS), the civilian Secretaries, Stimson and Knox, found themselves continuously bypassed by the President and their own staff. Their influence was eroded to such a degree that they were frequently unaware of what was going on in their Departments and between the Departments and the White House.

The true power of decision in Washington after 1942 rested with the President, with Harry Hopkins, and with the Joint Chiefs, General Marshall, Admiral King (who concerned himself mostly with the Pacific Theater), and Admiral Leahy, Roosevelt's Chief of Staff. There were other people, including members of the Cabinet, who from time to time were asked for advice in their respective fields, but, as an institution, the JCS overshadowed every other. This was perhaps inevitable. It has been noted that,

> The absence of a formal charter for the JCS facilitated the expansion of its functions since it was impossible for any

5. Cordell Hull was often kept in the dark about what went on in the White House in the field of foreign policy. Almost nine months after Teheran he confessed to Secretary Morgenthau that he " had never been permitted to see the minutes of the Teheran Conference." See Henry Morgenthau, Jr., " Our Policy toward Germany," *The New York Post*, November 26, 1947. Roosevelt so disliked to deal with the State Department that he instituted a special liaison office (with Charles E. Bohlen, a young career diplomat befriended by Harry Hopkins, in charge) through which necessary communications of the White House with that agency were handled. Robert E. Sherwood, *Roosevelt and Hopkins: An Intimate History* (New York: Harper, 1948), pp. 774–75, 756–57. Cf. Samuel P. Huntington, *The Soldier and the State: The Theory and Politics of Civil-Military Relations* (Cambridge: Harvard University Press, 1957), pp. 321ff.

> rival agency to argue that it was exceeding its authority. Tied in close to the President, the interests and power of the Chiefs tended to expand and become co-extensive with his. The formulation of the American position preparatory to the great inter-allied war conferences was normally done by the military and the President. The Chiefs themselves attended virtually all these conferences while the civilian secretaries were left at home. . . . Civil affairs and military government, at least with respect to overseas operations, were largely areas of military responsibility.[6]

This situation put the military, particularly the War Department, in a unique position in the planning of the occupation. The power of the Civil Affairs Division (CAD), under Maj. General Hilldring, was further enhanced by the fact that Hilldring represented the JCS in the Combined Civil Affairs Committee, and could thus negotiate directly with his British counterparts. The CAD used its power to assert the " military point of view " in the CCAC, where the State and Treasury Departments were also represented, and to resist attempts by " civilians " to get into the act of governing Germany.

At Hilldring's level the actual power was not accompanied by an acceptance of over-all responsibility. His immediate superior, General Marshall, advised the President and took part in decisions which extended well beyond military matters. But although he knew that civilian agencies were powerless and could provide neither the guidance nor the machinery of occupation, Marshall insisted that the Army should not be saddled with political and economic functions in occupied Germany. At one point, Marshall " indicated that he was going into civil affairs planning and administration with reluctance. He instructed Hilldring to get into it no farther than he had to."[7] Hilldring and his CAD shared this

6. Huntington, *The Soldier and the State*, p. 323. Chapter 12 of this enlightening study is helpful for an understanding of the rise of the military during the war. See also Elting E. Morison, *Turmoil and Tradition* (Boston: Houghton Mifflin, 1960), pp. 601–3.

7. Hammond, *American Civil-Military Decisions*, p. 320. Cf. Harry L. Coles and Albert K. Weinberg, *Civil Affairs: Soldiers Become Governors* (Washington: Department of the Army, 1964), p. 142. This early stage of development of the occupation policy is presented with great clarity by Walter L. Dorn in his article, " The Debate over American Occupation Policy in Germany in 1944–1945,"

unrealistic approach wholeheartedly. Operating on a limited liability theory, the CAD wanted to confine the military in Germany to the tasks directly related to the war. It wanted only short-term directives of the most general nature, allowing for a great deal of flexibility and improvisation. It insisted that no long-range political objectives should be entrusted to the military establishment. While shying away from larger specific responsibilities, the CAD did not hesitate to express its opinions on more general German questions and, though still voicing its disclaimers, became completely engrossed in policyplanning. The CAD preferred not to regard it as such; the level was considered "technical." But this was the only level which counted.

Meanwhile, President Roosevelt consistently disregarded the repeated requests for policy guidance which came to him from all sides. He seemed unwilling to show any real interest in the detailed problems of governing Germany after the war and preferred to postpone all relevant decisions until the next meeting of the Big Three (which eventually took place at Yalta), at which the basis for postwar cooperation was to be established.

It was against this background that in August, 1944, Secretary Morgenthau, after an inspection tour of the liberated part of France, went to England to see General Eisenhower. Both men apparently agreed that postwar treatment of Germany should be harsh. They felt that "talk of letting Germany off easy . . . came from those who feared Russia and wanted to strengthen Germany as a potential bulwark against any desires for expansion which Russia might some day have." Eisenhower thought that Russia would not want anything, "because she now has all she can digest, and she has problems of her own which will keep her busy until long after we are dead." [8] Morgenthau, an ardent advocate of the early withdrawal of American forces from Europe, was at

Political Science Quarterly, LXXII, No. 4 (December, 1957). In addition to the public record, Dorn relied heavily on his interviews with many key participants in the debate.

8. It is possible to reconstruct the developments which led to the emergence of the Morgenthau Plan by piecing together the recollections of the main actors in that episode. There are some minor discrepancies in the published accounts but they are largely irrelevant for the purposes of this study. The article by Fred Smith, former Assistant to the Secretary of the Treasury, "The Rise and Fall of the Morgenthau Plan," *United Nations World*, (March, 1947), quoted here, appears to be less accurate in some details than, for instance, the Penrose book.

that point much less interested in who would eventually control Germany than he was in making it tough for the Germans.[9]

Having come to the conclusion that Eisenhower (and perhaps Eden, with whom he discussed the subject in the next couple of days)[10] was on his side, Secretary Morgenthau suddenly called a policy meeting. Ambassador John G. Winant and his advisers, Philip E. Mosely and E. F. Penrose, represented the EAC; Colonel Bernard Bernstein, a former Treasury official, represented the European Civil Affairs Division of SHAEF; Harry Dexter White, Joseph Dubois, L. G. Aarons, and William Henry Taylor represented the Treasury. Bernstein criticized what looked to him like a "soft" approach to Germany on the part of SHAEF planners, but Winant pointed out that the planners had no idea what the official American attitude toward Germany was. Penrose summarized British views on the economic treatment of Germany, which, as far as he knew, were determined by pragmatic considerations rather than by vengeance.

Morgenthau then outlined a plan, later amplified by White,

9. Morgenthau told Hopkins on one occasion: "I've got only one object in my life and that is to see that Hitler gets licked." In recruiting personnel for the Treasury, Morgenthau's criteria was "Does [a candidate] want to lick this fellow Hitler, or does he want to sit down and do business with him . . . does this fellow hate Hitler's guts or does he like him." John Morton Blum, *From the Morgenthau Dairies: Years of Urgency, 1938–1941* (Boston: Hougton Mifflin, 1965), pp. 267, 338. At the same time, Morgenthau relentlessly fought those who expressed doubts about American relations with the Soviets. See one of the earlier drafts of his article, "Our Policy toward Germany," in U.S. Congress, Senate, Committee on the Judiciary, *Interlocking Subversion in the Government Departments*, Part 30, 84th Congress, 1st Session, p. 2704. Morgenthau's anti-German feelings reached their peak during his trip to Europe where he learned about the extent of the atrocities committed against the Jews by the nazis. His "pro-Soviet" sentiments were greatly intensified by his hatred for the Germans. He felt that of all the Allies, the Soviets could do the best job in suppressing Germany. See Morgenthau, *Germany Is Our Problem*, pp. 192ff.

10. See the excerpts from the memorandums by White of August 13 and 15, 1944, in the U.S. Department of State, *Foreign Relations of the United States. The Conferences at Cairo and Teheran: 1943* (Washington: U.S. Government Printing Office, 1961), pp. 881–84. Hereinafter cited as *Teheran Papers*. Eden said that he had been waiting for the EAC to come up with a program for reparations and controls over postwar Germany and acquainted Morgenthau with the discussions which had taken place at Teheran and which, presumably, had to serve as a basis for EAC planning. When White mentioned that the British Treasury wanted a restoration of German economy "because prior to the war Germany had been the most important customer of Great Britain. . . . Eden appeared shocked."

to permanently destroy Germany's economic and military capacity to wage war. In order to convert Germany into a "pastoral country," it would be necessary to eliminate German industry, particularly in the Ruhr, Rhineland, and Saar and to resettle a large part of the urban population on farms. To a remark by Penrose that there was not enough arable land in Germany to support all the Germans, Morgenthau replied that "the surplus population should be dumped into North Africa."[11]

Immediately upon his return to Washington, Morgenthau went to the President with his plan. Roosevelt was "shocked that we were apparently so close to victory with no plan in hand to eliminate Germany as a potential war power." The substance of the program outlined by Morgenthau apparently "had a strong emotional appeal to the President, who is reported to have told Morgenthau: 'If I had my way, I would keep Germany on a breadline for the next twenty-five years.'"[12]

On the same day Secretary Stimson received a message from General Eisenhower. Probably suspecting, after his talk with Morgenthau, that the discussion of the future treatment of Germany might develop into a major interdepartmental row, Eisenhower requested the Secretary to relieve SHAEF of its "responsibility for establishing law and order and maintaining economic controls" in occupied Germany.[13] But before this request could be considered Morgenthau, in support of his plan, decided to make sure that Roosevelt received a report from an "independent" source. Colonel Bernstein was flown in from England and given an audience in the White House during which he exposed the

11. Smith, *United Nations World* (March, 1947), p. 35. Cf. Penrose, *Economic Planning for the Peace*, pp. 243–48.

12. Smith, *United Nations World* (March, 1947), p. 36.

13. Quoted by Case, "The Development of the Morgenthau Plan through the Quebec Conference," *The Journal of Politics*, XVI, No. 2 (November, 1954), 335. In another message of August 23, General Eisenhower returned to the subject. Stating that the Allies would certainly have to fight their way into Germany, he suggested that the "soft" pre-surrender CCS-551 directive was no longer applicable. Since it was evident that there would not be any German central government with which to cooperate in the restoration of normal conditions, Eisenhower repeated his request to relieve SHAEF of the responsibilities to control the economy and maintain law and order, because it was ill-equipped for the task. He recommended no alternatives, apparently feeling that "the Germans should be permitted and required to make their own living," the best they could. See Hammond, *American Civil-Military Decisions*, p. 352.

" softness " of the SHAEF planners and gave Roosevelt a copy of the *Basic Handbook*.[14]

On August 26, the President sent a long memorandum to Secretary Stimson, with a copy to Secretary Hull, in which he called the *Basic Handbook* " pretty bad " and ordered that " all copies should be withdrawn." He emphasized that " it is of utmost importance that every person in Germany should realize that this time Germany is a defeated nation." The President continued:

> I do not want them to starve to death, but if they need food to keep body and soul together beyond what they have, they should be fed three times a day with soup from Army soup kitchens. . . . I see no reason for starting a WPA, PWA, or CCC for Germany when we go in with our army of occupation. Too many people here and in England hold to the view that the German people as a whole are not responsible for what has taken place—that only a few Nazi leaders are responsible. That unfortunately is not based on fact. The German people as a whole must have it driven home to them that the whole nation has been engaged in a lawless conspiracy.[15]

To all concerned, this memorandum—which was copied and widely circulated in the State, War, and Treasury Departments—could mean only one thing: the President had adopted Morgenthau's approach to the treatment of postwar Germany. His blast, ostensibly aimed at the SHAEF planners, " certainly had the effect, as it may have been intended by the President, of supporting Mr. Morgenthau's hand in his forthcoming meetings with Secretaries Hull and Stimson." [16] The President had set up a Cabinet committee consisting of Hull, Stimson, and Morgenthau, and coordinated by Harry Hopkins, to work out United States policy for Germany.

14. Harold Zink, *American Military Government in Germany* (New York: Macmillan, 1947), pp. 131–32. Another version has it that Morgenthau gave the *Handbook* to the President himself. According to Drew Pearson, the Secretary went to the White House accompanied by Harry Dexter White (*New York Daily Mirror*, September 21, 1944). Cf. Hammond, *American Civil-Military Decisions*, p. 354.

15. Hull, *Memoirs*, pp. 1602–3.

16. Case, *The Journal of Politics*, XVI, p. 337. Cf. Hammond, *American Civil-Military Decisions*, p. 356.

The deputies of the three Secretaries met on September 2, 1944. Harry Dexter White, who together with several other Treasury officials took charge of developing the Morgenthau Plan, presented a detailed and comprehensive scheme for permanently reducing German power by dismembering the country, destroying its industrial capacity, and by forcibly holding the German people to a subsistence level. The full Committee convened on September 5, and Morgenthau again expounded the Treasury program. Hull, apparently thinking that Morgenthau was reflecting Roosevelt's views, suddenly abandoned the State Department's own moderate plans. Stimson found himself in a minority of one and later recorded in his diary that he had never had "such a difficult and unpleasant meeting." He bitterly opposed Morgenthau, Hopkins, and Hull, and noted his objections in the memorandum which the four addressed to the President after the meeting. "My basic objection to the proposed methods of treating Germany," wrote Stimson, "was that in addition to a system of preventive and educative punishment they would add the dangerous weapon of complete economic oppression. Such methods, in my opinion, do not prevent war; they tend to breed war." [17]

The next day the three Secretaries met with the President. Although remarking that, as far as he was concerned, he would reduce Germany to an agricultural country, Roosevelt appeared to be considerably more restrained than Morgenthau. Encouraged, Hull gave cautious support to Stimson's views and later referred to the Treasury scheme as "a plan of blind vengeance" because "by completely wrecking German industry it could not but partially wreck Europe's economy." [18]

Morgenthau, fearing that Roosevelt was impressed by Stimson's arguments, promptly requested a rehearing. For the next meeting, on the 9th, he presented yet another memorandum, asserting that it was a fallacy that Europe needed a strong industrial Germany,

17. Henry L. Stimson and McGeorge Bundy, *On Active Service in Peace and War* (New York: Harper, 1947), pp. 571–73. Up to this meeting Stimson's position almost coincided with that of Hull. See *The Memoirs of Cordell Hull*, pp. 1606–7. Hull himself offers no explanation for the change in his position. Julius W. Pratt, *Cordell Hull, 1933–44* (New York: Cooper Square, 1964), II, 758, suggests that the harshness of the State Department's proposals presented at that meeting was due to the fact that those charged with the preparation of the draft worked closely with Morgenthau's aides.

18. Hull, *Memoirs*, p. 1606.

and arguing that its destruction would greatly help England by assuring her the domination of the European coal market. Stimson reiterated his views and asked the President not to make any hasty decisions. Roosevelt was about to leave for Quebec to meet the British Prime Minister.

Morgenthau, who since his return from England had "bombarded the White House with statistical and emotional material to fortify his plan, utilizing his genius as a salesman which was unexcelled when he wanted to promote a project with F. D. R.," happened to be on the same train as Roosevelt. He went with the President to Hyde Park—where he stayed overnight—all the while discussing the plan.[19] Three days later Roosevelt summoned Morgenthau to Quebec, where, in the absence of Hull and Stimson, he was invited to unveil his plan to Churchill.

Churchill's first reaction was bitter, and at the end of his speech he declared that he would not chain Great Britain to a dead Germany. The next day, however, the Prime Minister "showed himself more reasonable on the subject of weakening the German economy."[20] He restated the earlier Morgenthau memorandum in his own words and initialed it along with Roosevelt. Churchill's own laconic explanation of this turnabout was that Roosevelt and Morgenthau ("from whom we had much to ask") were so insistent that in the end he agreed to consider the Plan.[21] The gravity of England's economic situation was unquestionable, and Stimson later accused Morgenthau of dangling a six-and-a-half billion dollars' credit before Churchill as an inducement to attain his acceptance of the Plan. Another explanation is that Churchill, who had never been strong in economics, was simply sold on Morgenthau's idea that the destruction of German industry would bring great advantages to the British economy by

19. Smith, *United Nations World* (March, 1947), p. 37.

20. Morgenthau, "Our Policy Toward Germany," *The New York Post* (November 29, 1947). To Churchill, Morgenthau's recommendations were not novel: England had its counterpart of Morgenthau in the person of Sir Robert Vansittart, "a cross between an elder statesman and *enfant terrible*," who advocated a very similar treatment of Germany and the German people in his speeches and writings. See Dorn, *Political Science Quarterly*, LXXII, No. 4, 484–85.

21. Winston S. Churchill, *The Second World War, Triumph and Tragedy* (Boston: Hougton Mifflin, 1953), p. 156. For the text of Churchill's memorandum, see Morgenthau's 1946 article in *The Annals of the American Academy of Political and Social Science*, Vol. 246, p. 126. On Britain's financial distress, see R. S. Sayers, *Financial Policy, 1939–1945* (London: H.M. Stationery Office, 1956), pp. 427ff.

restoring its ability to compete.[22] In any case, Churchill was almost immediately overruled by his colleagues on the grounds that "the economic advantages to Britain of eliminating German industrial competition were largely illusory, and that the creation of chaos in Germany would react to the grave disadvantage of Britain." [23] The Morgenthau Plan was never accepted in London; its spirit remained alien to the officials who were responsible for formulating and implementing British policy toward Germany.

The Plan, albeit in a modified version, became the basis of American policy. Back in Washington, Morgenthau triumphantly handed to Stimson and Hull the directive on the treatment of Germany approved in Quebec by the two leaders. At the risk of irritating Roosevelt, Stimson wrote another appeal to the President, calling the Morgenthau Plan "an open confession of the bankruptcy of hope for a reasonable economic and political settlement of the causes of war." [24] Hull, who by then had again completely reversed his previous position, went to Roosevelt protesting against usurpation of the State Department's functions by the Treasury. He accused Morgenthau of blackmailing Churchill into joining "this extreme starvation plan" (which, if carried out, would mean death to "40 percent of the German population") in exchange for his support in obtaining the huge loan from the United States. And he warned the President that "if Morgenthau's proposals became known and the President were connected with them, it would greatly injure him politically." Roosevelt was at that time in the middle of the 1944 presidential campaign.[25]

Up to that point, very few people besides those directly involved knew about Morgenthau's proposals and the rift in the Cabinet. The President was not on public record as favoring the Treasury

22. Penrose, *Economic Planning for the Peace*, pp. 256–57. See also Hammond, *American Civil-Military Decisions*, pp. 204n, 453–54.

23. F. S. V. Donnison, *Civil Affairs and Military Government, North-West Europe: 1944–1946* (London: H.M. Stationery Office, 1961), p. 198. Cf. Penrose, *Economic Planning for the Peace*, pp. 248–50.

24. Stimson and Bundy, *On Active Service in Peace and War*, pp. 578–79. *Yalta Papers*, pp. 134–41.

25. Hull, *Memoirs*, pp. 1617–18. Yet even then Hull conceded something to Morgenthau's ideas; he proposed to Roosevelt that Germany should be kept under military control for twenty-five or fifty years and that the standard of living of the Germans should be kept below the average of neighboring countries until they gave evidence of devotion to "ideas of human rights, individual liberty, freedom and peace." Pratt, *Cordell Hull*, II, 761.

line, and the opposition could hope to persuade him to change his view. But on September 21 Drew Pearson reported in his column what was by then the month old "news" of Roosevelt's rejection of the *Basic Handbook*. "War and State Department officials are quaking," wrote Pearson, "since President Roosevelt blew up over failure of a plan for civil administration in Germany. British and American army units spent the summer rewriting a handbook for civil administrators to be assigned to Germany." Having listed some of the deficiencies of the *Handbook*, Pearson then described how Morgenthau and Harry Dexter White took the unsatisfactory product of the "army units" to Roosevelt and "tossed" it on the President's desk. Roosevelt ("already peeved because he wasn't consulted on appointment of Robert Murphy as political adviser to Eisenhower") read it and "threw it all down indignantly. 'Feed the Germans!' he said. 'I'll give them three bowls of soup a day, with nothing in them. Control inflation! Let them have all the inflation they want! Control industry! There won't be any industry to control!' He demanded that, within two days, Morgenthau, Stimson and Hull prepare a detailed plan, then wrote Stimson a letter, blistering the handbook."

The opponents of the Morgenthau Plan instantly realized that Pearson's report originated in the Treasury. It was also an evidence of Morgenthau's growing self-confidence and of his intention to commit the President to his policy. Fearful that unless this trend were checked the Morgenthau Plan would be implemented with what from their point of view seemed disastrous consequences, the opposition decided to strike back through the press. Having discussed the situation with Stimson, who apparently did not quite approve of the proposed course of action, Cordell Hull went into a strategy meeting with one of the President's assistants who, he knew, was also worried about Morgenthau's new role and who thoroughly disapproved of the Treasury Plan. Following this meeting, the sympathetic assistant called in Arthur Krock of *The New York Times* and acquainted him with all recent developments. On September 22 Krock reported in the *Times* that Morgenthau's participation in the Quebec Conference meant that the Secretary had become the President's adviser on the postwar treatment of Germany. Two days later, Krock described the split in the Cabinet Committee and outlined the Morgenthau Plan. On the same day, Alfred F. Flynn, who was probably briefed by the same assistant, reported the Morgenthau Plan in considerable detail in *The Wall Street Journal.* Simultaneously, the wire services spread the news all over the world. After that the storm broke.[26]

The Morgenthau Plan came under attack from the American and, particularly, the British press. It was roundly denounced in the House of Commons. It was immediately seized by Goebbels' propaganda machine and used to foster a last-ditch resistance to the Allies. Hitler himself told the German people that the Americans wanted to uproot 15 to 20 million Germans and enslave and starve the rest. From news reports it appeared that the German resistance to the advancing Allied armies had stiffened. The Allied military propagandists in SHAEF, who had been trying to soften the German will to fight by following a quite different line in their broadcasts to Germany, were dismayed. And the Republican presidential candidate, in the heat of the election campaign, called the Morgenthau Plan "as good as ten fresh German divisions." He declared that "the blood of our fighting men is paying for this improvised meddling which is so much a part and parcel of the whole Roosevelt administration." And he asserted that the war was being prolonged by Roosevelt's "own confused incompetence." As Hull had warned the President, his approval of Morgenthau's proposals became a political liability.[27]

Always sensitive to shifting political winds, Roosevelt tried to disassociate himself from the Secretary of the Treasury. On September 27, he telephoned Stimson and told him "that he didn't really intend to make Germany a purely agricultural country."[28]

26. Hull had perhaps an additional satisfaction from striking back because of his feud of long standing with Drew Pearson. Pearson's fierce attacks on Hull in which he accused the Secretary of being "anti-Russian" reached a high point in the summer of 1943, when Roosevelt was forced to fire Under Secretary Welles, Hull's adversary but a close friend of Pearson. See Pratt, *Cordell Hull*, II, 615–17. This episode was explained to me by Mr. Krock in letters dated May 13 and May 28, 1963.

27. For the reaction to the news about the Morgenthau Plan, see Stimson and Bundy, *On Active Service in War and Peace*, p. 580; John L. Snell (ed.), *The Meaning of Yalta* (Baton Rouge: Louisiana State University Press, 1956), p. 50, and his *Wartime Origins of the East-West Dilemma over Germany* (New Orleans: Houser Press, 1959), pp. 97–99; Friedrich, *American Experiences*, pp. 222–24; Chester Wilmot, *The Struggle for Europe* (New York: Harper, 1952), pp. 550–51. The Morgenthau Plan, within the context of the 1944 elections, is also discussed by Hammond, *American Civil-Military Decisions*, pp. 383–86.

28. Stimson and Bundy, *On Active Service in War and Peace*, p. 580.

On September 29, he wrote Hull that "no one wants to make Germany a wholly agricultural nation again," and that "no one wants 'complete eradication of German industrial productive capacity in the Ruhr and Saar.'" The President also indicated his suspicion that the leak which brought public fury down upon the Morgenthau Plan originated in the State Department. "Somebody down the line has handed this out to the press," he wrote. "I wish we could catch and chastise him." [29] In another diversionary move, he directed the Foreign Economic Administrator "to accelerate studies from the economic standpoint of what should be done after the surrender of Germany to control its power and capacity to make war in the future." [30] And he said that it was not the Secretary of the Treasury but the State Department which would "study and report upon the problem of Germany's future." [31]

Nevertheless, President Roosevelt never disowned the Morgenthau Plan. Disappointed with the whole affair he consistently refused to commit himself to any other long-range policy toward Germany. At the same time he let Churchill and Stalin, who were about to meet in Moscow, know that he would prefer that they should not make any decisions about Germany until he could discuss the subject with them.[32]

In an effort to postpone the matter further, the President wrote Hull that although "it is very well for us to make all kinds of preparations for the treatment of Germany," nonetheless "speed

29. Roosevelt to Hull, September 29, 1944, *Yalta Papers*, p. 155. That the President did suspect the State Department was confirmed by Stimson. But, according to Hull, by showing the President that Drew Pearson was in close contact with the Treasury, Stimson convinced him that the leak occurred elsewhere. Hull, *Memoirs*, p. 1620.

30. Roosevelt to Crowley, September 28, 1944. Quoted by Holborn, *American Military Government*, p. 41. This letter was made public by Roosevelt in his September 29 press conference.

31. Ratchford and Ross, *Berlin Reparations Assignment*, pp. 33–38.

32. Herbert Feis, *Churchill, Roosevelt, Stalin: The War They Waged and the Peace They Sought* (Princeton: Princeton University Press, 1957), p. 372. No decisions were made in Moscow but Churchill and Stalin discussed at length "the merits and drawbacks of the Morgenthau Plan" and Stalin expressed lively interest in various schemes for the partition of Germany. Informed by Churchill, Roosevelt found Stalin's ideas "most interesting" but reiterated his desire to postpone final decisions until all three could get together. See Churchill, *Triumph and Tragedy*, pp. 240–42. Churchill does not reveal precisely what Stalin's ideas were. As the talks at Yalta later showed, Stalin tried, with a measure of success, to take advantage of the Morgenthau spirit in the United States government.

on these matters is not an essential at the present moment." He disliked "making detailed plans for a country which we do not yet occupy." The European Advisory Commission, if it was anxious to do so, could "go ahead and execute some of the advice," although, "when the time comes, we may not like it at all."[33]

The meeting with Stalin and Churchill at Yalta did not lead to a clarification of United States policy toward Germany. Records of the formal meetings throw little light on Roosevelt's views in February, 1945. It is possible that they were more clearly defined in his private talks with Stalin and Churchill, but no record is available of them.[34] Several possible reasons may be advanced for Roosevelt's apparent indecision. It may have been the result of the contradictory pressures to which he had been subjected in Washington. Or it is possible that the poor state of his health prevented him from concentrating on all but immediate and clear-cut issues. In addition, the relations between Stalin and Churchill were already so strained that Roosevelt would be likely to avoid getting into the question of the general treatment of Germany because he feared the emergence of little else but three irreconcilable positions.

Besides the inconclusive discussion of dismemberment, the only topic that came up in several meetings was that of reparations. The Soviet proposals closely paralleled the corresponding features of the Morgenthau Plan and were firmly rejected by Churchill. When Churchill finally suggested relegating the question to a commission, Roosevelt decided to side with him. The President also made the point that Germany should be left enough industry to keep her from starving and that the United States would not finance the reparations program this time as it did in the twenties.[35] This was a considerable modification of his views of a few months earlier and suggested that Roosevelt's position may have changed before Yalta.

It has been implied or suggested by many students of the ques-

33. Roosevelt to Hull, October 2, 1944, *Yalta Papers*, p. 158.

34. James F. Byrnes, *All in One Lifetime* (New York: Harper, 1958), p. 259.

35. Byrnes, *All in One Lifetime*, pp. 26–28. Also *Yalta Papers*, pp. 193–97, 808, 909. The American position was that reparations were only a part of the over-all economic policy to be adopted toward Germany and should not be decided separately.

tion that the United States did not really have a policy toward defeated Germany. It has been pointed out that President Roosevelt, except for the Quebec episode, consistently shied away from making a formal decision in Washington and followed the tactics of postponement in his relations with the Allies. It has been further asserted that his shifting views on the issues brought into focus by Morgenthau's proposals did not add up to anything that could be called policy.

Formally, this might have been so. Indeed, what is known as the Morgenthau Plan was not one single document; Morgenthau himself modified his position more than once, and even the first White memorandum of September 1, 1944, was in some respects more moderate than the Secretary of the Treasury wished. Yet all the modifications, both in the Treasury stand and in Roosevelt's views, were only a matter of degree, and of a very small degree at that. With all the cross-currents in Washington, there was no serious disagreement among the participants in the debate on the substance of how Germany should be treated. Everybody agreed that the policy must be harsh and that peace must be punitive. The Treasury took an extreme position in that it wanted to assure, among other things, economic chaos in Germany, and the State Department contended that without maintaining control over the economy, the occupation authorities would not be able to meet their responsibilities in enforcing reparations and restitution. State was also more aware of the interdependence of the European economy and of the necessity of preserving Germany, if only as an economic unit ruled jointly by the Big Three. In this respect the Treasury took a devil-may-care attitude which eventually found its expression in the occupation policy directive.

The War Department, with the notable exception of Secretary Stimson, whose views were close to those of the Department of State, was willing to accept any policy which would have given the military government maximum freedom of action and an absolute minimum of responsibilities for governing the defeated nation. Like all other participants in the debate, the military did not consult the Hague Rules Respecting the Laws and Customs of War on Land;[36] the fear of being branded "pro-German" was

36. Violations of the Hague Rules by the Axis were severely criticized in the United States by international lawyers, economists, and other writers. See, for instance, Raphael Lemkin, *Axis Rule in Occupied Europe* (Washington: Carnegie

so great that it effectively silenced everyone who dared to challenge the Treasury extremists.

Finally, it seems to be established beyond reasonable doubt that President Roosevelt essentially shared Morgenthau's approach and supported at least tacitly his position in the interdepartmental wrangling which, to him, was over technicalities and not over the substance of the problem. If at one point or another his views appeared tempered, this was probably more a result of various pressures, domestic as well as international, rather than of a change of heart.

The question of whether the United States did or did not have a policy toward Germany as a whole is less relevant than it may appear. Since Germany was to be occupied not by the United States alone, and since it had already been decided that each victor would rule as sovereign in his zone of occupation, a meaningful and binding policy could emerge only as a result of a consensus among the Big Three. A consensus eventually emerged. It took the form of the Allied Declaration Regarding the Defeat of Germany, signed in Berlin on June 5, 1945, but it was binding only if enforced through the Allied Control Council, in which each participant held a power of veto. Yet to the extent joint decisions —including the declaration—were made, they were affected by the attitudes of the American policymakers. As the record shows, Roosevelt's sentiments on punishing the Germans were not lacking in clarity, and in the end it was not his (or Truman's) fault that the Morgenthau Plan, in one form or another, did not become law for the whole of Germany.

What is relevant to this part of my study is that to the extent to which the United States became a sovereign power in Germany (that is in its own zone of occupation), it *did* have a policy. This policy was officially approved by Roosevelt and later by Truman. It was spelled out in considerable detail in a document which came to be known as JCS-1067. This directive did not contain *all* the original provisions of the Morgenthau Plan. Dismemberment of

Endowment for International Peace, 1944), pp. 50ff. For the early evolution of official American attitudes toward the Hague Rules, see Friedrich (ed.), *American Experiences*, pp. 23ff. The existence of such a double standard might be understandable in view of certain nazi practices. Nonetheless, the fact that the Directive for the Treatment of Germany, which became the law in the United States zone, violated about nine articles of the convention duly ratified by the United States needs to be recorded.

Germany, flooding the coal mines, wrecking of the Ruhr and Rhineland industry, and the "pastoralization" of the German nation were not mentioned, perhaps because these measures were beyond American control anyway. But most of the rest remained.

The State-War-Treasury discussions of the text of the "draft interim directive," urgently requested by SHAEF, started on September 2, as a part of the proceedings of the Cabinet Committee on Germany. Several drafts were produced, with the Treasury team constantly trying to "stiffen" the punitive provisions. By September 17 the gap between the contending viewpoints had narrowed, but the State Department continued to oppose the economic policy sections of the draft prepared by the Treasury. The showdown came on September 22, four days before the Cabinet Committee on Germany was dissolved by the President in view of the public scandal developing around the Morgenthau Plan. When on that day,

> Harry Hopkins called the deputies of the members of the Cabinet Committee to meet in Mr. McCloy's office for an all-day session to draft the interim directive for General Eisenhower, the Treasury representatives declared that the original White memorandum had been approved by the President. This put an end to all further opposition on the part of their colleagues from the War and State Departments. Thus it happened that the original version of J.C.S. 1067 became largely a Treasury document. Although written in accordance with the limited liability theory of the War Department, its principal features were of Treasury origin and none of the basic State Department policy recommendations were incorporated in its clauses. By forbidding the American Army to maintain price, wages and market controls, it literally decreed, as a State Department official put it, economic chaos. In this way the Treasury's view that the extreme disruption of German economy was not in conflict with Allied interests became official American policy . . . the Cabinet Committee, including Mr. Hull, approved this directive. . . .[37]

37. Dorn, *Political Science Quarterly*, LXXII, No. 4, pp. 494–95. Dorn's report is corroborated by J. W. Riddleberger, who represented the State Department at that meeting. In his memorandum to Hull, Riddleberger wrote that the Treasury representatives present insisted that the Treasury Department "should be consulted on all phases of German problems, including both political and economic." They

Hull's approval, however, did not come easily. On September 25 he addressed a memorandum to the President in which he pointed out the necessity of consulting Great Britain and the Soviet Union before approving the directive and reminded Roosevelt that the European Advisory Commission existed precisely for the purpose of such consultations. Hull's appeal was not answered and consequently he had to bow to his Chief's wishes. The War Department, that is Stimson and McCloy, also accepted the directive. It was immediately cleared with Roosevelt, approved by the Joint Chiefs of Staff (JCS), and sent to Eisenhower and Winant. Simultaneously, it was recommended by the JCS for consideration to the Combined Chiefs of Staff (CCS). It was taken up by the CCS at the meeting on October 3 but was rejected by the British on the spot, "somewhat to the surprise of War Department officials, who anticipated difficulties with the British Cabinet instead."[38]

The directive was intended as stopgap policy guidance for the American and British forces in Germany, to be replaced at a later date by an agreed upon long-term policy. Because of British opposition, it could serve only as a policy guide to Eisenhower in his capacity as the ranking American military commander in Europe and would therefore apply only to the United States zone of occupation.

Not everything is clear about this episode. How did it happen that even Harry Hopkins did not know that Roosevelt approved the White memorandum? Why did Hull, who on that very day of September 22 was mapping his counterstrike against the Treasury, fail to devise some way to postpone the decision for another week or two? Of course, the odds against him were great and perhaps the atmosphere of what appeared to be Morgenthau's triumph was overwhelming. Stimson's and McCloy's later explanation was that they had been convinced that since Morgenthau had the President's

also "insinuated that the Treasury plan for the treatment of Germany had received the approval of the Cabinet Committee and the blessing of the President." *Yalta Papers*, p. 141.

38. Hammond, *American Civil-Military Decisions*, p. 376. It seems likely that Secretary Hull was less surprised by the British rejection of the directive. On September 27 he had sent a copy of the directive to London, with a note stressing that the document had "not yet been approved by the Combined Civil Affairs Committee" and informing that "it is not transmitted for submission to the European Advisory Committee." *Yalta Papers*, pp. 142–43. The implication, of course, was that the British still could veto it. If this message came into the British hands in time, they could instruct their representatives at the CCS to do just that.

ear, no other directive was obtainable. Their further justification was that in view of the military situation in Europe, they were willing to settle on *any* directive, even this one, which, as they well knew, was impracticable to say the least.

If such was the case, what followed becomes easier to understand. JCS-1067 remained the only official expression of American policy toward Germany. But to the participants of the meeting, the document agreed upon on September 22 was an interim directive and, at least in theory, subject to revisions. This left an opening which the State Department, in the aftermath of the public furor over the Morgenthau Plan and Roosevelt's retreat, attempted to exploit. The Department again tried to win over the President to its views. It argued its position with the War Department and in various committees, particularly in the State-War-Navy Coordinating Committee (SWNCC), established in December under the chairmanship of Assistant Secretary of State Dunn, where JCS-1067 was supposed to be " finalized." [39]

These efforts were of no avail. Although the Treasury was officially removed from the policyplanning for Germany, Morgenthau remained close to the President; he still had to be consulted on matters of economic policy and his general concurrence to any decision was indispensable. Far from being pushed into the background, Morgenthau pursued his goals with relentless energy. He was in constant communication with Stimson, McCloy, Marshall, and Stettinius (who by then had replaced Hull). He subjected the British draft policy directive for Germany to devastating criticism, complaining among other things that it failed to deal with " the elimination or destruction of heavy industry in Germany." He told Stettinius that the British were altogether too soft on the Germans and intended to give Allied commanders " too much responsibility for the well-functioning of the German economy." [40]

Although Stettinius was committed to the State Department's position he had few ideas of his own and was inclined to accommodate Morgenthau. Before long he started to advocate for the German people " the lowest standards of health, diet and shelter

39. SWNCC was charged with the formulation of recommendations to the Secretary of State on questions having both political and military aspects and with coordinating the views of the three Departments in matters of common interest. See Notter (ed.), *Postwar Foreign Policy Preparations: 1939–1945*, pp. 347–48.

40. *Yalta Papers*, p. 164.

compatible with the prevention of disease and disorder." [41] In addition to having to contend with the views of their own Secretary, the State Department representatives in SWNCC ran into heavy opposition from the War Department, which, fearing that the recently won compromise would be lost, insisted that nothing be done in the revision of JCS-1067 to alienate the Treasury and that changes from the original version should be modest. The revision, agreed upon in SWNCC on January 6, 1945, was still essentially the same document which the Cabinet Committee and Roosevelt approved in the previous September. It prescribed the "industrial disarmament" of Germany and the enforcement of the program of reparations and restitution. Economic controls were permitted only to the extent that they "may be essential to protect the safety and meet the needs of the occupying forces and assure the production and maintenance of goods and services required to prevent starvation or such disease and unrest as would endanger these forces." It stated that the execution of a reparations program should not be used as an excuse for supporting basic living conditions in Germany. In its special financial section, JCS-1067 forbade any steps "designed to maintain, strengthen or operate the German financial structure," except in the interests of the occupying power.[42]

The revised directive still contained the reservation that it was not "intended to be an ultimate statement of policies of this Government concerning the treatment of Germany in the postwar world." Although to the State Department this reservation looked less and less convincing, it continued its efforts to persuade Roosevelt to abandon his adherence to Morgenthau's program. These efforts produced only one victory, and even that was a short-lived one. After the Yalta Conference, Roosevelt unexpectedly directed Stettinius to prepare a policy paper based on Yalta decisions. Having received so direct a commission, the State Department "responded with unusual speed and decision, and, taking advantage of this opportunity to recast American occupation policy, drew

41. Stettinius to Roosevelt, November 10, 1944, *Ibid.*, p. 166. Cf. Morgenthau's memorandums to Stettinius, *ibid.*, pp. 163–65, 175–76.

42. For the full text of JCS-1067, see *Department of State Bulletin*, XIII (1945), pp. 596–607. Cf. Manuel Gottlieb, *The German Peace Settlement and the Berlin Crisis* (New York: Paine-Whitman, 1960), p. iii, and Friedrich (ed.), *American Experiences*, pp. 41ff.

up its own draft directive on March 10 and sent it on to the White House. Two days later, the President returned it to the State Department with his official approval. For exactly eight days this State Department directive, superseding the J.C.S. 1067, remained the official statement of American policy when it fell prey to the combined opposition of the War and Treasury Departments." [43]

The Treasury-War alliance was re-established on March 20 in Morgenthau's office when he conferred with McCloy and Hilldring. Whatever their differences, they agreed on their opposition to the State Department's March 10 directive. Morgenthau then went to the ailing President. The showdown came on March 23 at a meeting in the White House at which the three interested Departments were represented. (Leo Crowley, the Foreign Economic Administrator, who had been assigned by Roosevelt six months earlier to study the economic aspects of the occupation, was not invited.) Roosevelt stated that he had not read the State Department's draft which he had approved, that he did not like the March 10 directive now that he read it, and ordered it to be superseded by another document which, in effect, left JCS-1067 intact. This document, signed at Morgenthau's insistence by all present, contained instructions to the recently created Informal Policy Committee on Germany to proceed with the final draft of the directive.

After that Morgenthau took no chances. Although the Informal Policy Committee was presided over by Assistant Secretary of State Clayton, " it was perhaps of more than symbolic significance " that it held its plenary meetings in Morgenthau's office. Even after Roosevelt's death, Morgenthau continued to be recognized as " the guardian of the President's views." [44] The final draft of JCS-1067 was agreed upon on April 26, 1945, approved by President Truman on May 11, and issued to Eisenhower three days later.

By then Stimson and McCloy had abandoned all resistance to Morgenthau, mainly because they felt that it was too late to change

43. Dorn, *Political Science Quarterly*, LXXII, No. 4, 496. For a detailed account, see Hammond, *American Civil-Military Decisions*, pp. 408–21.

44. Dorn, *Political Science Quarterly*, LXXII, No. 4, p. 497. In 1946 Morgenthau argued, and not without reason, that the " pastoralization " of Germany was " an official policy of governments, not—as is so often alleged—a personal scheme of mine." He supported his argument with the pertinent passages from the Yalta and Potsdam agreements. Henry Morgenthau, " Postwar Treatment of Germany," *The Annals of the American Academy of Political and Social Science*, Vol. 246, pp. 127–28.

policy; the War Department's occupation instructions, based on JCS-1067, had been drafted, printed, and sent out. The prospect of renewing the argument with the still influential Secretary of the Treasury under the new administration was not appealing to them.

Stettinius did not argue either. At that time he was deeply involved in the preparations for the United Nations conference in San Francisco. In any case, he had never become very personally involved in the subject of the treatment of Germany. With the opposition to the Treasury viewpoint silenced, the State Department was effectively removed from policymaking with regard to Germany, at least until the 1947 Moscow Conference of the Foreign Ministers.

This was perhaps inevitable. Germany became subject to military rule, so much so that General Lucius D. Clay, United States Military Governor in Germany, went to his post without even thinking of consulting anyone in the State Department.[45] Clay's political adviser, Robert Murphy, could not obtain any guidance from the State Department. James F. Byrnes, who became Secretary of State under the Truman administration, had close personal ties with Clay, and his views on Germany were later greatly influenced by the General. But he was too deeply involved in a series of international conferences where the multitude of pressing questions dealing with peace settlements with countries other than Germany were debated and decided. For over a year after Potsdam, Byrnes paid little attention to the role of Germany; all in all, as Harry Hopkins put it early in the summer of 1945, "Germany was pretty far down on Washington's priority list." [46]

Because of British opposition, the CCS failed to agree on how to treat Germany. But it approved the recommendations of the CCAC based on the modification of its earlier directive on presurrender policies and, on October 6, 1944, sent orders to the Supreme Commander requiring the redrafting of the SHAEF handbook. The final text was based on the following principles: (1) that no steps involving economic rehabilitation of Germany were to be undertaken; (2) that no relief supplies were to be imported or distributed beyond the minimum necessary to prevent

45. Robert Murphy, *Diplomat among Warriors* (Garden City, N.Y.: Doubleday, 1964), p. 249.
46. *Ibid.*, pp. 260–61.

disease and such disorders as might endanger or impede military operations; (3) that under no circumstances should active nazis or ardent sympathies be retained in office for purposes of administrative convenience or expediency; and (4) that Germany should always be treated as a defeated and not as a liberated country.[47]

No further CCS directives were ever issued. The British and the French (who soon became the fourth party in the occupation of Germany) did not feel bound by the October directive; after the end of hostilities they modified their policies according to what they believed to be the requirements of an efficient administration. As was shown, the Americans had no such choice.

The final version of JCS-1067 was not even given to the British at the CCS for their approval. It was meant to be "a statement of United States policy to be presented simultaneously to the British and the Russians" through the European Advisory Commission in London. There it was opposed by representatives of the State Department and the Foreign Economic Administration of the United States.

The Americans presented British and the Soviet representatives in the Commission with a "spectacle of internal dissension."[48] Even after it became evident that no joint policy would emerge from that body, some officials in Washington continued to hope that in the Allied Control Council Eisenhower, Clay, and Murphy would urge other members to adopt JCS-1067 as a guide to their policies. The record of their efforts was slim and unrewarding.

JCS-1067 was a secret document to serve as guidance only to the top officials in the American military government in Germany; even its very existence was initially denied. It was published, rather suddenly, in the *Department of State Bulletin* in October, 1945. Although its publication was cleared through SWNCC, the reasons for this step are not clear. The likeliest explanation is

47. The *Handbook* was an important document, not only because it was accepted also by the British but because it served as guidance to each and every officer for his attitude toward the German people. In practical terms, however, perhaps its major significance was in that it meant the "almost complete withdrawal of the modest discretion allowed to the military government." Donnison, *Civil Affairs*, pp. 203, 198; Friedrich (ed.), *American Experiences*, pp. 37–38. The *Handbook for Military Government in Germany* was released in London by SHAEF in December 1944.

48. Lewis H. Brown, *A Report on Germany* (New York: Farrar Straus, 1947), p. 11.

that the State Department wanted to prove to the Soviets—Secretary Byrnes was at that moment attending the Conference of Foreign Ministers in Moscow—that the United States' "tough" attitude toward Germany had not changed.[49] Another explanation is that the publication of the directive was the result of pressures on the part of the more strongly anti-German elements within the government who wanted to reassure the public that the official attitude toward the defeated enemy remained the same, while putting General Clay on notice that his acts in Germany would now be watched by many eyes and that his deviations from the directive would be recorded.

If the latter explanation is correct, the publication of the directive had opposite results. As soon as it was made public, Clay flew to Washington to request that JCS-1067 be modified and that he be allowed greater leeway in its implementation. Although nothing was done at that time, "everyone he consulted, from President Truman down, conceded that drastic modifications were in order."[50] As will be shown later, these new sentiments had significant consequences for the United States zone of Germany.

49. One of the peculiar misconceptions under which American policymakers and military and civilian planners operated was the assumption of the implacable Soviet hatred for all things German. This misconception dated back to pre-Teheran days when the Western Allies feared a separate Stalin-Hitler deal and were anxious to prove to Stalin their determination to fight Hitler to the end. It persisted in Allied negotiations long after Stalin expressed criticism of the unconditional surrender policy and proclaimed that "the German people are not responsible for Hitler's crimes." See Hanson W. Baldwin, *Great Mistakes of the War* (New York: Harper, 1950), pp. 15–16. In this, the Western powers failed to take notice of the basically pragmatic elements in Soviet policy. The result was that the Anglo-American position in Germany was—and still is—weakened by the recurrent outbursts of anti-German emotions in various forms, emotions which have been skillfully played upon by the Soviet government.

50. Murphy, *Diplomat among Warriors*, p. 285.

CHAPTER VIII

SOVIET OCCUPATION FINANCE PRACTICES IN EASTERN EUROPE AND THE SOVIET ZONE OF GERMANY

The economic and financial aspects of Soviet occupation in the 1939–40 period in eastern Poland, Estonia, Latvia, Lithuania, and Bessarabia and, after 1944, in Rumania, Bulgaria, Hungary, Poland, and Czechoslovakia suggest that the Soviet government was guided by two major considerations: to secure benefits for the Soviet Union and to induce in the occupied countries a runaway inflation in order to lower their standard of living and to undermine the traditional socioeconomic structure. The induced inflation complemented the political and administrative measures which were carried out by the occupation authorities to the same end.

There was a significant difference between the two periods. The areas which were annexed as a result of the Stalin-Ribbentrop Pact were considered "liberated." The occupation period, before these areas were formally incorporated into the Soviet Union, lasted only for a few months. The Soviet army was subject to strict discipline, and although the troops benefited from the occupation, this was mainly a by-product; the Soviet government was primarily concerned with annexing these areas as quickly and painlessly as possible.

The occupation of Eastern Europe in 1944–45, on the other hand, had all the characteristics of a conquest. Soviet economic needs were far greater by then, and the troops were instructed to live off the land. At the same time, economic and financial policies of occupation were designed to serve the long-range plans of consolidating the Soviet position in every country of the expected Soviet sphere of influence. It appeared that both aims did not contradict each other and could be pursued simultaneously, in a fashion typical of the integrated communist *Weltanschauung*. It was several years before such factors as political and economic nationalism, ignored during the occupation, began to manifest themselves and complicate the relations within the communist bloc.

During the short Soviet occupation of 1939–40, the indigenous currencies of the occupied countries remained legal tender. The ruble, with which the troops were paid, was also declared legal tender and circulated alongside the local currencies. The occupation authorities relied on rubles for their general needs.

The Soviet government was aware that these areas were soon to become an integral part of the Soviet Union; such was the Soviet interpretation of the provisions of the secret protocol attached to the Stalin-Ribbentrop Pact. The transitional period of occupation was utilized for political and economic preparation for the final act of annexation. Monetary policy was designed to reduce the general standard of living of the local population drastically and as a means of dispossessing the wealthier classes who were violently opposed to the merger with communist Russia.

These goals were achieved by a combination of measures which included an induced inflation. Among the inflationary forces were: (*a*) the inflow of large quantities of Soviet rubles, (*b*) massive spending by the troops and Soviet officials which quickly reduced the supply of available goods, (*c*) Soviet procurement practices, and (*d*) large-scale wage increases for local labor.

The establishment of rates of exchange between the ruble and the local currencies which vastly overvalued the ruble—by maybe as much as 2,000–3,000 per cent—put tremendous purchasing power into the hands of the occupation army and the multitudes of Soviet officials who came swarming into the " liberated " territories. The availability of goods in the stores assured an almost uncontrollable inflow of Soviet paper currency. The retail stores in cities and villages were for a while crowded with Soviet customers who suddenly found themselves immensely rich and who could buy with their rubles and send to their families goods long unavailable in Russia. During that brief period anyone who was anybody in the Soviet Union was pulling strings in order to be sent on a "business trip" to "liberated" areas in the west.[1] Local merchants at first were happy to have such brisk business, but they soon discovered that their sources of supply were giving out, and that all they had to show for it were piles of worthless rubles.

The shortages were inevitable in view of the activities of the thousands of Soviet purchasing agents. They were everywhere and, by successfully outbidding local merchants, contracted the goods in warehouses as well as the current production from local factories for delivery to Russia. At the same time, production was disorganized by the deliberate policies of the occupation authorities which backed the newly created communist and pro-communist organizations in their demands for higher wages for workers and farm hands. Propaganda campaigns purporting to show Soviet interest in raising the standard of living accompanied these policies. Employers, aware of the changed political situation, were forced to increase wages, sometimes tenfold, but since they were forbidden to increase prices for their goods, mass bankruptcies followed and many businesses folded.

The disorganization of the economy, with the resulting acute shortages of food and all basic commodities, was obviously a consequence of Soviet occupation policies. But when a sharp increase in the cost of living and the appearance of the black market led to general discontent among the people, the communist propaganda blamed all economic difficulties on "capitalist elements" which presumably sabotaged the "liberators'" efforts to improve the well-being of the "working class." This propaganda set the stage for a gigantic purge of the "bourgeoisie" when the "liberated" areas were finally incorporated into the Soviet Union. The former "capitalists" had their stores and factories automatically nationalized; in the mass arrests which followed, they were stripped of their personal possessions (including the rubles which they had accumulated during the occupation) and, with their families, were shipped to Siberia by the trainload.

1. At the same time, the stores in the occupied regions were getting a fairly good supply of Soviet merchandise in order to demonstrate to the local population that things were not too bad in the Soviet Union. This information, as well as other data related to the Soviet occupation practices in 1939–40 was obtained in interviews with people who lived under the Soviet rule during that period and who now reside in the United States.

The old currency—which people still held at the moment of the annexation—was simply abolished.[2] Workers began to receive their wages in rubles; others had to adjust to the new conditions the best way they could.

The success of the Soviet policies of occupation fell short of their goal in one respect: in spite of all the upheaval which the occupation caused, the standard of living in the annexed territories still remained higher than that which prevailed in the rest of Russia. In order to obscure this fact from the masses of Soviet citizens—and to protect them from a possible contamination from excessive contact with a society which was so recently "capitalist"—a sort of informal boundary was established along the old Soviet frontier, with the police carefully screening the traffic in both directions. This state of affairs lasted until the German invasion of Russia in June 1941.

The experience with the occupation during the 1939–40 period was fully utilized by the Soviets when the Red army again crossed the Soviet borders toward the end of the war. The device of overvaluing the ruble to the same absurd degree was successfully employed in the occupations of Poland, Rumania, Bulgaria, Hungary, and Czechoslovakia.

The Soviets did not contemplate outright annexation of these countries. They were not sure to what degree, and for how long, they were going to exercise control there. This uncertainty lasted for the first two postwar years; it accounts, better than anything else, for many inconsistencies, as well as extremes, of Soviet behavior in Eastern Europe. During this period, the occupied countries had coalition governments in which the communists may or may not have played a leading role but where they were firmly, and increasingly, supported by Soviet administrations. It made no difference whether a country had a "friendly" government at the end of the war (anti-German governments appeared in all of them in due course) or not. Always mindful of history and deeply aware of the hostility toward communism (if not always toward Russia), a characteristic of the traditional Eastern Euro-

2. Because the annexed territories were by then flooded with Soviet paper money, the deflationary effect of this act was limited, especially since the shortages of goods were growing steadily.

pean societies, Stalin looked beyond tomorrow. He knew that the submissive leftist regimes could remain in power mainly, if not exclusively, as the result of the presence of Soviet troops. And he knew that in order to create more solid foundations for the Soviet domination, far-reaching social changes were required, which necessitated the destruction of the economic positions of the old ruling classes—something that all communists, regardless of nationality, enthusiastically welcomed.

Not all Soviet economic objectives in Eastern Europe were shared by the local communists. For example, there was an imperative necessity to lower the general standard of living in the occupied countries because it was still considerably higher than that of Russia. This disparity had to be reduced not only because it provoked unfavorable comparisons among the millions of Soviet soldiers pouring into Europe, but also because the Soviets held that a great power had to be better off economically than its satellites in order to assert its primacy. Such considerations justified harsh armistice terms as well as unrestricted requisitions and plunder, which were common in most occupied areas.

Consequently, the effects of Soviet occupation were, for the most part, very painful. The helpless governments of the occupied countries of Eastern and Central Europe, whether former enemies or not, had to pay reparations and shoulder all Soviet occupation costs, providing millions of Soviet soldiers with housing, transportation, food, and even clothing.[3] When Soviet authorities deemed it necessary to pay for such goods and services, their payments were made in rubles at a highly inflated rate of exchange imposed by Moscow.[4]

3. The most lenient treatment was probably accorded to Czechoslovakia, which leaned toward Moscow more than any other nation of Eastern-Central Europe. See, for instance, Paul E. Zinner, *Communist Strategy and Tactics in Czechoslovakia, 1918–48* (New York: Praeger, 1963), pp. 99–102. Nevertheless, Article 2 of the Soviet-Czechoslovak Agreement, signed on March 31, 1945, reads: "The Government of the Czechoslovak Republic undertakes to consider as its own military expenditures all its expenditures for the maintenance of the Red Army units, such as cash outlays, materials and services. It undertakes an obligation to place at the disposal of the Red Army units for the duration of war all necessary cash, materials and services, charging these expenditures against the budget of the Czechoslovak Republic." Ministerstvo Inostrannykh Del SSSR, Ministerstvo Inostrannykh Del ChSR, *Sovetsko-chekhoslovatskiye otnosheniya vo vremya Velikoi Otechestvennoi Voiny 1941–1945 gg.* (Moscow, 1960), p. 240.

4. The rate of exchange of the Polish zloty, for instance, in 1945 was 100 zloty

Local governments were obligated to furnish local currency upon request. Although there is no record that any Soviet request had ever been turned down, the original procedure was soon modified. By appointing either their own officials or trusted local communists to the appropriate positions, the Soviets acquired a more direct control over the note-printing facilities and helped themselves to paper money without restraint. Before long, it was often the local governments who were asking for their own currency for their needs. The amounts printed or issued can, at best, only be estimated. Soviet control over monetary circulation—soon extended to the banking systems—for all practical purposes turned indigenous currencies into occupation currencies. Although there probably were some Soviet economists who were horrified by the adopted practices, the policy, however inconsistent, aimed at the dispossession of the rich through a deliberate monetary inflation.

The pattern of monetary inflation was uneven throughout Eastern Europe. In addition to the overheated printing presses, many political and economic factors helped determine its severity: general Soviet policy toward the occupied country (which was often a function of the population's hostility to the communist "new order" and its capacity for sabotaging it); the number of Soviet troops stationed in the country and the duration of occupation; the size of indemnities and restitutions demanded by the Soviet government; the degree of decomposition of the old administrative machinery and the new regime's ability to administer budgets in which the outgo often exceeded the revenue by 400–500 per cent; the extent of mass evictions (like those of the Germans from Poland or Czechoslovakia, or of the Magyars from Rumania or Czechoslovakia), which meant a loss of many skilled laborers; and the extent of the labor market's disorganization owing to communist agitation for ever higher wages and radical land reforms, which was intended to win greater support of the masses.

Among these factors, the over-all Soviet attitude seems to have been crucial. In "liberated" and basically friendly Czechoslovakia, for instance, the Soviets exercised considerable restraint; the country was occupied for only six months. Although the total

to 1 ruble. Since the wartime rate of exchange between the reichsmark and the zloty was 1 to 2, and the dollar-mark ratio after the war was 1 to 10, the dollar-ruble cross rate was something like $5.00 to 1 ruble, an obvious absurdity.

of goods and services supplied by the Czechs is unknown, it probably had a substantial inflationary impact; by the time of the first postwar currency reform—October, 1945—there were an equivalent of 120 billion *krony* in circulation, reduced in the reform to 24 billion. But the inflation continued after the occupation had ended: by 1947 there were already 56 billion, and by 1948, 69 billion *krony* in circulation.[5] The 1945–48 increase was noticeable—about 2.9 times—but was attributable exclusively to internal factors and thus should be considered " normal " within our context.

In occupied Poland the situation was also relatively favorable. Poland was officially a " liberated " country and developments there were for a while closely watched in Washington and London. Poland paid no restitution to anyone; on the contrary, it received reparations from Germany and heavy infusions of UNRRA supplies. In addition, the relatively undamaged new provinces of the Oder-Neisse region, cleared of the indigenous Germans, allowed for an orderly solution to the population resettlement problem. Yet largely because of the presence of large numbers of Soviet troops, the monetary picture in Poland was noticeably worse than in Czechoslovakia. The currency reform of January 15, 1945, reduced the amount of zloty in circulation from about 27 billion to 13.6 billion. But a year later there were 36.7 billion and, by 1948, 130 billion zloty in circulation.[6] This represented a very substantial increase—about ten times the 1945 figure—but the situation was not nearly as bad as it was elsewhere.

Rumania was an " enemy " country which the Soviets felt free to punish. It was occupied by a large number of troops, but its government, which had purged itself of pro-nazi elements and, having joined the anti-Axis coalition, lost nearly 170,000 troops, tended to resist the kind of internal reorganization that the Soviets demanded.[7] This resistance explains the harshness of the occupa-

5. V. P. Komissarov and A. N. Popov, *Den'gi, kredit i finansy evropeiskikh stran narodnoi demokratii* (Moscow, 1960), pp. 18–20. Of course, like any other Soviet source, this one carefully avoids blaming Soviet authorities for economic disorders in the Soviet-occupied countries. The monetary chaos is usually ascribed to the " grave heritage " left by the old capitalistic regimes, and to the consequences of the war.

6. *Ibid.*, pp. 16–18.

7. Ghita Ionescu, *Communism in Rumania, 1944–1962* (Oxford: Oxford University Press, 1964), p. 91.

tion rule in Rumania better than anything else, while the harshness found its reflection in the monetary field. Although Rumania's economy had not suffered badly in the war and the transition to the new regime was gradual, inflation became rampant. The total monetary circulation in June, 1944, shortly before the beginning of the occupation, was 211.8 billion *lei.* A year later, it was already 649 billion, and by the end of the same year it was 1,232 billion *lei.* By the end of the following year, 1946, 6,397 billion were in circulation. In June of the next year the figure was 40,684 billion, 63 times more than the 1945 and 726 times more than that of 1939. At the same time, while the cost of living index in August, 1944, stood at 944 (August, 1939 = 100), in July, 1947, it was 525,688.[8]

No reliable figures are available for Albania and Bulgaria. Stalin thought that Bulgaria "deserved punishment,"[9] even though it had never declared war on the Soviet Union or hurt Soviet interests in any other way. The punishment, by the standards of the times, was mild. Ignoring the formation of an anti-German goverment in Sofia (which immediately declared itself no longer at war with Great Britain and the United States), the Soviet Union suddenly declared war on Bulgaria on September 5, 1944; its troops crossed the Danube three days later. But because the Red army encountered no resistance, and because the Bulgarians—except for pro-Western and, therefore, anti-communist elements—greeted Russian soldiers with great enthusiasm, the occupation regime did not develop the harshness typical of other places. Its mildness was evident in the soldiers' behavior; they were subject to rigid discipline and their offenses against the local population were kept within reasonable limits.

A quite different situation developed in Hungary, the country which remained loyal to the Axis until the end. Although the government created there under Soviet auspices was left of center, even the former opponents of the Horthy regime and confirmed antifascists regarded the Soviet Union and the Hungarian communists (who returned from their Moscow exile) with an ill-

8. *Ibid.*, p. 138. Komissarov and Popov, *Den'gi, kredit*, pp. 26–27. Cf. Bank for International Settlements, *Sixteenth Annual Report* (Basle, 1946), pp. 37–39. The figures given by these sources roughly correspond.

9. See Charles de Gaulle, *War Memoirs, Salvation: 1944–1962* (New York: Simon and Schuster, 1960), p. 77.

concealed abhorrence. The more caution the Soviet occupation authorities had to exercise in handling the potentially explosive political situation, the more they were inclined to take full advantage of their rightful spoils.

The armistice agreement authorized the occupation administration to print and issue local currency to be redeemed by the Hungarian government. Since the note-printing facilities were taken to Germany by the last pro-Axis regime, a minor snag developed until new equipment was procured. In the meantime, the Soviet authorities had to lend some of the money they seized in Hungarian banks to the government to keep it from complete collapse.

Once new bank notes started rolling off the presses, they became the main source of Hungary's revenue. For the first year of the occupation, the taxes covered a mere 10 per cent of the expenditures. After the government fulfilled its main function of supplying the occupation forces with goods and services and of delivering reparations to the Soviet Union, Czechoslovakia, and Yugoslavia, it had very little left to distribute among the civil servants and the rest of the population. Severe shortages caused severe price inflation. For example, between January and November of 1946 the price index increased 17,552 times.[10] The price of one dollar on the black market on April 1, 1945, was 250 *pengo;* on December 31, 1945, 265,000 *pengo*; on May 31, 1946, 52,000,000,000 *pengo*; three months later it was already 4,600,000 quadrillion *pengo*.[11] Price inflation and monetary inflation developed concurrently. The currency reform of December, 1945, reduced the amount of paper money in circulation from over 24 billion *pengo* to about 6 billion. But by June, 1946, the figure reached an astronomical 6,277,000,000,000 billion *pengo*.[12] In the Soviet-controlled money-printing plant an acute shortage of

10. Komissarov and Popov, *Den'gi, kredit*, p. 30.

11. Stephen D. Kertesz, *Diplomacy in a Whirlpool: Hungary Between Nazi Germany and Soviet Russia* (Notre Dame, Ind.: University of Notre Dame Press, 1953), pp. 154–55.

12. Bank for International Settlements, *Sixteenth Annual Report*, p. 27. Cf. Komissarov and Popov, *Den'gi, kredit*, pp. 29–30. The Basle source points out that only during the first two weeks in July, 1946, the amount of *pengo* in circulation increased more than ten thousand times. In the case of Hungary there is a noticeable discrepancy between the two sources. The Soviet account gives the amount of *pengo* in circulation " by the beginning of 1945 " as 24 billion, whereas the Swiss give, for June, 1945, only 15 billion.

paper was solved by adding zeroes to the nominal figures on the notes until one trillion (1,000,000,000,000) notes were issued. The first real stabilization took place in August, 1946, when a new monetary unit was introduced, backed by the Hungarian National Bank gold reserves, which had been seized in Germany by the United States forces and returned to the Hungarian government in the summer of 1946.

In the end, it can be added that—insofar as it can be established—the Soviets did not relinquish control over the issue of currency in the occupied countries until fully servile communist-dominated regimes had been safely established throughout Eastern and Central Europe and the social revolution they sought to effect had been essentially accomplished.

The Soviet government did not resort to a special military currency in Eastern Europe. The only exception was Rumania where Soviet-printed "military *lei*" were introduced for a short while in 1944. Quite obviously, it did not make any sense for the Soviets to go to the trouble of printing special currencies when they could seize the authentic printing presses. In any case, the ruble was legal tender everywhere, always at extremely favorable rates of exchange.[13] The governments of the occupied countries were eventually ordered to redeem whatever rubles were found in private hands and in the banks in local currency and to surrender them to the Soviet government free of cost. Thus the Soviets never faced the danger of having rubles which had been spent in foreign countries filter back to aggravate the monetary inflation at home, a danger which the Germans, in their occupation finance policies, had to guard against constantly. The absence of any measures to keep inflation manageable indicated that the Soviets expected it to produce the same sociopolitical effects as it had in the occupied countries in the 1939–41 period. Throughout

13. As the "people's democracies" became poorer, the purchasing power of their currencies started to approach that of the ruble and the rates of exchange became more equitable. With the end of the occupation régimes, local communist governments could resume trade relations with the Soviet Union. In the immediate postwar years, the terms of trade agreements heavily favored the Soviets; the picture changed noticeably after the 1956 uprising in Hungary. The trade within the communist bloc has been conducted on the basis of bilateral and multilateral clearing, with prices and balances since 1957 for the most part expressed in rubles. Soviet credits to "people's democracies" have been sometimes given in dollars. See Komissarov and Popov, *Den'gi, kredit*, pp. 218ff.

Soviet-occupied Eastern Europe, inflation greatly increased *after* the end of the war. Although more orderly supply procedures were established—the occupation troops were now supplied by the governments of the occupied countries—other factors entered the picture: troops were once again paid and developed a taste for the good life; deliveries to the occupation forces (and to Russia) increased sharply; and the disorganizing effects of the Soviet-induced social revolution began to be felt much more acutely.

The relationship between the economic policies of occupation and monetary inflation was obvious. In the countries of Western Europe which were spared the occupation altogether, or in which the occupation forces did not live off the land the way the Soviets did, monetary inflation tended to be much less pronounced, although some of these countries had suffered as much wartime damage as the countries of Eastern Europe.

CURRENCY IN CIRCULATION

(in millions of national currency units)[a]

Country	*December, 1945*	*December, 1946*	*December, 1947*
Belgium	71,798	73,891	79,761
Denmark	1,561	1,633	1,641
France	579,093	733,797	920,831
Netherlands	1,386	2,744	3,010
Norway	1,478	1,933	2,088

[a] Bank for International Settlements, *Eighteenth Annual Report* (Basle, 1948), p. 130.

To conclude: in terms of the inflationary pressures it generated, the Soviet occupation was the most burdensome employed in World War II. The Soviet occupation of East Germany was no exception.

The Soviet Union received a zone of occupation in Germany which was the most self-sufficient and best balanced economically of all four zones. Its industrial plant had suffered much less from Allied bombings than the Ruhr. More importantly, the Soviets held the provinces which had traditionally supplied the rest of Germany with agricultural products. In the critical year of 1945, the Soviet authorities retained the whole harvest for their zonal needs; only Berlin received some vegetables from the Soviet zone.

The Potsdam agreements placed no limit to what the Soviet government could take from its zone in the form of reparations.[14] In addition, it was awarded 25 per cent of "usable and complete industrial capital equipment" from the dismantled plants in the western zones; 15 per cent of such equipment was to be in exchange for an equivalent value of food, coal, and other products and commodities from East Germany; 10 per cent was to be taken without any compensation.[15] This was on paper. In fact the Soviets kept receiving dismantled machinery from the Western zones for a whole year without sending anything in exchange.

In addition to extracting material advantages from Germany, the Soviets made a positive effort in the political field, where they displayed a much greater sense of direction than the Western Allies. The official Soviet attitude toward the Germans started changing perceptibly even before Potsdam. The communist propaganda line softened and the threat of punishment was moderated. As one historian recorded, "The makers of Soviet policy seemed to have decided to leave the way open to a more positive and even half-friendly approach to the masses of the German people. . . . The Soviet spokesmen had carefully refrained from any indications of a desire to make the Germans suffer needlessly." [16] The implication was that the harsh policy announced in the name of the Big Three was adopted at the insistence of the Western powers and against the wishes of the Soviet Union.

The German communists did not fail to emphasize that in his victory speech on May 9, 1945, Stalin declared that the Soviet Union "does not intend either to dismember or to destroy Germany." Before long they had further evidence that the Soviets were the only friends of the German people. In a speech in Paris on July 10, 1946, Molotov said: "The Soviet Government has always held that the spirit of revenge is a poor counselor. It

14. The Soviet government never revealed, and probably never itself learned, the size of the reparations it took from its zone of occupation. At the London meeting of the Council of Foreign Ministers in December, 1947, Bevin estimated it at $7 billion. F. S. Northedge, *British Foreign Policy. The Process of Readjustment: 1945–1961* (New York: Praeger, 1963).

15. U. S. Department of State, *Foreign Relations of the United States. The Conference at Berlin, 1945* (Washington: U. S. Government Printing Office, 1960), II, 1956. Hereinafter called *Potsdam Papers.*

16. Herbert Feis, *Churchill, Roosevelt, Stalin: The War They Waged and the Peace They Sought* (Princeton: Princeton University Press, 1957), pp. 58, 235–38.

would be incorrect to identify Hitler's Germany with the German people. . . . It would be incorrect to adopt a course of Germany's annihilation as a state or that of its agrarization including the annihilation of its main industrial centers. . . . If the interests of peace and tranquility are dear to us the destruction of Germany should not be our objective."

This was an allusion to the Morgenthau Plan and an open bid for the allegiance of the German people. The words were accompanied by deeds. The National Committee for Free Germany which was formed in the Soviet Union in the summer of 1943 of exiled communists (and some German generals captured in Russia) appeared to be a ready nucleus for the future all-German government, the only such nucleus then in existence.[17] Its members, headed by Walter Ulbricht, started organizing local administration in the Soviet zone as early as May, 1945. Marshal Zhukov's order of June 10 permitted the establishment of trade unions and authorized the formation and activity of all antifascist parties, "placing political control in the Russian zone completely in the hands of the Free German movement." [18]

In order to expand the political base of the German Communist Party, the Soviet authorities arranged for its merger, in April, 1946, with the much more numerous Social Democratic Party to form the Socialist Unity Party (SED), which appeared as the only native political organization then functioning in Germany. It supplied the Soviet authorities with the cadres needed to govern the country. While the SED, clearly a tool of the conquerors, did not enjoy great popularity, its members were Germans, and in 1946 this counted for something.

Yet if the Soviet government's aim was to woo the entire German people and attract them to communism, the policies during the initial stages of the occupation in the east did not seem to be directed to this end. In fact, it seemed for a while that the Soviets had no hope of retaining even their own zone. The Soviet invasion was accompanied by rape and plunder on such a grand scale that one observer noted that "nothing like it has happened in Germany since the days of the Thirty Years War." [19] Requisi-

17. For the story of the National Committee, see Heinrich von Einsiedel, *I Joined the Russians* (New Haven: Yale University Press, 1953).

18. *Potsdam Papers*, I, 473.

19. Fritz Loewenthal, *News from Soviet Germany* (London: Gollanz, 1950),

tioning was unrestricted; in addition, each army unit had its quota for the collection and shipment to the Soviet Union of numerous items, ranging from foodstuffs to accordions. Dismantled machinery from German factories was shipped indiscriminately, and only a fraction of what was shipped could be put to use in Russia. The army "trophy brigades" roamed the countryside confiscating transport and equipment, and grain and farm animals (it has been estimated that no more than a third of the animals ever reached Russia). Soviet occupation policies were resulting in severe and seemingly senseless damage to the industrial and agricultural economy of their zone.[20]

Robbery by the troops was common. Few Germans could feel secure, either in their persons or their property. Furthermore, the official requisitioning served as a pretext for a large number of Soviet army officers to accumulate ("semi-officially") enormous stocks of property for their own personal use. In the early months of the occupation, high-ranking officers were sending their "trophies" back to Russia by the carload, but even as late as 1947–48 demobilized officers were permitted to send home up to two-and-a-half tons of personal property each; generals were allowed up to ten tons.[21]

Little is known about inner operations at the top of the Soviet apparatus during the first year of occupation. There was reportedly a continuous conflict between the technicians, interested in an orderly exploitation of German resources, and the military, who

p. 252. Little has been published on Soviet atrocities in occupied Germany. Except for the Germans most people seem shy to enter this lurid subject. Some documented data may be found in the publication by the Bonn Federal Ministry for Expellees, Refugees and War Victims, *The Expulsion of the German Population* (4 vols.; Bonn, 1955–60). Soviet brutalities in occupied countries differed apparently in degree only. Even in most friendly Czechoslovakia, "pillage and rape were the order of the day." Josef Korbel, *The Communist Subversion in Czechoslovakia, 1938–1948* (Princeton: Princeton University Press, 1959), p. 130. For a more descriptive account, see Jan Stransky, *East Wind Over Prague* (London: Hollis & Carter, 1950), pp. 27–37. The quasi-official Yugoslav accounts of Soviet exploits in Yugoslavia in 1945 indicate that even a communist-governed country was not spared. See Hendrick von Berg (ed.), *Genosse Feind* (Bonn: Bertoverlag, 1962). As Stalin told Benes, "Red Army men are no angels." Stransky, *East Wind Over Prague*, p. 27.

20. Robert Slusser (ed.), *Soviet Economic Policy in Potsdam Germany* (New York: Research Program on the U.S.S.R., 1953), pp. 1–9.

21. *Ibid.*, pp. 11–12. Also Gregory Klimov, *The Terror Machine: The Inside Story of the Soviet Administration in Germany* (New York: Praeger, 1953), pp. 117ff.

tried to retain their wartime power and to use it for their own improvement. This conflict was evidently aggravated by the indecision of the government in Moscow, which for a while was unsure how long its control over Germany east of the Elbe was going to last and could not decide what long-range policy would be the most advantageous.[22] This confusion contributed to a state of near-anarchy in the Soviet zone and undoubtedly affected, perhaps permanently, Soviet political fortunes in Germany. It was some time before the policy of wooing the Germans was firmly chosen, and the Soviet government, having reshuffled military leaders, passed the authority in Germany to a more intransigent and disciplined group headed by Marshal Sokolovsky. German attitudes toward the victor were not immediately affected by this new policy. As with other victorious powers, the transition from wartime psychology to what was to become normalcy was a long and tedious process.

In addition to fulfilling Soviet demands for reparations, the zone had to maintain an occupation army, which in the spring of 1946 still numbered over 700,000 troops and which lived entirely off the land. The economy also had to support the inhabitants of the zone, including millions of expellees from the territories east of the Oder-Neisse line. Since the Soviets adopted a system of indirect rule, feeding the people was a major problem for the German administration. There was little left after Soviet needs and desires had been satisfied. Rationing provided each German with 5–7 ounces of bread a day and some potatoes. In theory, the daily ration allowed up to 1,200 calories; in practice, it often provided much less. Black market prices were rising rapidly and even rationed goods tended to disappear.

Monetary inflation aggravated the situation. Some efforts were made early in 1946 to balance local budgets and to stabilize the value of the mark. The issue of new notes was apparently discontinued.[23] This, however, had little effect since the volume of currency in circulation was already very large and the occupation authorities and the army had stored plenty of cash. In the meantime, consumer goods were vanishing rapidly. With the exception

22. W. Friedmann, *The Allied Government in Germany* (London: Stevens, 1947), pp. 24ff.

23. Komissarov and Popov, *Den'gi, kredit*, p. 23. Available sources do not give actual figures on monetary circulation in Germany.

of a few goods and services still supplied at fixed prices, practically nothing could be bought in the market places. Since money was rapidly losing its original value and therefore most of its meaning, a new universal medium of exchange replaced it: the cigarette. The price of *one* cigarette during the first three years of occupation was about 7 marks, that is, 70 cents at the official rate of exchange in the United States zone, or over $2.00 in terms of the legally frozen price-wage level.[24]

The remarkable value attained by the cigarette provided the Soviet authorities with a new means of extracting from the German population formerly hidden assets. They started selling Russian-made cigarettes for gold; sixty cigarettes for one gram of gold. When no more gold was obtainable in the zone, the Soviets decided to sell cigarettes for paper money, but at prices close to those of the black market. Over 3,000 tons of tobacco, largely booty from Vienna, was delivered to local cigarette factories; 1,800 million cigarettes were sold at prices ranging from 2.5 to 3.15 marks apiece. This operation netted about 5 billion marks in profit. It helped to reduce the amount of marks in circulation, and, for a while, depressed the black market prices of cigarettes.[25]

The first material signs that East Germany was beginning to be treated as a long-range economic asset to the Soviet Union appeared late in 1946. The dismantling of factories stopped and some plants, which had earlier been shipped to Russia, were returned.[26] Industry was organized through Soviet-controlled corporations, and efforts were made to increase production. Finished goods were shipped either to Russia, at prices dictated by Moscow, or exported to "hard currency" countries such as Sweden, England, Denmark, Holland, and Switzerland. Hard currency went to Moscow; the factories and the corporations received what was due to them in marks.[27]

24. Gordon Schaffer, *Russian Zone* (London: Allen and Unwin, 1947), p. 23.

25. Loewenthal, *News from Soviet Germany*, p. 297. A reorganization of banking in the Soviet zone carried out in February, 1947, permitted the reduction of the monetary mass by the end of the year by another 10 billion. Komissarov and Popov, *Den'gi, kredit*, p. 23.

26. Schaffer, *Russian Zone*, p. 51.

27. Loewenthal, *News from Soviet Germany*, pp. 296–97. In their efforts to obtain hard currencies, the Soviet authorities even organized tours of their zone for the Western military, gladly accepting dollars and Military Payment Certificates in payment for hotels, restaurants, and other services—and often discriminating against nonconvertible Western currencies.

Nothing was brought into East Germany except the raw materials unobtainable locally and needed for industries working for export. In order to keep the economy functioning, the Soviets had to provide it with operating capital. The only source for this capital was the Soviet reserve of AM marks. This method of financing made marks the cheapest commodity in the Soviet zone. One puzzled Western economist, uninformed about the mechanics of the Soviet occupation practices, noted that "the most important as well as the most imponderable factor governing the economic situation in the Eastern zone was inflation. The position of currency, and of the prices governed by it, gave way almost completely." [28]

The truly remarkable feature of the situation was not that it was so bad but that it was not worse. Had the Soviets introduced a distinct and separate currency there would have been runaway inflation like that which developed in Rumania and Hungary during the same period. In fact it would have probably been worse because the German economy had been damaged more than the economies of those countries and because the occupation costs imposed on the Soviet zone of Germany were much higher, in relative as well as absolute terms. Yet while the Rumanians and Hungarians counted their money in billions and trillions, the note of the highest denomination in Germany remained 1,000 marks. Moreover, even when the inflation was at its worst, paper money retained some value.

There is only one explanation for this anomaly: the currency used in the Soviet zone was the same as in the rest of the country. In great amounts it kept drifting westward, to the American, British, and French zones, and to Berlin, where conditions, though bad, were considerably better, and where valuable goods were available.

When the Western Allies first suggested that one currency should be used in occupied Germany, the Soviet government had to pause

28. J. P. Nettl, *The Eastern Zone and Soviet Policy in Germany, 1945–50* (London: Oxford University Press, 1951), p. 242. Nettl's analysis contradicts Manuel Gottlieb's assertion (*The German Peace Settlement and the Berlin Crisis* [New York: Paine-Whitman, 1960], p. 105) that the Soviets "plainly desired to eliminate inflationary pressures." If they did, they did little about it, especially in the 1945–46 period.

and weigh the possible advantages and disadvantages of such an arrangement. Early in 1944 the future of Germany was still clouded in uncertainties. Agreements on postwar settlements in Europe and the Far East were still to be reached. Soviet military successes were dependent on lend-lease deliveries and the opening of the second front. The Soviets had enough incentive to court Allied goodwill.

Stalin knew that the United States and British governments ardently hoped for postwar collaboration with the Soviets and attached considerable importance to having a single currency in Germany. At that point he himself was probably willing to accommodate his allies. After some hesitation, the Soviet government consented to the proposed arrangement. There appeared to be nothing wrong with Allied military marks as long as the Soviet Union retained complete control over their issue in the Soviet zone of occupation. In fact, it promised certain material benefits. It would never be too late to introduce a new separate currency. Generally speaking, the preservation of the identity of the currency is important, but only to a government which is interested in maintaining a stable currency. Stalin showed little interest in such a policy for any of the Soviet-occupied countries.

The set of the duplicate plates, with formulas, inks, and other materials arrived in Moscow late in April, 1944. The advancing Soviet armies were well supplied with AM marks by the time they entered Czechoslovakia and Germany. The Soviets spread the marks " like fall leaves over the country. Their troops were paid salary accumulations of up to six years in these marks, and Russian purchasing missions with satchels of these bills roamed the country buying anything salable." [29]

The abundance of AM marks in Russian hands quickly came to the attention of the American High Command. Late in May, 1945, Eisenhower reported to the War Department that the " Russians distribute A.M. marks . . . to their troops without accountability, without regard to scales of troop pay, and in any quantities troops request. Such A.M. marks are distributed by handful with rations. . . . Our troops are receiving large quantities of Russian A.M. marks from Russian troops, civilians and displaced persons

29. Jack Bennett, " The German Currency Reform," *The Annals of the Academy of Political and Social Science*, Vol. 267 (January, 1950), p. 44.

for cigarettes, candy and even gratis." [30] A few months later the American headquarters in Berlin reported again that "Russians have great quantities of marks in their possession. . . . Considerable amounts of Russian-printed marks are being converted into dollars through the medium of United States finance offices." [31]

The monetary inflation in the Soviet zone was beginning to affect Berlin and the Western zones. What originally looked like a "seepage" of Soviet-printed marks, soon became a deluge. In Berlin, along the East-West zonal border and in Czechoslovakia—wherever the Americans and the British were in contact with the Russians—the marks were moving in one direction, westward. They were brought into the Western zones by the masses of German refugees and expellees from the east and by the thousands of black marketeers of all nationalities. Instances were recorded of the utilization by the Soviets of Polish displaced persons who were sent into the Western zones with suitcases of marks "to pursue their voracious acquisition of German property. This spending was so loose that the Soviet officials themselves could not reckon or reasonably estimate the number of marks they placed in circulation." [32]

The flow of currency westward was prompted by a substantial difference in the purchasing power of the mark between the Soviet zone, where the only commodity supplied by the occupying power was the currency itself, and the American zone, where the occupation forces were lavishly provided with everything from the home country. Even when the mass movement of people fleeing to the west had slowed down, the currency traffic was continued by thousands of German smugglers. It lasted at least until the summer of 1947, when the Soviets, in view of the political changes represented by the Truman Doctrine and the Marshall Plan, greatly strengthened the frontier controls. After that, Berlin and a few border-crossing points remained the only places where currency transactions continued unabated.

This largely spontaneous outflow of marks (as well as inflow

30. U.S. Congress, Senate, Occupation Currency Transactions, *Hearings before the Committees on Appropriations, Armed Services and Banking and Currency*, 80th Congress, 1st Session, June 17–18, 1947, pp. 327–28.

31. *Ibid.*, pp. 384–85.

32. Bennett, *The Annals of the Academy of Political and Social Science*, Vol. 267, p. 44.

of goods from the Western zones and sectors of Berlin) was an economic factor of the greatest importance for the Soviet zone, for it artificially preserved a much higher purchasing power for the mark than would otherwise have been the case. It is difficult to say whether this effect was fully expected in Moscow when the decision to accept the Western offer for a single currency for occupied Germany was taken. More likely, the move was viewed as the one which could not possibly hurt Soviet interests and promised instead tangible benefits, political as well as economic.

Chapter IX

MONETARY INFLATION IN GERMANY

There were two major reasons for introducing military currency in occupied Germany: the invading armies needed a locally acceptable currency to pay the troops; second, it was intended that Germany, both at that time and in the future, should be made to pay for the cost of the Allied occupation, a cost above and beyond the direct occupation costs (in the form of labor, housing, transportation, and other services). The easiest way to assure the transfer of occupation costs to Germany was to establish total control over monetary circulation. As a first step, practically all public and private accounts in German banks were blocked and the banks' cash reserves placed at the disposal of the occupation authorities. For the United States zone, the JCS-1067 directive specified that "The German authorities may be required to make available Reichsmark currency or credits free of cost and in amounts sufficient to meet all the expenses of the forces of occupation, including the cost of Allied Military Government and including to the extent that compensation is made therefore, the cost of such private property as may be requisitioned, seized, or otherwise acquired, by Allied authorities for reparations or restitution purposes." There were no "German authorities" in Germany at the time of the invasion, and some banks were looted by Allied soldiers, displaced persons, and German civilians during the initial phase of the occupation. Otherwise, the military governments of all four zones assumed control over the banks.

The Allies rightly anticipated that their currency needs would not be satisfied by the reichsmarks in German banks. Military (or occupation) currency was to supplement these assets and to remove physical limits from the spending capacity of the occupying powers.

From the point of view of the occupation authorities, there was little difference between Allied military marks and reichsmarks.

They were declared interchangeable at the rate 1 to 1, while the *Reichskreditkassenscheine*, as a symbol of the Reich's former power over other countries, ceased to be legal tender. For strictly psychological reasons American personnel were paid in Allied military (AM) marks; it was feared that victorious troops would resent being paid in the currency of the defeated enemy.[1] The British, French, and Soviets had no qualms about using reichsmarks for paying their troops.

The Allied occupation planners in Washington further decided that no general rate of exchange between the mark and the home currencies of the occupying powers, or for that matter *any* foreign currencies, should be established. The mark, in effect, became an " outlaw " currency. This decision precluded any trade with Germany and sealed the country off economically from the rest of the world, making it totally dependent on Allied policies. Such an economic isolation, however, was probably beneficial—at least for the American zone—during the first years of occupation. Some enterprising businessmen in the United States were anxious to take advantage of the situation and develop the German market, but were opposed by General Clay who " was determined that no potential carpetbaggers should enter this devastated land until appropriate measures could be taken to safeguard the German people against such an invasion." [2] In resisting these pressures from home, Clay successfully used the argument that the absence of the general dollar-mark rate of exchange made such trade impossible.

Instead of general rates, special military rates of exchange were introduced, rates which also deliberately undervalued the mark and gave the Allies additional purchasing power. These rates were " special military " in the sense that only Allied personnel

1. *Hearings before the Committees on Appropriations, Armed Services and Banking and Currency*, 30th Congress, 1st Session, June 17–18, 1947, p. 300. Hereinafter referred to as *S-47*. The European Theater fiscal director attempted in April, 1945, to prohibit the acceptance of the reichsmarks from the troops for remittances home on the grounds that these notes were illegally acquired, but was quickly overruled by Eisenhower's Chief of Staff, General Walter Bedell Smith. For details, see Walter Rundell, Jr., *Black Market Money: The Collapse of U.S. Currency Control in World War II* (Baton Rouge: Louisiana State University Press, 1964), pp. 33ff. Rundell's presentation of the Army's ambivalence in meeting the problem of currency control both in the European and the Pacific Theaters is valuable.

2. Demaree Bess, " American Viceroy in Germany," *The Saturday Evening Post* (May 10, 1947), p. 82.

were permitted to exchange currencies. This, as we recall, was the exact opposite of the German practices with military currency: the Germans had general rates of exchange but no special military rates in the countries occupied by them. In the United States zone the rate of exchange was 10 marks to $1.00. This rate was adopted and introduced at the insistence of Harry Dexter White despite strong opposition from the British who proposed a rate of 5 marks to $1.00 (and 20 marks to £1) as more reasonable.[3] Once the 10 to 1 rate was established in the American zone, however, the British had to go along. Early in 1946, General Clay reported to Washington that " present legal prices and present legal wage scales in Germany reflect a value for the mark closer to 40 cents than to 10 cents." [4] This meant that even one year after the end of the war the 10 to 1 rate overvalued the dollar (and, correspondingly, the pound and franc) by approximately 300 per cent. The dollar-ruble cross rate led to an automatic overvaluation of the ruble by well over 2000 per cent.[5]

Such an overvaluation of the dollar (which was, incidentally,

3. Minutes, Ad Hoc Committee on Financial Planning, *S-47*, pp. 240–42. At that meeting the " importance of the effect of lack of a general rate on German psychology " was stressed. A 40 cent rate was also discussed and opposed by the army representative who felt that this rate would excessively tax the appropriations' equivalent of the army expenditures. This meeting was held in July, 1944, but the rate of 10 cents was cabled to SHAEF only in September. *Ibid.*, p. 253.

4. *S-47*, p. 579.

5. It has been argued that troop spending is similar to tourist trade and that relative purchasing power of currencies, in establishing rate of exchange, was rather meaningless since troop spending was not competitive with the spending by the local population; the troops did not compete on the market with the natives for basic commodities but bought souvenirs, objects of art, luxury items, etc. See Andrew M. Kamarck, " Allied Financial Policy in Italy " (unpublished MS, Harvard University Library), p. 125. This argument has some virtue, but it is not conclusive. For one thing, the troops also bought such things as fresh food, wine and liquors, frequented restaurants, etc. In addition, " tourist trade " can only benefit countries whose economies are geared to it. An avalanche of tourists into areas not economically prepared for taking care of them can be disastrous. The pumping of excessive amounts of money into such areas inevitably results in inflation. And in the Soviet zone, the troops could not be classified as " tourists " by any stretch of imagination. In addition, there was a difference between Soviet and American practices, a difference, the significance of which emerged before long: the Soviet personnel in Germany were paid in marks and were forbidden to either have rubles or to exchange their marks into rubles. The official rate of exchange existed only for the calculation of the pay and of the value of reparations extracted from Germany, and for general accounting purposes. This arrangement gave the Soviet economy full protection from the consequences of inflation in the countries occupied by the Red army.

decided upon even after the negative effects of similar action in Italy had been fully felt) was a manifestation of Morgenthau's triumph. The Army wholeheartedly concurred, because this overvaluation boosted the spending capacity of the military establishment in Germany, while at the same time it promised to make the troops happier by increasing their purchasing power. Such considerations were clearly secondary in the Treasury thinking, but since the War Department was the Treasury's important ally in the formulation of occupation policies, the Treasury accepted the soldiers' happiness as an unwelcome but inevitable by-product of a decision whose central purpose was to punish the Germans. Monetary inflation in occupied Germany was an explicit policy of the United States Treasury. Secretary Morgenthau and his advisers " held that since the Germans were responsible for bringing on inflation in the occupied areas, they should be given a taste of their own medicine." [6] In a lengthy statement of March 14, 1945, the United States Treasury declared: " The wide geographical scope of military operations in this war and the great development of techniques of economic warfare have made money an important offensive and defensive weapon of war. Providing this weapon in its most efficient form has required careful and detailed planning far in advance of military operations. Just as we need many varieties of military weapons, of ships and planes, so we have found that the effective conduct of war on the financial side requires a variety of currency measures designed to meet varied and changeable situations." [7] This view of money as an " offensive weapon of war " had many aspects, one of which was the ability to induce inflation in a conquered land. It was this aspect that was incorporated in the financial section of JCS-1067 and later permeated actual experiences in the monetary field in the American zone of occupation.

Defeated Germany could not escape inflation. At the end of the war organized economic activity was at a standstill. Germany had lost vast territories in the east, but at the same time some 10 million people, refugees and expellees from East Prussia, Pomerania, Silesia, Poland, Czechoslovakia and other places, had been

6. E. F. Penrose, *Economic Planning for the Peace* (Princeton: Princeton University Press, 1953), p. 247.

7. *Annual Report of the Secretary of the Treasury: 1944–1945* (Washington: U.S. Government Printing Office, 1946), p. 389.

added to the population of "Potsdam Germany." [8] German cities and industrial centers were in ruins. A large part of the remaining industrial equipment was to be dismantled and taken away as reparations. There were virtually no forms of transport. Agricultural production was at its lowest, and the system of civilian supply, which the Reich government operated almost until the end, had broken down. There was an acute scarcity of everything —except money.

At the time of the invasion, the German people were in possession of an unusually large amount of cash. Over 53 billion marks were in circulation in territories under German control in February, 1945; 54.4 billion was the last officially recorded figure, as of March 7, 1945. In addition, in the vaults of various German banks there was another 15–16 billion.[9] This was an increase of over 50 per cent since the end of 1943. This increase was a result of the return to Germany of great numbers of soldiers (who were allowed to convert into reichsmarks a part of their foreign notes) and refugees fleeing from the territories taken by the Soviet army. Continuous bombings and the general insecurity of the people had induced many of them to withdraw their savings from the banks so that they would always have some cash on hand,[10] although such withdrawals were restricted by the existing regulations. However, because of the rigid price controls, the shortage of goods on the market, and the habitual discipline of the German people, these great amounts of currency in circulation did not result in price inflation. Rationed food supply, even in the heavily bombed areas, continued almost until the surrender. The black market, although it existed, played a minor role.

The collapse of the Reich changed the situation drastically. The division of the country into four national zones of occupation destroyed its natural economic balance. The denazification program caused an almost total disintegration of the administrative machinery. For the American zone, JCS-1067 permitted control of the economy only to the extent necessary to assure deliveries of reparations and to prevent economic rehabilitation. JCS-1067

8. *Germany Reports* (Bonn, 1955), pp. 145, 222.

9. Bank for International Settlements, *Fourthteenth Annual Report* (Basle, 1944), p. 297.

10. *Ibid*., p. 298. See also, Otto Pfleiderer, "Waerungsreform in Westdeutschland," in *Enzyklopaedische Lexikon fuer das Geld-, Bank-, und Boersewesen* (Frankfurt a/M, 1957).

specifically forbade any "steps designed to maintain, strengthen or operate the German financial structure."

It is impossible to establish exactly the extent of the inundation of occupied Germany with the AM currency. It should be remembered that until the June, 1948, reform, the same currency (reichsmarks and AM marks) existed in all four zones of occupation. Some reliable figures are available. It is known, for instance, that altogether 15,216,780,000 marks were printed in the United States and delivered to the War Department for distribution among the three Western powers. Of this amount, 4,532,000,000 marks were in 1,000 mark notes, which American officials said they never placed in circulation. This reduces the maximum amount of AM marks that could have been issued in the Western zones to about 10.5 billion. The actual amount is more difficult to establish. As of September 30, 1946, the French in their zone issued 580 million AM marks and the British issued 1,795 million.[11] In the summer of 1947 American officials estimated that the total issue of AM marks in the United States zone had not exceeded 2.5 billion. A year later the amount issued by the Americans could have reached 5 billion, but the total amount for the three Western zones was still well within the maximum of 10.5 billion marks. Yet according to General Clay, the currency in circulation in the Western zones exceeded 73 billion marks early in 1946.[12] By June, 1948, when the currency reform was announced in West Germany, the total was "well above" 118.7 billion marks.[13]

It is difficult to estimate the currency circulation in the Soviet zone. The Soviet authorities have never revealed how much currency they printed or issued. The figures published in the West reflect either the estimates of German statisticians, or impressions gained from discussions with Soviet Military Government officials in Berlin by their Western colleagues.[14] These figures tend to

11. *S-47*, p. 137.

12. Lucius D. Clay, *Decision in Germany* (Garden City, New York: Doubleday, 1950), p. 203. Fred H. Klopstock, who participated in the preparation of the 1948 reform, in his article, "Monetary Reform in West Germany," *Journal of Political Economy*, Vol. 57 (1949), gives the figure of 119 billion marks of currency in circulation at the time of the reform. These figures probably also include demand deposits in the banks. They exclude the cash in the hands of the occupation personnel and authorities.

13. Henry C. Wallich, *Mainsprings of the German Revival* (New Haven: Yale University Press, 1955), p. 64.

14. Hans Moeller, *Zur Forgeschichte der Deutsche Mark, Die Waerungsreformplaene 1945–1948* (Tuebingen: 1961), p. 476.

be very conservative, usually within the 5–6 billion mark range. To approximate the true figure, therefore, we would approach the problem differently.

According to a Soviet statement, a total of 28 billion marks (reichsmarks and AM marks) was exchanged in the Soviet zone currency reform which immediately followed that in the Western zones. This total does not include the sums in the possession of the Soviet troops (which still numbered in 1948 over 600,000), Soviet civilian personnel, or the military government.[15] Nor is it likely that the people brought all their cash for exchange. Whereas each citizen could exchange 70 old marks (roughly the price of a pack of cigarettes) at the rate of 1 to 1, the rest was exchanged at the rate of 10 to 1 but in total amounts up to 5,000 old marks per person. Those who accumulated large amounts—peasants and numerous black marketeers—often found it unprofitable to declare their holdings and face the questioning of police. Savings accounts (again, up to 5,000 marks) were exchanged at the rate of 5 to 1 but in the Soviet and Western zones savings did not amount to much since the high rate of circulation resulting from growing inflation discouraged saving.

Soviet personnel were allowed to exchange their old marks for new ones at the rate of 1 to 1. It is not known whether there was any limit to the amount each person could exchange. Nor do we know the total amount of AM marks in Soviet hands, private or official; it probably ran into billions.[16]

15. Bank for International Settlements, *Nineteenth Annual Report* (Basle, 1949), p. 48. See also, V. P. Komissarov and A. N. Popov, *Den'gi, Kredit i Finansy Evropeiskikh Stran Narodnoi Demokratii* (Moscow, 1960), pp. 25–26.

16. There were rumors that, having seized the Leipzig mint, the Soviets also printed reichsmarks. See *S-47*, pp. 27, 32. These rumors have never been confirmed, although one Soviet source hints at such a possibility: Komissarov and Popov, *Den'gi, Kredit*, p. 23, say: "By the middle of 1946, with the budgetary deficits eliminated, the issue of notes, *including military marks*, for the purpose of covering these deficits, was discontinued in East Germany." (Italics added.) The Soviet official announcement in the Allied Control Commission stated that as of November, 1946, the Soviets discontinued the printing of AM marks. Even if taken at face value, this allows for all sorts of possibilities: that notes continued to be printed for purposes other than covering budgetary deficits; that only reichsmarks were printed after that date; that the Soviets had already piled up a reserve of either or both currencies sufficient for all imaginable needs and purposes. It appears unlikely to me that the Soviets printed reichsmarks in any sizable amounts; for one thing, the reichsmarks required a much better paper and a more complex technology for their production; for another, printing and issuing the nazi currency from the old plates must have looked, even to the Soviets, as a sort of political liability.

Among other unknowns is the amount of AM marks circulating in the West at the time of the currency reform. Many people with large amounts could not exchange them because of the terms of the reform and got stuck with the worthless currency. Some AM marks were lost by foreign holders (including foreign banks) because there was no provision to compensate them. Sizable amounts undoubtedly drifted into the Soviet zone in the first few days of confusion following the reform before the Soviets established strict border controls. Finally, we do not know how much was exchanged to the Allied personnel in the city of Berlin and in the Saarland. This was outside the jurisdiction of the German financial institution which administered the reform.[17]

All we can do is to make a very conservative estimate of the extent of the Soviet contribution to inflation. Three pertinent figures, which we have already established, ought to be considered: [18]

a.	Currency in circulation plus private demand deposits in June, 1948, in the three Western zones (except the Saar)........	120 billion marks
	Cash exchanged in the Soviet zone in the June–July, 1948, currency reform.......	28 billion marks
	Total in circulation	148 billion marks
b.	Currency in circulation plus cash in banks in March, 1945, 70 billions, less the currency left in Austria and other provinces now detached from Germany (10 billions)[19]	60 billion marks
c.	The maximum amount of AM marks which could have been issued in the Western zones	10 billion marks

17. This author communicated with the Deutsche Bundesbank on this subject, but to no avail: no joint German-American statistics have ever been compiled; no American, French, or British figures for their share of cash in AM marks have been released. There is no way of finding out how successful was the presumably absolute blockade of the Soviet zone (and of Berlin) clamped down by the Soviets immediately following the announcement of the reform.

18. For the date on reichsmark balance in Austria, see Bank for International Settlements, *Sixteenth Annual Report*, p. 35. The *Nineteenth Annual Report*, although stating that it has no positive knowledge or information on the total amount of currency in circulation in Germany as a whole, is inclined to believe that during the three postwar years it had been largely static.

19. Out of this amount, 8 billions were left in Austria and an estimated 2 billions in Alsace-Lorraine, Saar, Czechoslovakia, Luxembourg, and in the territories east of the Oder-Neisse line. See Moeller, *Zur Forgeschichte der Deutsche Mark*, pp. 444–45.

Even if we take the figure of 28 billion in the total (a) as representing the amount of marks in circulation in the Soviet zone before the reform, the minimum total amount put into circulation by the Soviets would be $a - (b + c)$, or 78 billion.[20] Since we do not know the exact composition of the amounts (a), and the amounts held by the four occupying powers and the German population of Berlin at the time of the reform, this is admittedly a very rough estimate.

Two conclusions can be drawn on the basis of these figures. First, the amount of currency in circulation, already excessive at the end of the war, increased three or four times during the following three years, creating monetary inflation of immense proportions. Its impact was powerful, particularly in view of the extreme scarcity of goods on the market. It fostered the black market and helped to disorganize whatever existed in the rationing system. More significantly, the deluge of currency made the economic recovery of Germany impossible. The hopes of those who wanted the German people to "stew in their own juice" were largely fulfilled.[21]

The second conclusion is that the device of common currency allowed the Soviet government to draw heavily upon the resources of the Western zones of Germany. This drainage continued long after the political split between the wartime Allies became clear, and after all hopes for at least the economic unity of Germany, as envisaged in Potsdam, were abandoned. Thus the decision of Secretary Morgenthau to supply the Soviet government with a set of duplicate plates for the manufacturing of marks deprived the United States, Great Britain, and France of one method of defending their interests in the drastically changed postwar world.

It is interesting to speculate on what would have happened had the United States refused to give the Soviet government the facilities to manufacture AM marks independently. We recall that General Marshall and Secretary Morgenthau offered to supply the Soviets with an "unlimited" amount of AM marks printed

20. If one takes into account that every Soviet soldier stationed in Germany in 1945 was paid his pay for three or more years, and that all officers received substantial cash bonuses, this figure would become realistic. At one time or another, at least 2 million Soviet troops were brought to Germany, and although the pay scale was low, the rate of exchange was very favorable.

21. Manuel Gottlieb, "Failure of Quadripartite Monetary Reform 1945–1947," *Finanzarchiv* (Band 17, Tuebingen, 1956/57), p. 404 n. 2.

in America. There is no question that, had this offer been accepted, the Soviets would have initially been given a very large amount, probably exceeding the number issued to the forces of all three Western Allies combined. The Soviet government could have rightfully claimed that, having the largest occupation army, and having suffered badly as a result of the German occupation of Russia, it was entitled to a more generous remuneration. However, once it became clear that it was not Germany, but the United States, that was in effect rewarding the Soviets, a thought might have been given to the necessity of making the notes issued to the Soviets sufficiently identifiable to isolate them and restrict their circulation outside the Soviet zone. As will be shown later, very early in the occupation, the army finance officers (but not the German banks!) were forbidden to honor the 1,000 mark notes, which were issued solely by the Soviets.

There is disagreement among Americans who were in Germany after the war and Treasury officials over the identifiability of Soviet-printed notes. In fact, the serial numbers initially identified all four zones. The notes issued in the U.S. zone had " 1 " before the number; in the British it was " 0 "; in the French " 00 "; and in the Soviet it was the dash. However, when worried American officials began to suggest that the notes issued in the Western zones be made identifiable, the Treasury instructed the Bureau of Engraving and Printing to put the dash on *all* the notes routinely printed for the replacement of the withdrawn worn out currency, thus confusing the picture completely.[22] This decision can only be ascribed to the Treasury's determination not to allow the calamitous consequences for the United States of the flood of the Soviet-printed currency to interfere with the political considerations. It was quite another for the Western Allies to try to discriminate against Soviet-printed AM marks as a matter of policy in their zones. This would have required a decision to carry out a comprehensive currency reform, for the reichsmarks would have had to be banned simultaneously. Such a decision, which would have infuriated the Soviets, was not psychologically possible in 1945. It certainly could not have been made on the grounds that the Germans living in the Western zones were the charges of the corresponding Western powers

22. Rundell, *Black Market Money*, pp. 44–46.

and were thus entitled to their rulers' protection; in 1945 (and, for many, until a much later date) *all* Germans, East and West alike, were considered "bad." Nor was it possible to deny the Soviets some benefits at the expense of the American taxpayer until the whole political picture in Germany had changed and until the hopes for friendship with Russia had faded in the United States. Finally, in the absence of other means of correcting the situation, any drastic step aimed at cutting the Soviets off from this indirect American aid required drastic decisions at the highest government level of the kind which would have frightened most policymakers in Washington. This illustrates the danger inherent in such an essentially irreversible step as the transfer to the Soviets of a set of duplicate plates which provided for no corrective mechanism by routine bureaucratic means.

The Soviet government had powerful motives in insisting on an independent capacity to produce AM marks. For all practical purposes, occupation marks were a levy on the German economy which could be justly classified as a form of reparations. If the United States had retained the monopoly of printing the AM marks, the Western Allies would at least have been in a position to know the extent to which the Soviets were benefiting by issuing this currency and to take it into account in the discussions of reparation deliveries. Even if all Soviet requests for occupation currency were granted by the United States, this procedure would at least have placed a limit, if only in psychological terms, on these requests. This occurred in Austria where the allocation of occupation schillings was subject to the decision of all four commanders.[23]

23. The situation in Austria was different in many other ways, mainly because of the existence of the Austrian government (in spite of its subordinated status). There were two currency conversions there, and after the second conversion (from AM schillings to Austrian schillings), the government was in charge of issuing currency. Its allocation, however, still depended on the joint decisions of the commanders-in-chief. By and large, the monetary circulation in Austria seemed to be under better control, although the developments there in many ways paralleled those in Germany. Some information on the Austrian experience was supplied to me by Arthur W. Marget, formerly with the U.S. headquarters in Vienna, in a letter dated May 28, 1962.

CHAPTER X

AMERICAN BLACK MARKET AND ARMY OVERDRAFT

In the minds of the American political and military leaders, the American occupation was to come to Germany as an avenging sword of justice. Following the spirit and letter of the JCS-1067 directive, the occupation authorities would mete out punishment to the nazis. They would insure that the German economy would not recover. They would seal the German nation off from the rest of the world and make it pay for atrocities and injustices that had been committed under Hitler. They would rule the enemy country (or, at least, their zone of occupation) justly but firmly. There would not be any fraternization with the " indigenous population "; the American soldier would carry out his duty sternly, unexcelled in his military and moral superiority.

Perhaps the main defect of United States economic plans for Germany was that they were unrealistic. They were an outgrowth of a crusading spirit which had permeated a large segment of the American public but which had not significantly affected the American military overseas. Few soldiers took the pronouncements of the High Command seriously and fewer officers of the Army of Occupation had any idea of how to implement the directives prepared in Washington.

It soon became apparent that the JCS-1067 directive was unenforceable in several important respects. One of the first breakdowns occurred in the field of the nonfraternization, which the GI's came to resent as a strictly " Brass Hat " idea. The incidents of rape were rare, but many hungry German *fraulein* were willing to entertain the troops in exchange for food, a couple of candy bars, or a pack of cigarettes.[1] This collapse of the " race barrier "

1. Julian Bach, Jr., *America's Germany* (New York: Random House, 1946), p. 75. " Considering the background of the American fighting men," says Bach, who was a military correspondent during that period, this policy " never had a

was embarrassing and, for a while, the occupation authorities tried to compensate for the damage done to the American image by additional displays of animosity toward the Germans. Some zealous War and Navy Department officials went so far as to prohibit German employees in the Military Establishment in Germany to use the same toilets as the Americans. Others put stress on denazification, so that at least those Germans obviously compromised under Hitler's régime would not be seen around. There was some resistance to denazification on the part of those generals in Germany whose main concern was with "getting things done." Their influence, however, was minimal, and the denazification campaign intensified after General Patton, Military Governor of Bavaria, was relieved of command for having declared that the difference between nazis and antinazis was no greater than the difference between Republicans and Democrats in the United States.[2]

Another breakdown was looting. Convinced that "Krauts were all alike," many GI's—and officers—did not hesitate to "liberate" individual Germans of their more valuable possessions. The looting was never as bad as in the Soviet zone—Americans were not interested in sewing machines, secondhand civilian clothing, or door knobs—but it was widespread nevertheless. In a few celebrated cases, the generals and colonels involved in thefts of jewelry and other valuables were court martialed. The great majority, however, have never been brought to trial. The inability of the Army to enforce discipline was also noted in the British and French zones. But it was in the American zone where the defiance of orders was most common.

The fighting was over. German cities were no more than piles of rubble, with starving and frightened people crowding the basements of the ruins and the few tenements which remained. Army recreation programs were still far off. The GI's, who did not care about the American "image," needed outlets for their energies. Such outlets were provided by wine, women, and the black market. One American official recorded that "overindulgence in any one of these three can demoralize an organization; when they

---

chance of working. . . . The final hypocrisy—not lost to the Germans—was the appearance in large communities and at all headquarters of neat Prophylaxis Station signs at a time when intercourse of any sort was banned."

2. Robert Murphy, *Diplomat among Warriors* (Garden City, New York: Doubleday, 1964), pp. 293–95.

are combined as they were in Berlin they constitute a major threat to continued operations." [3]

Wine and women no doubt had some adverse effects on the discipline and efficiency of the American military establishment in Germany, but it was the black market that proved to be the most insidious, the most widespread, and the most demoralizing factor of all. In Berlin, as elsewhere in Germany, the black market centered around the Americans who suddenly discovered themselves in the enviable position of being monopolistic suppliers. The British had little to sell. The French had nothing; their occupation troops lived off the land in much the same way the Soviet troops did. But the American rations were bountiful; Post Exchange (PX) stores and commissaries were overflowing with precious goods from the United States, supplemented by Swiss watches, Dutch cheese, French wine and cognac.

In order to turn the American black market into what it became, two other elements were needed: customers with plenty of cash, and the opportunity to convert profits into American dollars and other assets of permanent value. Both of these elements were present in the United States zone of Germany and in Berlin, ruled jointly by all four powers.

Customers on the black market were Russians, Germans, and masses of displaced persons. The Germans and the refugees needed food and cigarettes; the Russians needed other items, mainly whisky, watches, and cameras. All had money in abundance, especially the Russians who were amply supplied with crisp AM marks.

The American black market operator had four principal sources of supplies. One of them was "legal," in the form of packages he received from home. The other three were illegal: the weekly PX ration (the sale of which was, in theory, prohibited), the quartermaster's warehouse, and the mess halls. The chief commodity, accounting for the bulk of black market operations, was cigarettes, for Germany neither produced nor imported tobacco.

3. B. U. Ratchford and William D. Ross, *Berlin Reparations Assignment: Round One of the German Peace Settlement* (Chapel Hill: University of North Carolina Press, 1947), p. 10. Such a great lack of discipline in postwar Germany can be at least in part explained by the disorganization which resulted from the wholesale transfers home and reshuffling of established army units after the end of the war. See Lt. General L. K. Truscott, Jr., *Command Missions* (New York: Dutton, 1954), pp. 513–14.

A pack of cigarettes bought by a GI at a United States Army Post Exchange for five cents sold on the black market for at least 100 marks, or $10; a five cent candy bar sold for $5; a pound of coffee, for $25; a bottle of whiskey, for $100; a Mickey Mouse watch, which cost $1.98 at a PX stores, sold for $150–$200. Fancier Swiss watches brought anywhere between $600 and $2,500.[4] Thus, a GI stationed in Berlin for one year, who could sell all his ration of cigarettes, candy, and liquor on the black market would make a profit of about $12,000. A few parcels from home could easily bring his yearly income to $25,000–$30,000, not counting army pay and allowances. On August 2, 1945, *Stars and Stripes* reported that " approximately $4,000,000 has been sent home during July by 33,000 American troops in Berlin. . . . During the same period the soldiers in the United States Berlin garrison were paid a total of only about $1,000,000 in cash."

This extra income (tax free) was something an average GI found difficult to resist. In the beginning, there were about 1 million troops in Germany; and even a year later, there were still over 300,000. Trade was briskest in Berlin, but it was also good elsewhere. Operations on the black market were by no means limited to privates and noncoms peddling their wares on street corners of ruined cities; a great many officers were making money as well, and often on a much larger scale. The few who did not were considered crackpots.

There was no specific prohibition of black marketeering in JCS-1067, but this activity was obviously violating the spirit of the directive, which aimed at creating a noble, if stern, image of the conquerors and providing a sharp contrast with the nazis. The blurring of this image greatly disturbed the more idealistic Americans (including some Treasury officials). At the same time, some officials entrusted with administrative duties began to see the

4. C. R. Jordan, *From Major Jordan's Diaries* (New York: Devin-Adair, 1952), p. 230; Bach, *America's Germany*, pp. 54–70; Walter Rundell, Jr., *Black Market Money: The Collapse of U.S. Currency Control in World War II* (Baton Rouge: Louisiana State University Press, 1964), pp. 46ff. The cigarettes were rationed, but an American could buy any quantity of them at $0.95 per carton through an American firm which was advertising in the Paris edition of the *New York Herald Tribune*. Observers agree that 95 per cent of the Americans in Germany participated in black market operations, although maybe only 10–15 per cent of them carried out operations of truly commercial dimensions.

influence of the black market on the general decline of discipline. One report noted: "The greed it inspired, the extent to which it interfered with the work of military government, the distorted sense of values it created, and the extent to which it discredited Americans in the eyes of the Germans—all of these were more important than the monetary cost. From personal observation, it can be reported that a man who was badly bitten with the black market bug was of no value to military government. Not only did he spend much of his time planning and carrying out his deals; but also, if he did decide to devote some of his time to his duties, he was in no frame of mind to do effective work." [5]

The top army command attempted to counteract black marketeering in a variety of ways. Several orders were issued by General McNarney, the first Military Governor, pointing out the immorality of profiteering and the necessity to strengthen discipline and to encourage those soldiers who abstained from illicit activities. Army psychologists attempted to rationalize the situation by explaining that the "GI resented controls and restrictions which he considered an interference with individual rights and liberties. . . . He believed in democracy and individual human rights. . . . He could see no reason why he should not make a small profit, for he believed that the enemy would pay the cost. He could even justify the sale of equipment issued for military purposes." [6] Army equipment, including firearms, was in fact sold on the black market. The army records show that pilfering of depots and warehouses by thousands of locally employed displaced persons and Germans, with the complicity of the American personnel, reached sizable proportions.[7]

These extra-legal exploits were by no means limited to the army establishment. Scores of thousands of civilians attached to the military government and to UNRRA, the American Red Cross, the American Joint Distribution Committee, and other charitable missions which operated in occupied Germany also participated.

5. Ratchford and Ross, *Berlin Reparations Assignment*, pp. 15–16.

6. U.S. Congress, Senate, *Hearings before the Committees on Appropriations, Armed Services and Banking and Currency*, 80th Congress, 1st Session, June 17–18, p. 59. Hereinafter referred to as *S-47*.

7. Until the spring of 1946 the total value of items pilfered every month averaged 2 per cent of theater depot stocks, or more than $2 million. Oliver J. Fredricksen, *The American Military Occupation of Germany, 1945–1953* (U.S. Army in Europe, 1953), p. 65.

They were entitled to use Army Post Exchanges and commissaries and had every opportunity to convert their black market profits into dollars. Finally, there were the "guests" of the American military government: newspaper correspondents and businessmen traveling in Germany, and members of military missions, both from Eastern and Western European countries, who not only shared in the banking privileges of the American military but also helped themselves to the American supply of marks.[8]

Many officials in the military government and officers in the Army were alarmed by what was going on but were helpless to reverse the trend. Only a massive concerted effort could correct the situation. This effort could not come from within the occupation establishment which had already developed a deep vested interest in the preservation and further development of the black market. To reverse the trend, a great pressure from without was needed; from public opinion at home, from Congress, from the United States government in Washington. Such pressure was distinctly lacking. The American press remained strangely silent on the subject of military behavior in Germany, and in any case, other problems were absorbing the attention of the politicians.[9] In the United States the public image of the American GI remained that of a hero. In Europe newspapers soft-pedaled criticism of Americans; there was no independent German press.

For quite a while there was no check to the black market activities of the American personnel. Eventually, however, the United States government became aware of the dangers of the situation and the need for corrective action. This awareness was not the result of the deterioration of discipline or general demoralization in the ranks, but was rather a consequence of a serious drain on the army's financial resources, a drain which resulted in a rapidly growing deficit. This deficit was caused by the black marketeers. When the profits they remitted home in dollars were in excess of pay and allowances appropriated by Congress, they were paid out of the United States Treasury, at the expense of the American

8. *S-47*, pp. 607, 685, 567–68. As an example, the Polish military mission obtained in the form of "advances" 103,205,000 AM marks, which it never bothered to repay.

9. Marshall M. Knappen, *And Call It Peace* (Chicago: University of Chicago Press, 1947), pp. 5–6. Cf. Freda Utley, *The High Cost of Vengeance* (Chicago: Regnery, 1949).

taxpayer. Inasmuch as the War Department was accountable to Congress, this deficit—and the circumstances under which it accrued—threatened to explode into a political issue of no mean dimensions.[10]

When it was decided to introduce special military currency in Germany, congressional leaders were made to believe that the issue of the billions of AM marks would relieve the United States of a great part, if not all, of the occupation costs. Consequently, these sums, as well as those seized in the German banks, were treated by the United States Treasury as congressional appropriations to the War Department, with the dollar outlays reduced accordingly.[11] This was the same procedure as the one that had been followed in the occupation of Italy. Congress, jealous of its prerogatives, was not prepared to look kindly upon loose spending by the Army after war had ended. The following exchange took place during the 1947 Senate hearings in which John H. Hilldring, now Assistant Secretary of State, appeared as a witness:

SENATOR TYDINGS: To make it crystal clear, by the medium of the Allied mark . . . we were in a position to impose upon Germany the cost of keeping our Army over there?

MR. HILLDRING: The internal costs are visited upon Germany, and to do it certainly aided tremendously by the use of the military mark.

SENATOR TYDINGS: To come down to specific figures, if 250,000,000 dollars worth of these Allied marks have been

10. The Treasury and War Department officials first displayed a mild interest in currency control questions late in the spring of 1944. Certain possibilities in this direction were discussed by various officials during the following year but no meaningful steps were even planned until a full-scale crisis developed in Germany. For detailed information see Rundell, *Black Market Money*, pp. 31ff.

11. See *Annual Report of the Secretary of the Treasury: 1944–1945*, pp. 97, 393. "The United States military forces should, when they obtain A.M. marks . . . for such of their expenditures as would normally be charged to their appropriations set aside in earmarked accounts with the United States Treasury Department the dollar equivalent, at the decreed rate of exchange, and the relevant United States appropriations will thereupon be debited accordingly." Basic Accounting Guide for Germany, *S-47*, p. 244. It was amended later to read "A.M. marks and Reichsmarks." The amendment was proposed by SHAEF and approved by the Combined Chiefs of Staff. *Ibid.*, pp. 250–51. Accounting was to be kept in marks. Unlike the Americans, the British and the French considered the marks issued to them by SHAEF, as well as those they collected from German banks in their respective zones, as net cash income. In other words, these funds were *in addition* to their budgets for the occupation.

put in circulation in Germany, there is 250,000,000 dollars that have been saved to the Treasury?

MR. HILLDRING: Something like that. I would not say to the dollar.[12]

This was wishful thinking. Even if there had been a German government which could have been made to assume the responsibility for AM currency, the American way of handling the occupation finance ruled such savings out. The army accountants soon established that the so-called troop pay overdraft was running into millions of dollars every month. The injection of AM marks into the German economy simply intensified inflation and created conditions favorable to the black market operators. At the same time, the existing provisions for exchanging marks into dollars had the effect of transferring the intended United States benefits to the individual soldier.

From the accountant's point of view, there would have been no problem if the black marketeers had kept their profits in local currencies and spent them locally. But since so many of them remitted their cash profits home in dollars through the facilities of the army post offices, army finance offices, American Express, and Western Union,[13] the overseas military establishment ended up holding huge amounts of nonconvertible currencies, while the sums remitted home were automatically charged against the War Department's appropriations. Although army accountants made strenuous efforts to reduce this deficit, its major component—the troop pay overdraft as it was reflected by the accumulated holdings of foreign notes—stood as of December 31, 1946, at $530,775,400. More than one-half of the overdraft, $270,909,788, had accrued in Germany, mostly in AM marks of Soviet issue.[14] The actual

12. *S-47*, pp. 117–27.

13. One scheme for transferring large sums from Berlin to the United States, which was very popular for the first six months of occupation, was cabling home money for flowers to be delivered to the GI's sweethearts and families. For a substantial commission, certain florists would accumulate dollars for their clients instead of delivering flowers. The amounts thus transferred were reportedly very large, but this channel was tracked down fairly quickly and closed in November, 1945. See Rundell, *Black Market Money*, pp. 48–49. Those soldiers who for one reason or another failed to convert their occupation notes into dollars while overseas had no difficulty in exchanging them on their return home, either on shipboard or at the finance offices of the army camps in the United States.

14. Rundell, *Black Market Money*, pp. 36, 88. The next largest deficit,

loss caused to the United States by financial activities of both the military and civilian American personnel in Germany was probably in the vicinity of half a billion dollars. This amount does not include black marketeers' profits converted into jewelry, gold, fine china, cars, real estate, or German stocks. Here the loss was to the German economy and not the American taxpayer.

The figures of the army overdraft do not, of course, correspond to the size of the infusion of AM marks into the German economy, a major factor in the postwar inflation. Since the marks collected in the army post offices, PX stores, commissaries, etc. were put back into circulation by the Army, the American contribution to monetary inflation cannot be estimated exactly. The same, of course, should be said about the other three occupying powers which, for three years, issued and reissued AM marks in their respective zones and in Berlin.

The initiative for introducing controls over remittance procedures came from the Treasury and War Departments, when they realized that they had to explain to Congress the causes of the deficit in the costs of the occupation of Germany. Since the Soviet contribution to the black market and monetary inflation was already an established fact, there was no longer any talk about the advantage of having common currency with the Soviets. As was noted earlier, the army finance officers were ordered very early not to accept the 1,000-mark notes put in circulation by the Soviets but never issued by the Western Allies. This was hardly an effective measure, but it was something. To institute remittance controls, however, was not an easy matter. The Army, which had been acting as a sort of international banker during the war, took the view that "the facility of transmitting funds to any person, bank, or agency in the United States on a moment's notice . . . contributed in large measure to [the soldier's] peace of mind and [his] effectiveness as a combat soldier."[15] The very suggestion of limiting these transactions brought protests from the field. Having the soldiers' interests in mind, General Eisenhower felt that "cur-

$73,037,246, was accumulated in the Far East, in Japanese, Korean, and Ryukyus yen. The remainder was in the currencies of other European and Asian countries in which the U.S. Army acted as the chief financial institution for the Americans overseas.

15. *S-47*, pp. 6, 96.

rency control, if necessary, should be world wide and not applicable solely to [the European] theater, as our personnel would suffer by comparison with other theaters." [16] Unfamiliar with accountancy problems, the General recommended charging the deficit to Germany (!) and imposing no restrictions on the currency transactions of the troops.

If the Commanding General felt that way, the resistance of his subordinates was easy to understand. Insisting on a measure of autonomy "the local top brass created a variety of feudal kingdoms in which they ruled supreme," presenting their superiors with all sorts of arguments in favor of the preservation of the existing system. It was very difficult for the command "to draw the line between legitimate leeway and discretion and the assumption of unwarranted authority" by the military.[17]

On still lower levels, control measures against black marketeering were almost impossible to enforce. "Even a blind man could not have been unaware of the traffic going on in the offices and homes of American personnel; yet the Army officials who controlled the PXs and commissaries gave little or no heed," writes an Army historian, adding that, "It almost seemed that these officials must themselves be so involved that they were unwilling to do anything about correcting the situation." [18] This seems like a fair guess.

In November, 1945, after several unsuccessful attempts, the War Department ordered the issue of the Currency Exchange

16. *Ibid.*, p. 393.

17. Harold Zink, *American Military Government in Germany* (New York: Macmillan, 1947), p. 200. Ambassador Murphy recalls that Colonel Bernstein, the financial "czar" of OMGUS (Organization of the Military Government of the United States), already disturbed by the Army overdraft, argued strongly in favor of instituting early controls over the remittance procedures. On the other hand, General Walter Bedell Smith, Eisenhower's Chief of Staff, just as strongly—and much more successfully—argued against such controls on the grounds that they would represent a discrimination against the troops in the European Theater. It was perhaps not by accident that General Cobbs, the theater fiscal director, who tried to institute some controls, found his office quietly eliminated in July, 1945. Rundell, *Black Market Money*, pp. 39, 51. General Clay claims that outside of Berlin, where the military establishment was dominated by OMGUS, no controls ever worked well because various commanding officers were anxious to perpetuate the gainful activities of the military personnel. Clay also points out that similar activities of the American military outside of Germany (and Italy), i.e., in France, were never subject to any controls, then or later, and that their participation in the black market continued unabated.

18. Harold Zink, *The United States in Germany: 1944–1945* (Princeton: Van Nostrand, 1957), p. 139.

Control Books.[19] From then on, a soldier's pay and allowances were to be recorded and his remittances home be limited to the recorded amount. At first this control system caused alarm, but soon a number of loopholes were discovered. In the first place, it did not apply to the thousands of nonmilitary "authorized" personnel who were also doing a lot of business. Second, it did not affect officers above field grade. Many such officers were willing to help their comrades-in-arms for a modest commission. Finally, no control books were initially issued to the dependents who were already coming to Germany; thus, wives could send home dollars for their uniformed husbands.

The GI's regarded control books as "interference with their personal affairs" and did not hesitate to alter figures in them or declare them lost and apply for duplicates. In addition, some enterprising GI's started counterfeiting the control books and selling them to anyone who was in distress. Even the law-abiding soldiers found out that the new system was not so bad after all; purchases from PX stores and commissaries, for instance, were not recorded in the books; goods could still be sold, providing the speculators with the opportunity to live lavishly—while saving their pay to the last penny.

The control books produced some change in the pattern of soldier savings. From 1946 on the stress was less on converting the profits into dollars and more on the acquisition of German valuables. In February, 1946, the army command reported that "military personnel are using marks they cannot transfer into dollars for purchase of German manuscripts, jewelry, fine china, et cetera, which are then sent through army post offices to the United States for resale. Although the morale problem of limiting such transactions is understood, serious thought should be given to the eventual implications of such operations with respect to the reputation of the United States Armed Forces." [20]

The reputation of the United States Armed Forces suffered another setback when in the summer of 1946, in its efforts to combat the black market, OMGUS instituted official barter marts. In these marts the Germans traded secondhand goods for Ameri-

19. For details, see Rundell, *Black Market Money*, Chapter 6; also *S-47*, pp. 51, 447, 458.

20. *Ibid.*, pp. 475–577.

can cigarettes, personal effects, and foods. The marts helped to bring out a great supply of German goods wanted by Americans (many conservative Germans had stayed away from black markets but were willing to part with their possessions in an officially approved place). Americans also welcomed this novel way of doing business, for it saved them the trouble of dealing through professional black marketeers and middlemen yet preserved the same high profit margin.

The presumed purpose of the barter marts was to reduce the velocity of monetary circulation by reducing monetary transactions and perhaps give the Germans a chance to receive a better price for their valuables. The first reason was economically naïve: any prevention of goods reaching the market could only intensify the inflation. The second advantage was also dubious, since the Germans parted with their goods when the "prices" for them were most depressed. Some finance officers who observed the barter marts also noted that they led to a sharp increase in speculation, both among the Germans and the Americans, and involved a large-scale evasion of the German custom duties introduced by OMGUS. They also were a political liability, for by that time the United States government was in the process of changing its attitude toward Germany, and the German opinion of Americans was beginning to matter. Nevertheless, it proved difficult to abolish this innovation from which so many Americans profited. Barter marts were not closed down until the end of 1947.[21]

While the War Department was torn between a desire to protect "the current and future financial interests of the American soldier" and the necessity of dealing with its growing deficit, the Treasury Department watched the developments with growing apprehension. As Secretary of the Treasury Fred M. Vinson pointed out to the War Department in his letter of February 18, 1946, the situation was of the utmost gravity. "The inability of the United States Army to prevent the conversion into dollars of foreign currencies acquired by personnel through unauthorized channels," wrote Vinson, "and the unwillingness of the War Department to impose effective controls which the Treasury has in the past suggested, has resulted in a serious worsening of the situation and the Treasury now feels it necessary to propose a more

21. Fredricksen, *American Occupation of Germany*, p. 117.

drastic measure, which would render unnecessary and thus eliminate the Army's conversion system." [22]

This measure was the introduction of Military Payment Certificates (MPC), or scrip, as a special currency for paying the American troops abroad. Reluctantly, the War Department accepted the scheme and, after protracted consultations in which the objections from the field were finally overcome,[23] stopped paying troops in occupation currencies. The MPC's, which were introduced in Germany in September, 1946, were denominated in dollars; they could be converted into marks (at the same rate 10 to 1) on request, but the marks had to be spent locally. Only MPC's could be accepted for remittances home.

This was a system of "canteen money" similar to the one the Germans used in the Balkans during the war—and it produced results. As one student put it, "Canteen money was the belated recognition of the fact that in an invasion or occupation three separate foreign exchange areas are involved: the invaded country, the home country, and the military community. The military community is a society of its own with its own system of economic and financial transactions. The transactions between these three communities must be controlled effectively if the foreign exchange reserves of any one of them are not to be needlessly depleted." [24]

The introduction of MPC's did not stop American participation in the black market, but made it difficult to convert profits into dollars. Now the profits had to be invested either in local businesses (in partnership with the Germans, since the Americans were legally banned from acquiring interests in German economy and from buying real estate) or in valuables. The main accom-

22. Quoted by Rundell, *Black Market Money*, p. 81.

23. *S-47*, p. 5. Among the objections raised against MPC's, Colonel R. A. Koch, theater fiscal director, listed the following: "Relations with friendly nations (particularly Russia) sharing in the German occupation would be adversely affected. Negotiability of Russian-issued marks would virtually disappear, inasmuch as U.S. redemption of such marks through currency control leaks would stop." *S-47*, p. 515. An important factor in the American decision to introduce MPC's was the shift to a similar device by the British early in 1946. This channeled to the United States zone the marks earned on the black market by British operators who could no longer convert into pounds their profits and had to ask their American comrades-in-arms for help. Thus, the U.S. Treasury started financing British black marketeers as well.

24. Andrew M. Kamarck, "Allied Financial Policy in Italy" (unpublished MS, Harvard University Library), p. 40.

plishment of the MPC reform was that it essentially halted the increase in the troop pay overdraft. From then on, the profits of American black marketeers were paid out of the German economy only.

Some economists familiar with occupation finance have suggested that the MPC reform came so late because in the experience of the occupation of Italy (on which Washington planners presumably relied), the problem of overdraft never arose. If this was the case, the Treasury experts had obviously overlooked a point of crucial importance: that experience in Italy in this respect was not in fact a useful guide for other areas; on the contrary, it was positively misleading.

It is important to recall that since the end of 1944 the United States was reimbursing the Italian government for " net troop pay " which the soldiers were spending in Italy. The " *net* troop pay " was the remainder left after deducting from gross pay and allowances (1) all deductions for allotments and rations, (2) all purchases in the PX stores, and (3) all savings deposits, purchases of war bonds, payments on war insurance, and all remittances home.[25] It follows that in Italy, American black market operators were raiding not the United States Treasury, but the foreign exchange resources of the Italian government, which in the end received in reimbursement from the United States about $160 million less than it would have received had not the Americans transferred their black market profits to the United States.[26] Inasmuch as that was the case, the conscience of the War and the Treasury Departments was clear.

The question as to what to do with the deficit already accumulated was not answered by the MPC reform. The normal course would have been to ask Congress for additional appropriations. The War Department, however, chose not to follow this course, since the Republican-controlled Congress was not expected to react kindly to such a request.[27] The hearings in the appropriations

25. Frank A. Southard, Jr., *The Finances of European Liberation, with Special Reference to Italy* (New York: King's Crown, 1946), p. 18.

26. Kamarck, " Allied Financial Policy in Italy," p. 38; *S-47*, p. 10. Italy's additional loss due to the fact that the Americans drew their cash from the black market, rather than by exchanging their dollars at the official rate of exchange, is impossible to estimate.

27. The British government had acknowledged a deficit of £58 million accumulated in a similar fashion. Most of this deficit was covered by an appropriate parliamentary action. Rundell, *Black Market Money*, pp. 89–90.

committees would have been conducted publicly and would, therefore, have attracted attention to the financial enterprises of the troops in Germany and Japan. This the War Department was most anxious to avoid. Instead, by arrangement with the Treasury —which was also becoming publicity-shy—it decided to get rid of the deficit by "internal means." One such means was to increase prices for commodities in PX stores and commissaries. Another was to charge the American personnel in Germany (and Japan) for services which had been supplied by the German administration as part of the occupation costs. The Allied personnel which had been provided with free maids, gardeners, valets, chauffeurs, etc., and who had lived in rent-free houses and villas, now were made to pay, albeit modestly, for the luxuries of life. This novelty created a great furor, particularly among those who had not participated in the black market and for whom it meant an increase in living costs. The deductions, however, were automatic; besides, by then the American military establishment in Germany had already lost most of its glamor and, with it, most of its capacity for resisting change. The funds thus collected were used for the reduction of the deficit. They were relatively small, and it was feared that the process would be a long one.

The solution was found suddenly in the War Department, where somebody came up with the idea of making German and Japanese prisoners of war pay for the profits of the American black marketeers. According to Article 23 and 24 of the Geneva Convention of 1929, German prisoners of war in American camps were entitled to a certain amount of pay. Some of the prisoners while in the United States earned additional sums by working on farms and elsewhere.[28] None of the German prisoners of war was actually paid, but the accounts were kept, and the needed

28. Article 23 prescribed paying the officers "the same pay as officers of corresponding rank in the armies of the detaining Power. . . . This pay shall be granted them in full, once a month if possible, and without being liable to any deduction for expenses incidental on the detaining Power." Article 23 also stipulated that in these payments "the rate [of exchange] adopted shall be that in force at the opening of hostilities." Article 34 prescribed the rules for paying prisoners of war (other than officers) doing work for the state or private employers while in detention, ordering that "the pay remaining to the credit of the prisoners shall be delivered to them at the end of their captivity." See *U.S., Statutes at Large*, XLVII, Part 2, 2038–42. In practice German soldiers working in the United States while in captivity were credited about 90 cents per work day. The officers also received credit rather than cash as provided in the Convention.

amount—about $150–$200 million—was duly appropriated by the Congress. When, early in 1946, the released prisoners of war started returning to Germany, each one of them was given a Treasury certificate stating the amount, in dollars, due to him.

Had they been paid in dollars, some of the prisoners would have been well off; the price of a dollar on the German black market was by then well above 200 marks. Instead, it was decided to pay them in marks and to use the dollars due to them for covering the army deficit. The question arose at what rate the prisoners' dollars were to be converted into marks. General Clay strongly objected to using the troop pay rate (10 to 1) because "it would give ex-POWs undue purchasing power" and "add to inflationary threat." He recommended the rate of 2.5 to 1 as more accurately reflecting the relative purchasing power of the two currencies.[29] He did not suggest changing the troop pay rate.

The War Department readily agreed with the General and ordered former prisoners paid at a rate of 2.5 marks to $1. However, the army finance officers discovered that the British were paying the former prisoners of war returning to their zone at a rate 50 per cent higher than that. Since this was creating difficulties in public relations, General McNarney asked the War Department to reconsider the rate and to permit him to pay for the Treasury POW certificates on the basis of 10 marks for every $3.00 of the face value. After much argument back and forth, the consent was given.[30] Despite the sizable contribution made by POW's toward reduction of the army deficit, it took American authorities in Germany and elsewhere several years before they

29. *S-47*, p. 579. Cf. OMGUS, *Economic Data on Potsdam Germany: Special Report of the Military Governor* (September, 1947), p. 34.

30. *S-47*, pp. 582–84. The "German solution" was also applied to the Italian POWs. In Memorandum of Understanding, signed on August 14, 1947, the United States and Italy agreed that the United States would honor—in lira (at the "prevailing rate of exchange")—American obligations to the Italian prisoners of war. *U.S., Statutes at Large*, LXI, Part 4, 3962–68. The action in the Pacific Theater was taken earlier and the enforcement of currency controls in Japan was better. On August 9, 1946, Associated Press report from Tokyo indicated that the deficit due to a "lucrative yen-dollar traffic" reached $70 million and that the Army planned to get rid of the deficit by purchasing commodities and services from the Japanese in the next thirty-five months. *S-47*, p. 624. Strictly speaking, using the overdraft to pay for official expenditures of the occupation establishment was illegal since it violated armistice terms. The vanquished, however, were in no position to protest, and President Truman approved this procedure. See Rundell, *Black Market Money*, p. 89.

disposed of the accumulated piles of currencies and wiped out the rest of the deficit.

Two more aspects of the experience with military currency in Germany should be mentioned. As had been the case with Allied military lire and supplemental francs, Allied military marks were easily counterfeited because of the poor quality of thc notes. The first counterfeit notes came to the attention of the occupation authorities in Germany as early as November, 1945, but no record is available that efforts were made to catch the counterfeiters. The same thing happened to Military Payment Certificates. Although MPC's were supposed to be a dollar instrument they were printed with even greater carelessness: the bills had no watermarks, and the first fake notes appeared only three weeks after the MPC's were introduced. No counterfeiters are known to have been caught; the counterfeiting of MPC's was on such a large scale that the Army had to call the old issues in and exchange them for new issues several times. The loss which resulted from counterfeiting was impossible to assess.[31]

Another aspect was currency traffic. MPC's had a premium value on the black market where they were brought for hoarding purposes, for conversion by devious means into dollars, or for illegal acquisition of PX and other army supplies. Despite army claims to the contrary, this demand for MPC's had not been seriously affected by the several conversions, on short notice, into new issues. The regular dollars commanded about 5 per cent premium over the MPC's; local black marketeers were willing to pay up to 300 marks per one yellow seal dollar and slightly more for a regular silver certificate. The regulations against dollar transactions were strict but the prospect of making a 3,000 per cent profit was irresistible. Dollars were brought into occupied areas by mail and in person, by "authorized" civilian personnel, including UNRRA and other officials, as well as by the military.[32] Sold to local operators, the dollars constituted a claim against the United States Treasury, thereby adversely affecting the country's

31. *Ibid.*, pp. 77ff. Also, Fredricksen, *American Occupation of Germany*, p. 116.

32. Arthur I. Bloomfield, *Speculative and Flight Movements of Capital in Postwar International Finance* (Princeton: Princeton University Press, 1954), pp. 29–30. Some displaced persons in UNRRA camps also actively engaged in currency transactions.

balance of payments. As in the case of counterfeiting, the extent of the dollar traffic in American-occupied areas cannot be measured.[33]

33. A lively currency traffic developed in the Pacific by soldiers and officers of various Commonwealth nations who exploited certain variations in the rates of exchange vis-à-vis military currencies of the Far East and of their "home" currencies, to a considerable profit to themselves. Similar traffic was carried out in Western Europe by the Allied personnel who had the opportunity to travel from country to country, or to send their agents on trips to proper places.

Chapter XI

DISCORD OVER GERMANY AND CURRENCY REFORMS

There is, of course, an essential difference between wartime and postwar occupation of an enemy country. Territories which are subjected to military occupation while the war still continues can be ruled in almost any manner. The assumption is always present that the fortunes of war may be reversed. Soldiers who risk their lives fighting the enemy are not expected to give much consideration to the people from whose ranks the enemy army is drawn. The overriding objective of the occupation authorities is to facilitate the victory. The interests of the occupied country are usually considered only insofar as they affect the security of the fighting troops and tend to foster developments which might weaken the war effort.

The moment the victory is secured, the nature of the occupation changes. The element of temporariness, implicit in a wartime occupation, disappears, and the long-range objectives of the occupying power begin to determine its occupation policies. A principal objective usually is to make it difficult, if not impossible, for the former enemy to rise again. This objective predetermines the introduction of a variety of punitive economic and political measures which, as history shows, may or may not accomplish their purpose. Such measures can be carried out successfully, but only up to a point. The victor's insistence on utilizing his power for the maximum destruction of the vanquished's economic potential and social structure leads to an increase in the financial and political costs of the occupation. The moment finally comes when these costs become so prohibitive as to make the continuation of a strictly punitive regime a self-defeating operation.

Short of outright annexation, the victor eventually must—whether he wants to or not—abandon policies based on an attitude of total hostility. Whether he has succeeded in accomplishing his original objectives or not, he is compelled to make the occupation regime look palatable and even beneficial to the occupied nation in order to achieve an acceptable peace settlement and to assure that the former enemy re-enters the international scene as a friendly, rather than a hostile, power.

The Western powers were more successful in effecting such a transition in the part of Germany they controlled than the Soviet Union was in its part of the country. The credit for this success belongs primarily to a few determined and far-sighted individuals in charge of the United States zone of occupation who eventually convinced their British and French colleagues, and the government in Washington, that the time to reconsider the Western attitude toward Germany had arrived. The transition was neither easy nor painless, and it can hardly be doubted that it would have been delayed even longer had it not been for the crude tactics adopted by the Soviet government in its drive for domination over Germany. The price for the emergence of a strong and Western-oriented West Germany was the division of the country and the ever-vulnerable position of the West in Berlin. This price, it seems, was worth paying.

Economic Developments in the Western Zones

In the summer of 1945 Germany lay prostrate in total defeat. Having defeated the Axis, the nations of the victorious coalition began the traditional return to normalcy. American soldiers in Italy and Germany staged mass demonstrations demanding to be sent home immediately. In secret meetings of the Allied Control Council in Berlin, the conquerors argued over reparations, displaced persons, food deliveries, disposition of the Reich's gold reserve, and denazification. The Germans themselves had ceased to participate in their country's affairs. Bewildered by the collapse of the *Vaterland*, they did not even attempt to assess the extent of their defeat, let alone to think about the future. A glimmer of native political life was visible in the Soviet zone, but the Soviets were hated more than other conquerors, and communist politics were so evidently an extension of the occupation regime that they inspired very few. In the Western zones, no political activities were tolerated.

The military governments faced a number of pressing problems. One of the most important was rebuilding. German railroads, destroyed by bombings, did not function; only military trucks maintained communications between towns and cities. Less than a half of the buildings in the Western zones were undamaged; more than a third, including most of the public utilities, were ruined beyond repair. The ruins were overcrowded; the population of the American and British zones was increased by several million refugees from the east and by displaced persons of all nationalities. There was no coal for heating and industry, and there was little food.

The depression of the standard of living of the " indigenous population " was a calculated Allied policy. This policy was successfully carried out from the beginning of the occupation. A system of rationing in urban centers allowed about 1,200 calories a day per person, but during 1945–46 the actual distribution often was as low as 600 calories. It never exceeded 1,500 anywhere until the summer of 1948, and generally averaged between 1,000 and 1,200 calories.[1] It soon became apparent that occupation authorities did not have to make strenuous efforts to keep the productivity in the country down. The apathy of the German people, the destruction of the means of production, and the hardening of the zonal boundaries successfully prevented any upsurge of economic activity. Special teams of experts still traveled in the United States zone sampling the degree of malnutrition and determining the maximum amount of food which could be " safely " given to a particular place. Their reports usually resulted in requests for supplies needed to prevent imminent starvation rather than for withholding food.

The maintenance of the subsistence level for the German city dwellers turned out to be a major headache for the British and the Americans. Importing food from outside was politically explosive, and the very idea of feeding the Germans was unbearable to many officials, particularly in the American zone. But unlike the occupation planners in Washington, General Clay, who was charged with the implementation of the directives, could not avoid the responsibility of keeping the Germans alive as long as the

1. Lucius D. Clay, *Decision in Germany* (Garden City, New York: Doubleday, 1950), pp. 263–73; F. S. V. Donnison, *Civil Affairs and Military Government, North-West Europe: 1944–1946* (London: H.M. Stationery Office, 1961), pp. 327–31; Lewis H. Brown, *A Report on Germany* (New York: Farrar Straus, 1947), p. 43; Victor Gollancz, *In Darkest Germany* (London: Gollancz, 1947), *passim.* Farmers, of course, remained relatively prosperous.

occupation continued. When Clay first read JCS-1067, he was shocked by it; " shocked not so much by its exclusively punitive provisions as by its failure to consider the basic economic realities which confronted the Army of Occupation in a ruined country." [2] His early efforts to obtain more discretionary powers and flexibility were frustrated in Washington, both in the government and in Congress where the Senate Military Affairs (Kilgore) Committee provided a forum for " tough-peace " advocates and critics of those American officials in Germany who tended to deviate from JCS-1067.[3] A large section of the press was more vociferous than ever before in demanding severe punishment for the German nation, and within his own organization, Clay encountered powerful opposition to any manifestations of " softness."

Military governors in the Western zones did not always see eye to eye with the army commanders. From their point of view, the armies of occupation were a heavy drain on zonal resources. Although the American and British troops received their food from abroad, they still drew on local supplies of fresh fruits and vegetables, while French troops relied on local food supplies entirely. The military governors were not concerned with costs: the financial reserves of the occupation were inexhaustible. By issuing as many AM marks as they wanted, Allied authorities could take care of all zonal expenditures and transfer the occupation costs to the population by further inflating the currency in circulation. The legal base for this procedure was worked out soon after Potsdam; the Allied agreement *On Certain Additional Requirements to be Imposed on Germany*, signed on September 20, 1945, stated in part:

> 20. The German authorities will supply free of cost such German currency as the Allied Representatives may require, and will withdraw and redeem in German currency, within such time limits and on such terms as the Allied Representatives may specify, all holdings in German territory of currencies issued by the Allied Representatives. . . .
>
> 21. The German authorities will comply with all such direc-

2. Walter L. Dorn, " The Debate over American Occupation Policy in Germany in 1944–1945," *Political Science Quarterly*, LXXII, No. 4 (December, 1957), 481.

3. Hammond, *American Civil-Military Decisions*, p. 438. For more on American reaction to the attempts to improve the state of the German economy, see Ratchford and Ross, *Berlin Reparations Assignment*, pp. 82–85.

> tions as may be issued by the Allied Representatives for defraying the costs of the provisioning, maintenance, pay, accommodation and transport of the forces and agencies stationed in Germany by authority of the Allied Representatives, the costs of executing the requirements of unconditional surrender, and payment for any relief in whatever form it may be provided by the United Nations.[4]

In the absence of " German authorities "—local administrations did not exist above the township level and even there they were closely supervised by Allied officials—their functions were assumed by the respective military governments. Payments for goods and services were made by German banks; if their funds were insufficient (as they usually were, despite the resumption of tax collections), the military government paid the balance in AM marks, charging the payments to " German authorities."

The difficulty was that AM marks had no value outside Germany, and military governors initially had no funds to pay for food which had to be imported in order to maintain even a 1,200 calories-a-day starvation ration. At the beginning, about 1 million tons of wheat were released from SHAEF stocks, and more was later supplied by the United States army. Great Britain, during its financial crisis of 1946–47, spent some £100 million on foodstuffs delivered to the British zone, one-third of which had to be paid for in dollars.[5] The United States Congress, however, was in no mood to shoulder the burden of German relief. Pointing to the lack of economic relations between the zones and the adverse effects of the further stripping of German industry for reparations, a House committee warned that the continuation of the present policies " can mean only one of two things, (a) That a considerable part of the German population must be ' liquidated ' through diseases, malnutrition, and slow starvation for a period of years to come, with resultant dangers to the rest of Europe from pestilence and the spread of plagues that know no boundaries; of

4. U.S. Congress, Senate, Committee on Foreign Relations, *A Decade of American Foreign Policy, Basic Documents: 1941–49*, 81st Congress, 1st Session, p. 518. Hereinafter referred to as *Basic Documents.*

5. After December, 1947, the United States assumed all costs which required payment in dollars, and the British contribution was estimated at about 20 million pounds annually, exclusive of the cost of occupation forces. F. S. Northedge, *British Foreign Policy. The Process of Readjustment: 1945–1961* (New York: Praeger, 1963), pp. 71, 82.

(b) the continuation both of large occupying forces to hold down 'unrest,' and the affording of relief mainly drawn from the United States to prevent actual starvation." [6]

The American and British occupation authorities thought that at the core of their difficulties were the absence of an inflow of food from the Soviet zone and the general violation of the principle of economic unity for Germany, which had been formulated in Article 14 of the Potsdam agreements:

> During the period of occupation Germany shall be treated as a single economic unit. To this end common policies shall be established in regard to:
> (a) mining and industrial production and allocation;
> (b) agriculture, forestry and fishing;
> (c) wages, prices and rationing;
> (d) import and export programs for Germany as a whole;
> (e) currency and banking, central taxation and customs;
> (f) reparation and removal of industrial war potential;
> (g) transportation and communications.

The Potsdam agreements, however, were not enforceable. Their implementation depended on the consent of each of the four powers. When, both for political and economic reasons, the Soviets refused to integrate their zone to any extent with those of the Western powers, the latter could do little more than protest in the meetings of the Allied Control Council. The effects of this breakdown of Germany's economic unity were most severe in the British zone, which had the largest urban population and an inadequate agricultural base. It soon became evident to the British authorities that "The hardening of occupational boundaries into final administrative zones created a host of problems unforeseen in the preparation of plans. The zones now had to be envisaged as separate economic units. This would have been a major upheaval even if the zones had been chosen according to economic principles, in view of the close integration of Germany. The actual division of the zones increased the problem a hundredfold, since none approached self-sufficiency." [7]

6. U.S. Congress, House of Representatives, Special Committee on Postwar Policy and Planning, Eighth Report, *Economic Reconstruction in Europe*, 79th Congress, 1st Session, pp. 36–37.

7. W. Friedmann, *The Allied Military Government in Germany* (London: Stevens, 1947), p. 18.

To the Soviets—and to the French—self-sufficiency was a relative thing. Their troops lived off the land and had priority in supplies coming from the zonal economies; the Germans had to be satisfied with what was left. French objections to any measures leading to German unity were prompted by considerations very different from those which motivated the Soviets; in addition, the French were in no way bound by the Potsdam decisions in which they had not participated. But since the French zone was the poorest of all (and supported a relatively small population), the French position in the Allied Control Council was of minor importance.

General Clay, fully backed by Sir Brian H. Robertson, the British Military Governor, tried very hard in the Allied Control Council to break down zonal barriers, but his efforts were to no avail. In May, 1946, he reported to Washington, "After one year of occupation, zones represent airtight territories with almost no free exchange of commodities, persons and ideas. Germany now consists of four small economic units which can deal with each other through treaties. . . . Economic unity can be obtained only through free trade in Germany. . . . A common financial policy is equally essential. Runaway inflation accompanied by economic paralysis may develop at any moment. Drastic fiscal reforms to reduce currency and monetary claims are essential at the earliest possible date." [8] Simultaneously, on his own initiative, he ordered the cessation of further dismantling of reparations plants in the American zone "until such time as Germany is treated as a single economic unit." The British followed this lead, but neither the Soviets nor the French were impressed, and the former continued to refuse to deliver food and other supplies which were due the American and British zones in exchange for the equipment already sent to Russia.

JCS-1067

The JCS-1067 directive was an official expression of the United States' attitude toward Germany as of the spring of 1945. It provided guidance to the Military Governor and the OMGUS establishment in the American zone. Like any other government directive, JCS-1067 was not a gospel; its effectiveness was deter-

8. Clay, *Decision in Germany*, p. 73.

mined not only by the efficiency of the personnel, but also by the individual judgments, views, likes, and dislikes of its numerous executors. Since no policy guidance can foresee every situation, a great deal must necessarily be left to the discretion of officials, and what may be called " real " policy (i. e., the sum total of the measures carried out by the officers in charge) is often quite different from what was in the minds of the policyplanners.

JCS-1067 was somewhat unusual in that it left the man responsible for governing the American zone, General Clay, little room to maneuver. Even more important was the fact that many officials of OMGUS shared the spirit of vegeance which permeated the directive and were prepared to enforce to the hilt its punitive features, consistently interpreting specific provisions of the document in such a way as to further aggravate conditions in Germany and to make life as difficult as possible for the Germans. These sentiments deprived the military government of operational flexibility much more than the reluctance of the agencies in Washington to revise JCS-1067 in accordance with the requirements of the situation in Germany.

Most implacably anti-German were the officials whose function was to enforce the economic and financial clauses of the directive. The credit for this goes to the Treasury Department which had succeeded in creating a very effective, albeit informal, administrative substructure in Germany. For almost two years this substructure ensured the strictest possible implementation of JCS-1067 and frustrated the attempts of many top administrators, from General Clay down, to modify the policies so as to enable the military government machinery to discharge its responsibility for governing the American zone.

The Treasury's organization in Germany consisted of the financial experts in the Army who had been Treasury officials until they were " loaned " at Eisenhower's request for the purpose of administering the financial and general economic needs of the occupation. These officials were noted for their loyalty to the Treasury, a loyalty which was also pronounced in Washington and gave Treasury officials, fighting for their cause in various interdepartmental committees, a peculiar advantage over other departments. Their determination and aggressiveness may not have been liked by others, but these qualities enabled them to score one success after another.

Although they wore army uniforms in Europe, the " Morgenthau boys," as they were commonly called in OMGUS, in effect were Treasury representatives in the Army, maintaining direct and private contact with the Treasury Department despite the sometimes violent protests of the military, who were unused to the by-passing of official channels. Their recognized leader was Colonel Bernard Bernstein, Director of Finance Division at SHAEF and later the financial " czar " of the occupation. From the time of his commission in October, 1942, until his resignation three years later (following that of his Treasury chief), Bernstein remained the repository of the Morgenthau spirit in the Army of Occupation. His constant and intimate contact with Morgenthau, and thus with the White House, gave him an advantage in negotiations in England before Germany's defeat.[9] It also gave him power well beyond his official status to enforce JCS-1067 during the first crucial months of the occupation.

The general political climate in Washington began to change even before Potsdam. This change had certain effects on the military government in Germany. By the fall of 1945, some of the more controversial personalities had resigned; others became less conspicuous. However, due to the " Morgenthau boys' " perseverence in the early period, " the policies of the [JCS-1067] directive were applied zealously and acquired sufficient cumulative momentum to delay a basic shift in policy." [10] Perhaps even more important was the fact that the United States as a nation was still quite content to see the German people pay for the sins of the defunct nazi regime. The shift started slowly, and only when it was discovered that a large and growing part of the bill had to be footed by the American people and that the old policy was becoming a serious liability to the United States in the rapidly changing international scene.

9. It was a result of Bernstein's efforts that the planning for occupation done by SHAEF's Germany Country Unit was largely discarded. Carl J. Friedrich (ed.), *American Experiences in Military Government in World War II* (New York: Rinehart, 1948), pp. 224–25. For more on Bernstein's role, see Hammond, *American Civil-Military Decisions*, pp. 349, 396, 405–6; also Russell Hill, *Struggle for Germany* (New York: Harper, 1947), p. 111.

10. Manuel Gottlieb, " Failure of Quadripartite Monetary Reform 1945–1947," *Finanzarchiv* (Band 17, Tuebingen, 1956/57), p. 404.

THE STUTTGART SPEECH AND THE MOSCOW CONFERENCE

The address which Secretary of State Byrnes delivered at Stuttgart on September 6, 1946,[11] has usually been regarded as a turning point in the United States policy toward Germany. In this address, Byrnes pointed out the failure of the Allied Control Council to effect economic unity of Germany and stated that "the time has come when the zonal boundaries should be regarded as defining only the areas to be occupied for security purposes . . . and not as self-contained economic or political units." He called for higher production levels, for the fusion of the zones, and for "the early establishment of a provisional German government for Germany." Even before this is done, said Byrnes, the German people should "be given the primary responsibility for the running of their own affairs."

Touching upon certain international aspects of the German problem, Byrnes reminded his audience (which, unprecedentedly, included many German officials) that the Oder-Neisse line was only a temporary eastern border of Germany, and that at Potsdam "the heads of government did not agree to support at the peace settlement the cession of this particular area." Byrnes ruled out subjecting the Ruhr and the Rhineland "to political domination or manipulation of outside powers." And although he was in favor of the economic integration of the Saar with France, he stated that "the United States will not support an encroachment on territory which is indisputably German or any division of Germany which is not genuinely desired by the people concerned." Finally, Byrnes warned that Germany should not become "a pawn or a partner in a military struggle for power between East and West." Occupation forces, he said, "will probably have to remain in Germany for a long time," and he emphasized that "as long as there is an occupation army in Germany, American forces will be part of that occupation army."

There have been many interpretations of the Stuttgart speech, but little is known of the motivations behind it. The most common interpretation is that the United States took a stand on Germany with the intention of counteracting the Soviet bid for the allegi-

11. U.S. Congress, Senate, The Committee on Foreign Relations, *Documents on Germany: 1944–1959*, 86th Congress, 2d session, pp. 35–42. Hereinafter referred to as *Documents on Germany*.

ance of the German people. This is possible, and there is some evidence to support such a view. For instance, when Molotov, a month earlier in Paris, made one of his major speeches denouncing those who out of the spirit of revenge favored the annihilation of Germany as a state and its agrarianization, Byrnes was obviously alarmed. Later he noted that Molotov's speech "was confirmation of our fears that unless forced by world opinion to do so, the Soviet Union would not agree to a treaty of peace with Germany for years to come. They would utilize their veto power on the Allied Control Council and in the Council of Foreign Ministers to secure adoption of their conception of 'democratic' government; to secure a part in the control of German industries . . . and to enforce the payment of 10 billion dollars in reparations."[12]

It is also known that Byrnes' views on the German problem were influenced to a considerable degree by Clay, a close personal friend whom he had personally promoted for the position of Military Governor in Germany.[13] And at that time, through daily contact with his Soviet counterparts in Berlin, Clay probably understood the problem better than anyone else. But other considerations were doubtless also present in Byrnes' mind: namely, the desire to cut down the growing cost of feeding the Germans and the necessity to limit French demands for the internationalization of the Ruhr by questioning the finality of other Potsdam decisions regarding Germany's boundaries.

The Stuttgart speech was interpreted as "pro-German" by a large segment of the American press. This interpretation seemed to be confirmed when Secretary of Commerce Wallace, who publicly attacked Byrnes' policies as too harsh on the Soviet Union, was subsequently fired by Truman.[14]

12. James F. Byrnes, *Speaking Frankly* (New York: Harper, 1947), p. 181.

13. Murphy, *Diplomat among Warriors*, p. 251. Initially, Clay was Deputy to General Eisenhower and, later, to General McNarney, in charge of OMGUS.

14. Clark Clifford, Truman's adviser, stated that the firing of Wallace was unrelated to Byrnes' sharp protest against Wallace's ventures into the field of foreign policy. Jonathan Daniels, *The Man of Independence* (Philadelphia: Lippincott, 1950), p. 314. Wallace, however, told me that the relation was most direct, as Truman himself had told him that Byrnes' position was strongly supported by Senators Connally and Vandenberg. On this episode, see also Byrnes, *Speaking Frankly*, pp. 239–43, and *Memoirs by Harry S. Truman* (Garden City, N.Y.: Doubleday, 1955), I, 556–61. The Stuttgart speech raised a storm not only in Moscow but also in France and, to Byrnes' evident surprise, even in Warsaw; the Secretary had not thought that his questioning of the finality of the Oder-

Yet the conclusion that by this time the United States had already decided to take a strong stand against the Soviets and to start wooing the Germans was rather premature. President Truman's attitude toward the Soviets had hardened considerably, but although he let Byrnes speak for the United States on European issues, "his relationship with and his dependence on his Secretary of State at that time was not entirely satisfactory," [15] and there is no evidence available to show that he supported Byrnes specifically on the German issue.[16] Moreover, there were no sufficient grounds to present Byrnes either as "anti-Soviet" or "pro-German." As nearly as can be established, Byrnes' main objective was to stimulate the Germans to revitalize their economy, and at the same time to induce the Soviets to produce a compromise solution (the Secretary was known to be fond of compromise solutions) in promoting interzonal economic relations.[17] A more reasonable conclusion is that by the fall of 1946 the United States had realized that (*a*) it did not want to pay the growing costs of the occupation and that (*b*) it did not want to allow the

---

Neisse line might infuriate the Poles. Upon his return to Paris, Byrnes sought to put French fears at rest by declaring that "the United States is firmly opposed to the revival of Germany's military power" as well as to "a struggle for the control of Germany which would again give Germany the power to divide and conquer." Byrnes, *Speaking Frankly*, p. 193. See also Dorothy Pickles, *French Politics: The First Years of the Fourth Republic* (London: Royal Institute of International Affairs, 1944), pp. 189ff. The British government, which was most concerned with the costs involved in the occupation of its zone, wholeheartedly approved Byrnes' position. Cf. James F. Byrnes, *All in One Lifetime* (New York: Harper, 1958), pp. 370–80.

15. Daniels, *The Man of Independence*, p. 312.

16. It might be worth recalling that earlier in the war Senator Truman was rather skeptical about the European powers. On the occasion of Hitler's attack on Russia in June, 1941, he "suggested that the United States help whichever side seemed to be losing: If we see that Germany is winning we ought to help Russia and if Russia is winning we ought to help Germany and that way let them kill as many as possible, although I don't see Hitler victorious under any circumstances. Neither of them think anything of their pledged word." *The New York Times*, June 24, 1941. The evolution of Truman's views on the Soviet Union in later years may be a matter of conjecture. But there is plenty of evidence that he retained an "aloof and distrustful attitude" toward the Germans. See Murphy, *Diplomat among Warriors*, pp. 283–84.

17. The evidence that, despite this limitation of his objectives, Byrnes was somewhat ahead of the attitudes prevailing in the government is offered by a senior State Department official who recorded that only by the end of 1946 "it began to be apparent that concentration upon the unattainable Potsdam goal of economic unity for Germany was blocking all other approaches to the problem." Joseph M. Jones, *The Fifteen Weeks* (New York: Viking Press, 1955), p. 219.

Soviets to gain a dominant position by exploiting the moral and economic decomposition of the defeated country.

The Stuttgart episode had important consequences. With explicit support from Byrnes (and from Senators Connally, Vandenberg, Russell, and George), Clay felt freer than ever to run the affairs of OMGUS in his own way, even if this meant considerable deviation from the spirit and even the letter of JCS-1067. He received further encouragement when a month after the Stuttgart speech, Congress approved the so-called GARIOCA program (Government and Relief in Occupied Areas) for the prevention of hunger and famine in Germany and Japan.[18]

Even more important was Great Britain's response to Byrnes. Negotiations with the British were quickly concluded and on December 2, 1946, the birth of "Bizonia" was officially announced.[19] Soviet sponsored communist propaganda attacked this decision vigorously, claiming that it was an Anglo-American scheme to resurrect "German militarism." It was perhaps even more bitterly criticized in Paris. French politics dictated that France should oppose anything which even remotely suggested the reappearance of a strong and unified Germany. In addition, the French left-of-center governing coalition was in no mood to challenge the Soviet Union.

The search for new approaches to the German problem started in earnest early in 1947. It was prompted by a series of developments of which perhaps the most important was a sharp and sudden economic crisis in Europe. One off-shoot of this crisis was Great Britain's decision to withdraw from Greece, which was then involved in the second round of its civil war. This decision led to the Truman Doctrine. Once committed to aid Greece and Turkey, the United States was rapidly assuming responsibility for the state of affairs in Europe. However, still wishing to avoid

18. In Germany it lasted until 1950 and eventually cost $1,620,200,000. *Germany Reports* (Bonn, 1955), pp. 282–83. There were some UNRRA supplies coming into Germany but these went exclusively to displaced persons of non-German origin and nazi victims. Practically all UNRRA personnel were bitterly anti-German.

19. The negotiations were started in July when Byrnes, seven weeks before his public address at Stuttgart, instructed the American Military Governor to make a formal proposal for the merger of the zones at the Allied Control Council. See John H. Hilldring, *American Policy in Occupied Areas*, Department of State Publication No. 2794 (Washington: U.S. Government Printing Office, 1948), pp. 7–8.

the division of the world into two rival camps, the government made one more attempt to settle its differences with the Soviet Union.

The meeting of the Council of Foreign Ministers in Moscow, which opened on March 10, 1947, lasted six weeks and accomplished nothing.[20] It was the first conference at which the Great Powers dealt directly with the question of peace with Austria and Germany. The Soviets took an uncompromising stand on the issue of reparations; they rejected the old American offer to conclude a twenty-five to fifty years' treaty to guarantee the continuing disarmament of Germany; they indicated time and again that they hoped the United States would leave Europe and go home; and they categorically insisted that there should be a strong central German government in Berlin, in the middle of the Soviet zone, because (as the Americans surmised), "they were confident that they could penetrate and dominate its politics and its trade unions through local Communists and turn Germany into a workshop for the Soviet Union while avoiding the danger that German power would ever be turned against them." The Americans, with the full support of the British and French, opposed such political and economic centralization. They did not want "a Germany that would be a projection into Western Europe of the totalitarian system." [21]

The Marshall Plan, born largely out of the failure of the Moscow Conference, caused a major shift in Soviet policies. Communist parties either left or were excluded from the coalition governments of Western Europe, in which they had participated since the war; they adopted a policy of stimulating labor unrest which further aggravated the economic situation. In September, 1947, a new communist organization, the Cominform, was founded and declared unequivocally that the world was divided into two camps: the "imperialist," headed by the United States, and the "peace-loving," headed by the Soviet Union.

20. See Walter Bedell Smith, *My Three Years in Moscow* (Philadelphia: Lippincott, 1950), Chapter X. Also, report by Secretary Marshall, April 28, 1947, *Basic Documents*, pp. 97–106. For the background, see Byrnes, *Speaking Frankly*, pp. 166ff. Also, Redvers Opie, *The Search for Peace Settlements* (Washington: The Brookings Institution, 1951), pp. 173–97. France joined the Council of Foreign Ministers in the spring of 1946. For the official American reports on the Council meetings, see *Basic Documents*, pp. 51–116.

21. Jones, *The Fifteen Weeks*, p. 217.

The fifth and the last meeting of the Council of Foreign Ministers convened in London on November 25, 1947. During October, Soviet attacks on American and British bizonal policy took particularly violent forms. The deputies of the Foreign Ministers, who came to London to prepare the agenda for the conference, struggled for three weeks, and at the end found themselves unable even to issue a joint report on their disagreements.

At the meeting, Molotov insisted that the establishment of a strong German government must precede a peace settlement with Germany. Marshall, on the other hand, stressed the importance of achieving economic unity. While also favoring the early establishment of a provisional German government, Marshall argued that "it was necessary first to agree in principle on the prerequisites to [its] effective functioning. . . . These included the establishment of basic freedom for the individual, the free movement of goods, people, and ideas throughout Germany, and the determination of the economic burdens to be borne by the German people." [22]

Although continuing to stress Soviet reparation claims, Molotov directed most of his lengthy speeches to the German people in an effort to persuade them that only the Soviet Union had their welfare at heart. He charged the Western Powers with perfidy and with having secret plans to divide Germany. The tension became so great that on December 15 the American delegation moved for adjournment.

Reporting on the meeting four days later, Marshall said: "It finally became clear that we could make no progress at this time—that there was no apparent will to reach a settlement but only an interest in making more speeches intended for another audience. . . . No real ground was lost or gained at the meeting, except that the outlines of the problems and the obstacles are much clearer. We cannot look forward to a unified Germany at this time. We must do the best we can in the area where our influence can be felt." [23]

Whatever hopes for a settlement still existed in the West did not last long. There were no indications in Moscow, or in the Allied Control Council in Berlin, that the Soviet government was

22. Opie, *The Search for Peace Settlements*, p. 236.
23. *Basic Documents*, p. 109.

willing to alter its positions. On the contrary, everything suggested that the Soviet Union had decided to retain its hold on East Germany and to force the West to accept the fact that all Europe east of the Elbe had become an inseparable part of the Soviet empire. In order to demonstrate the weakness of the Western powers—and to sabotage the implementation of the Marshall Plan—the communist parties staged a new wave of strikes and public disorders throughout Western Europe. This unrest was accompanied by an unprecedented outburst of anti-American propaganda.

At the same time, the Soviet Union greatly tightened its hold over the satellites of Eastern and Central Europe. The policy of a greater integration of the communist bloc led to a communist coup in Czechoslovakia in February, 1948, and in March, after Tito had refused to submit to full Soviet control, to the break in Soviet-Yugoslav relations. This break, completed with the expulsion of Yugoslavia from the Cominform in June, was accompanied by a series of bloody purges of " Titoists " in the satellite countries, in which the last vestiges of their independence, and the remnants of pro-Western elements, were destroyed.

By this time, very few people in the West continued to hope that the division between the wartime Allies could still somehow be narrowed and that peace could be secured for the world. The Berlin Blockade, the origins of which will be explored next, demolished the remaining hopes and made it obvious that the division of Europe was final.

CURRENCY REFORMS AND THE BERLIN BLOCKADE

To General Clay, the Moscow conference (which he attended) had one important consequence: it paved the ground for the rejection of the JCS-1067 directive. By mid-May, the reactivated SWNCC in Washington had prepared an official draft of a revision of the document which was based on Clay's suggestions. Two more months were required to overcome continued resistance. The new directive, JCS-1779, was approved at a meeting of SWNCC on July 10, 1947, and in its final form, the document " was purged of the most important elements of the Morgenthau Plan." [24]

24. Hammond, *American Civil-Military Decisions*, p. 443. For the text of JCS-1779, see *Germany 1947–1949*, Department of State Publication No. 3556 (Washington: U.S. Government Printing Office, 1950), pp. 34–37.

The liberalization of the occupation policy was welcomed, but at this late date it could produce no miracles. Nor was much accomplished by the creation of "Bizonia." In the summer of 1947 economic indices reached their lowest levels since the end of the war, amounting to a mere one-third of the 1936 level.[25] Major obstacles to economic revival were the lack of effective incentives to production and the continuing dominance of the black market, which was thriving on inflation. The financial situation was aggravated further by the destruction of the old German banking system, the last accomplishment of the "Morgenthau boys" who resigned *en masse* following the approval of JCS-1779.

The German banking system suffered probably more under the occupation than any other area of business activity in the American zone. In part this was due to the arrangement which put each division of the military administration in charge of the process of denazification in its own field. Since the finance division was the most actively anti-German, bankers and accountants formed a disproportionately large group of the former nazi officials who were removed from their jobs and put into prison.[26] However, the main problems of German finance resulted from certain provisions in the economic part of JCS-1067, such as the one prescribing the decentralization of the German banking system (the brainchild of Harry Dexter White). Opposition to this measure had been strong within OMGUS, and since the wording of the directive allowed for different interpretations, it was not enforced at the beginning of the occupation.

The importance of centralized financing (which had been traditional in Germany as well as in other European countries) was that it allowed for a greater flexibility in the flow of credit; short-term seasonal credits in agriculture, short and long-term credits in commerce, and long-term credits in industry were all drawn from the same pool of financial resources, managed by *Grossbanken* with branches all over Germany. To break that system meant cutting off this flow of credit and limiting banks exclusively

25. OMGUS, *Economic Data on Potsdam Germany: Special Report of the Military Governor* (September, 1947), p. 17.

26. The following is based on interviews I had with several former finance officials in OMGUS who were concerned with the banking reform, especially A. T. Warner, then Deputy Chief, Financial Institutions Branch, OMGUS. For the official view, see Rodney C. Loehr, *The West German Banking System* (Historical Division, Office of the U.S. High Commissioner for Germany, 1952), pp. 5–14.

to short-term financing, thus preventing the rehabilitation of German industry. This was exactly the objective of the remaining followers of Morgenthau in the decartelization division of OMGUS, which had been originally headed by Bernstein. They accomplished this objective in the spring of 1947 (when, as they well knew, policy toward Germany was under revision in Washington), with full knowledge of the disastrous consequences it would produce.[27]

Unknown to the other divisions of OMGUS, the experts from the decartelization division composed the text of what became known as Military Government Law 56; they waited until General Clay went away on a trip and then submitted the text for approval to one of his less sophisticated assistants. Law 56 was published on the eve of the arrival of JCS-1779. The law ordered banks in the American zone not to solicit or take instruction from any bank outside of the zone, and to manage their assets and business on a *Land* (i.e., province) basis. Special custodians were appointed to direct the banks' affairs " free from influence by stockholders or bank officials." Each *Land* unit " was required to adopt a name that differed from the parent *Grossbanken* and from other units. The Giro systems of these banks were broken up and even their names changed." As an official historian relates, there was no attempt to conceal that " this action was aimed at the *Grossbanken* which were the particular targets of American efforts to break up excessive concentrations of financial power." [28]

The British occupation authorities (and later the French), not wanting to create the impression of dissent, enacted similar orders. But they did not implement these orders. They limited action in their zones to changing the names of the banks, and in fact left the system virtually intact. But decentralization in the United States zone was carried through with great speed and had immediate adverse effects on the economy. Because the new JCS-1779 directive was not retroactive, the situation remained unchanged through the remainder of the occupation rule.

As economic conditions continued to deteriorate, the occupying powers realized that no significant improvement would occur

27. To many uninformed Americans, who since the Great Depression sincerely believed in the virtue of breaking up *any* concentration of financial power, this measure appeared logical and even beneficial.

28. Loehr, *The West German Banking System*, p. 9.

without a reduction of the money supply and drastic measures designed to restore public confidence in money. But they also were aware that in view of the differences in their objectives any such measures were bound to have grave political repercussions.

The necessity for some kind of monetary reform had been obvious from the very beginning of the occupation. The abnormal supply of currency left by the Reich and increased by the injection of AM marks had to be reduced if any financial order was to be re-established in Germany. Discussions in the Allied Control Council at Berlin in the winter of 1945–46 revealed a great diversity of views.

The French, as usual, opposed any move suggestive of the centralization of the German economy. They were engaged in a massive requisitioning in their zone; their occupation forces were large relative to the size of their zone; and they did not like the idea of limiting the amounts of currency they could spend on their needs. The Soviets had adopted a similar attitude: they would not renounce the right of unlimited access to free purchasing power provided by AM marks. They also objected to the legitimization of the nazi war debt (a measure favored by the British), and they demanded a sweeping capital levy on the more well-to-do sections of the German population. The British proposed to inflate the national income by artificially boosting both prices and wages and, by increasing tax revenue, to balance the budgets of the zones. They also were opposed to any monetary reforms at that time. The American position seems to have been characterized by a " nihilistic radicalism " which stemmed from the Treasury's attitude toward Germany. The American experts during this round of negotiations were opposed to monetary reform and to any steps which could have prevented runaway inflation. The discussions in the Allied Control Council were discontinued in the spring of 1946.

The growing cost of supporting the German population kept the problem of monetary reform alive. The United States finally created a special committee to devise an effective anti-inflation program which would at the same time be politically acceptable to all the occupying powers. The resulting Colm-Dodge-Goldsmith report was completed by September, 1946, and talks were resumed.

The report called for the regularization of the financial obligations of the future German government in regard to claims for war losses, for property taken for reparations, etc. The American program provided for a special equalization tax on all real property, of the order of 50 per cent *ad valorem*, which would become the main source of revenue; the proceeds from it would then be used for paying off German indebtedness. This capital levy meant a drastic redistribution of the ownership of property in Germany, a course favored both by the the Soviets and by the United States Treasury. It was hoped that such "massive inroads on property would appeal to Soviet predilections." [29]

At first it seemed as if the Colm-Dodge-Goldsmith report reconciled the various conflicting positions. The re-created Allied Control Council finance committee devised the details of the reform. However, a deadlock ensued when the discussions reached the subject of the preparation of the bank notes required for the reform. The Soviet representatives demanded that two sets of plates be made, one to be used at the Berlin mint, another at Leipzig in the Soviet zone. The Soviet government, mindful of its interests and distrustful of its partners, wanted to have custody of the plates.[30] The British and the French were willing to run the risk, but General Clay vetoed this step, explaining later that "theirs was not the financial burden for the support of West Germany which we had assumed. Moreover, we had enough of Soviet promise in the printing of Allied military currency. We had paid dearly for the set of plates we made available to the Soviet government. We did not intend to be placed in such

29. Manuel Gottlieb, *The German Peace Settlement and the Berlin Crisis* (New York: Paine-Whitman, 1960), p. 110. Eventually, the provision for the capital levy was striken out on orders from Washington, where it came to be regarded as an "anticapitalistic" measure. See also Murphy, *Diplomat among Warriors*, pp. 310–11.

30. One may speculate that this insistence was the result of the experiences in Austria which were referred to elsewhere. There the military currency, printed in the United States, was allocated to each of the four occupying powers by mutual agreement among the commanders in chief. Although there is no record of any Soviet request for money being turned down, the established procedure placed an automatic limit on what the Soviets could request. Ever anxious to preserve an outward respectability, they could not ask for more currency, for instance, than the rest of the Allies combined. The same limitation continued to be in effect after the Austrian government assumed control over the issue of currency; any unreasonable Soviet demand for cash would have encountered a joint veto of the Western powers, who tried to attain and maintain monetary stability in Austria, which they considered to be a "liberated" country.

position again and our government was firm in this view." [31]

The American counteroffer to have the notes printed in Berlin under the strict supervision of all four powers was rejected by the Soviets. By then, some members of the American delegation concluded that the Soviet government had lost interest in the agreement, "for they no doubt feared that economic recovery in Germany would ill serve the purpose of first bringing the people into a state of economic chaos." [32] Once again the talks broke down, seemingly for good.

At the November–December, 1947, meeting of the Council of Foreign Ministers in London, the United States and Great Britain warned the Soviet Union that unless Soviet cooperation was forthcoming they would go ahead with a separate monetary reform in the Western zones. The Soviet delegation replied with a dramatic walkout. This was a grave error, and it seems likely that Molotov would not have staged this demonstration had he known preparations for a separate monetary reform in the West were well under way.

Shortly after the Moscow Conference, General Clay succeeded in convincing his superiors in Washington that it was of extreme importance to be ready to carry out this reform at a moment's notice. His arguments were based on intelligence reports which alleged that the Soviets were printing new bank notes with the intention of introducing a separate currency in their zone. Had this action been taken before the Western Powers were ready with *their* separate currency, disaster would have been likely to follow: the outlawed notes would have immediately crossed the zonal border and the amount of notes circulating would have been swelled enormously. In what has been claimed as a purely defensive move (a claim which convinced very few), the Western Powers resolved to prepare themselves for such a contingency. A silent race toward a separate currency reform started. "Opera-

31. Clay, *Decision in Germany*, pp. 208–9.

32. Lowell Bennett, *Berlin Bastion* (Frankfurt a/M: Rudl, 1951), p. 45. Gottlieb, who covers the quadripartite talks on the currency reform much more extensively than Bennett, takes exception to this view and seems to ascribe the failure of the talks to the lack of persuasiveness on the part of the Americans. Bennett (who also participated in the negotiations) appears, however, more convincing to me; he does not attempt to ascribe too much importance to this episode and seems to be more aware of the political cleavage between the two sides which, in the end, decided the outcome.

tion Bird Dog"—as the manufacture of the new deutsche mark (DM) currency was called—was planned and carried out with outstanding efficiency. The Bureau of Engraving and Printing of the Treasury Department went to work around the clock. By the end of the year the new notes began to arrive in Frankfurt a/Main.

The preparation of the reform was probably one of the best kept secrets in postwar history. The details were known only to a dozen American, British, and French experts—plus a score of leading German economists who did most of the planning. In order to prevent any leaks, these economists were kept incommunicado at a United States Air Force base at Rothwesten, near Kassel. They stayed there for six weeks, complaining of long work hours, excessively rich food, and inadequate furnishings in the barracks. Several important bank officials were finally allowed to go home just before the currency reform was announced. The Allied officials kept the secret equally well. Even the guards, guarding unmarked boxes in the vaults of a Frankfurt bank, had no idea that they were full of the freshly printed deutsche mark currency.[33]

The fateful decision to proceed with the reform was taken in London following the collapse of the Council of Foreign Ministers. At a gloomy gathering at the American Embassy after Christmas, Marshall, Bevin, Clay, Robertson, Murphy, Ambassador Lewis Douglas, and Frank K. Roberts of the British Foreign Office discussed what to do next in Germany. Clay and Murphy urged that the currency reform be started without delay. Clay also warned that if the reform were carried out, the Soviets might make trouble in Berlin. Marshall and Bevin finally approved Clay's plans but urged him to try once more to obtain a four-power acceptance of the reform at the Allied Control Council.[34] Nothing was put on paper. Clay promised to make a final effort but was sure that no compromise with the Soviets was possible on the crucial issue of control over the printing of the new currency. Clay suspected that the currency to be introduced in the reform would be the one already stored at Frankfurt.

The Soviets were, of course, aware that the currency reform in

33. This information was supplied by Ed Tennenbaum, then Special Assistant to the Finance Adviser to the United States Military Governor in Germany and a co-author of the currency reform.

34. Murphy, *Diplomat among Warriors*, pp. 312–13.

the West was being prepared; they were not misled by a "last compromise proposal" on financial reform introduced by General Clay into the Allied Control Council in January, 1948. What they did not know was the timing, the specific terms of the reform, and the degree of Western preparedness to carry it out.

It seems probable that the Soviets counted on their ability to forestall the currency reform in the Western zones. For three years they had observed the Allies' eagerness for compromise solutions and their great desire to preserve the façade of unity. It must also have seemed highly improbable to them that the reform would be carried out at a time when the Western position in Berlin was rapidly deteriorating.

Sometime toward the end of the winter, in its greatly intensified drive to consolidate the communist bloc, the Soviet government evidently decided to try to squeeze the Western Powers out of Berlin. As usual, no announcement to that effect was made in Moscow, but the appropriate instructions were given to the Soviet High Command in Germany. On March 5, General Clay cabled to Washington: "Within the last few weeks, I have felt a subtle change in Soviet attitude which I cannot define but which now gives me a feeling that it may come with dramatic suddenness. . . . It is a feeling of a new tenseness in every Soviet individual with whom we have official relations. I am unable to submit any official report in the absence of supporting data but my feeling is real." [35]

Clay's premonitions were well founded. On March 20, with the predicted "dramatic suddenness," the Soviet delegation led by Marshal Sokolovsky walked out of the Allied Control Council meeting. Beginning on April 1, the Soviets unilaterally introduced a number of the increasingly strict control restrictions on civilian and military traffic between Berlin and the Western zones, reducing the flow of supplies to the city to a mere trickle. In the next dramatic move, the Soviet delegation, on June 16, walked out of the Allied Kommandatura of Berlin.

There is no question that in subjecting the Western Powers to one test after another, the Soviet government was encouraged by the apparent passivity of their responses. It was no secret in Berlin that many Allied officers and officials, conscious of Berlin's strategic vulnerability, were recommending the evacuation of the city

35. Walter Millis (ed.), *The Forrestal Diaries* (New York: Viking Press, 1951), p. 387.

before its abandonment was forced by Soviet pressure. The British, and more particularly the French, regarded Berlin as a political liability to be discarded as soon and as gracefully as possible. Clay's determination to resist this attitude was effective in preventing the mass evacuation of Americans.[36] The Soviets, however, seemed to be in a very strong position in Berlin, and it is likely that the Allied announcement of the currency reform in the Western zones came to the Soviets as a severe shock.

General Clay decided to proceed with the reform shortly after the Soviet withdrawal from the Allied Control Council. He persisted in this decision in spite of the growing tensions, fully aware that a separate currency reform represented a challenge to the Soviets and could easily lead to further aggravation of the situation. The Defense Department was informed of Clay's plans but avoided any decision; at such a critical time the United States government was not prepared to assume responsibility for any move which could have led to an explosion.[37]

The reform was scheduled originally for June 1. Preparations were completed by May 31, but then the French, who had up to this point expressed disapproval of any "provocative steps," suddenly informed Clay that they wanted the reform to include the French zone as well. Such inclusion necessitated certain changes in the plans, and the currency reform was not finally announced until June 18, 1948.

36. W. Phillips Davison, *The Berlin Blockade: A Study in Cold War Policies* (Princeton: Princeton University Press, 1958), p. 74. Murphy, *Diplomat among Warriors*, p. 313. Despite the growing tension, "no top level decision about what to do in the event of a Soviet blockade had been made in Washington, London, or Paris." Davison, p. 75. In the United States, the crisis over Berlin coincided with the 1948 presidential campaign, and with the peace propaganda pressures injected into it by Progressive candidate Henry A. Wallace. Truman insisted that the defense budget be limited to $15 billion and feared the label of "warmonger" if he took a more militant stand. The Army and Air Force reserves were at their lowest point, and an estimate of "Soviet intentions" prepared by Ambassador Smith in Moscow gave the Soviet armed forces the "capability" of overrunning Europe. Millis, *The Forrestal Diaries*, pp. 409, *passim*. Clay and Murphy in Berlin were convinced that the Soviets were bluffing; Clay also pointed out that the United States had a monopoly of atomic bombs and that the Soviets would be unlikely to risk even a minor military operation until Russia had recovered from its war losses. Millis, p. 460; Murphy, pp. 314–15. Insofar as I was able to determine by interviewing former Soviet officers, the feeling that the Kremlin was in fact bluffing also prevailed at Karlshorst, the Soviet headquarters near Berlin.

37. Or so it appeared to Clay and Murphy in Berlin, who had sought positive guidance from Washington.

Helpless to prevent the measure in the Western zones, the Soviets made a determined effort to stop it in Berlin. On June 19, the Soviet government said that as far as currency was concerned Berlin was an integral part of the Soviet zone. On the pretext of protecting East Germany from a flood of devalued currency, Marshal Sokolovsky ordered passenger travel into Berlin by train, car and truck, and even on foot stopped immediately. Freight was to be subjected to rigorous inspection. On June 21, a somewhat improvised currency reform in East Germany was also announced: special stickers were affixed to old notes. The reform was completed in four days—which suggests a great deal of preparation by the Soviet side, and that Western suspicions may not have been entirely without foundation.

For a few days both reforms left the question of currency in Berlin open. Clay knew that the Defense Department in Washington had felt that this issue was negotiable, and on June 20, he suggested to Sokolovsky that the financial experts' discussions should be resumed. The meeting was arranged for the next day. In an effort to find a compromise solution, the Western representatives were willing to accept an economic separation of Berlin from West Germany by introducing into the city a separate currency to be managed by all four powers. The Soviet representatives rejected this offer, stating that Berlin was located in the Soviet zone and was economically a part of that zone. The West's next offer was to declare the Soviet mark currency legal tender for all Berlin, with the provision that it bear an overprint and that its circulation be governed by all four powers through the Kommandatura. This was also rejected, the Soviet negotiators again reiterating their contention that Berlin was economically a part of the Soviet zone and that in the Soviet zone only Soviet regulations were valid.

While the finance experts were still in session, Marshal Sokolovsky issued an order to Berlin's acting mayor stating that Soviet mark currency was to be the only legal tender in the city. The Western governors then informed the German authorities that the Soviet order applied to East Berlin only. Caught between these conflicting orders, the Berlin Magistrate resolved, despite SED opposition, that the Soviets could not issue orders for the whole of Berlin. Their decision was followed by a series of communist-directed riots.

The Western governors were anxious to avoid a division of the city on the currency issue. The western deutsche mark currency with an overstamped " B," was introduced into the Western sectors of the city only. Soviet marks were also declared " limited legal tender "; that is, they could be accepted in the Western sectors in certain cases (in payment for rent, utilities, taxes, and the like) at 1 to 1 parity, although the free market rate was 1 to 4 and even 1 to 5, in favor of the DM currency.[38]

The Soviets, apparently still hopeful that the differences within the Western camp (especially due to the " soft " French position) would work to their advantage, increased the pressure by establishing a total blockade of the city on June 24. The next day, Clay, who had expected this move, ordered the beginning of the Berlin Airlift. The Soviets reacted by officially withdrawing their representatives and staff from the Berlin Kommandatura, thereby ending the quadripartite Allied rule in Berlin.

A full record of the developments of those days is not available. It is not known, for example, under what circumstances the British government—whose first reaction to the blockade was either to reach a " compromise " with the Soviets or to abandon the city—decided to go along with Clay. Clay himself was doubtless apprehensive of the consequences; there was a definite prospect of great shortages in Berlin and the possibility of civil disorders. In addition, in view of the menacing Soviet posture, the likelihood of an armed clash could not be ruled out. But he was deeply convinced that it " would be politically disastrous for the United States to abandon Berlin." [39] Before proceeding with the airlift, he consulted with Ernst Reuter, the leader of the Berlin Social-Democrats, who had been elected mayor of the city (but vetoed by the Soviets). Reuter assured Clay the population was ready to fight for Berlin's freedom and would not capitulate to the Soviets.

These assurances were well founded; the Berliners were swept with excitement. Fearful of a Soviet takeover, hopeful that the Americans would finally take a stand, and more than willing to

38. The acceptance of the Eastern currency at 1 to 1 parity lasted until March 1949; it amounted to a fairly costly subsidy but was probably justifiable in view of the political battle developing in the besieged city.

39. Davison, *The Berlin Blockade*, p. 104. It is a fair guess that General Clay welcomed the showdown over Berlin. The situation had become intolerable, and the chances for a reasonable compromise seemed nil.

take all the risks, they greeted the airlift enthusiastically. Their feelings were shared by the German people in general, in the east as well as in the west. Once the airlift had started, and it became evident that the Soviets were not prepared for a military showdown, public opinion in Europe and the United States gave growing support to Clay's actions. The British government's position became much firmer within a few days. The position of the United States, where the dangers of war were emphasized by a number of politicians, and by a large section of the press, remained less clear. Nevertheless, at a White House meeting on June 28, President Truman (who was renominated to run for the presidency on the same day as the Berlin Blockade went into full effect) overruled his Service Secretaries and said the United States would stay in Berlin, " dealing with the situation as it developed." He also approved, despite Marshall's misgivings, the sending of a group of B-29 bombers to Germany and two other groups to England. The Battle for Berlin had started.[40]

The year-long blockade of the German capital served the political needs of the Soviet government well. Without an adequate power base and totally unprepared for a military showdown, the Soviet Union challenged the West's position in the heart of Europe. By dramatically demonstrating its ability to put the Western Powers on the defensive, it dealt a crushing blow to the still powerful opposition to communist rule in Poland, Czechoslovakia, Hungary, Rumania, and Bulgaria, and consolidated its position in East Germany (undoubtedly the most urgent of Soviet objectives).

40. Millis, *The Forrestal Diaries*, pp. 455–56; Davison, *The Berlin Blockade*, p. 111. On the developments in Berlin, see Davison, pp. 78–112 *passim*. Also Bennett, *Berlin Bastion*, and Curt Riess, *The Berlin Story* (New York: Dial, 1952), Part III. How far Truman was prepared to go may never be known. On July 19 he said to Marshall and Forrestal that " our policy would remain fixed: namely, that we would stay in Berlin until all diplomatic means had been exhausted in order to come to some kind of accommodation to avoid war." Millis, p. 459; Truman, *Memoirs*, II, 122–28. The British government did not equivocate at all. On June 30, Foreign Minister Bevin and Harold Macmillan, who was speaking for the opposition, pledged that Great Britain would maintain her position in Berlin even at the risk of war. Donnison, *Civil Affairs*, pp. 116–17. Truman never went that far. Clay and Murphy, who flew to Washington on July 22 to plead that the attempt should be made to break the blockade of ground access to Berlin, found the reception cold. The military and " the Great Design people " bent on the accommodation with the Soviets favored negotiations. Engrossed in the election campaign and unwilling to take extra risks, Truman backed them. Murphy, *Diplomat among Warriors*, p. 316.

Yet the Soviet victory was incomplete. For one thing, it has to be measured against the prevailing expectations and fears. By June, 1948, there were many people who expected the West to evacuate Berlin, and who genuinely feared the Soviets might " overrun " continental Europe. The former was not entirely unfounded, but the later probably was not even considered in Moscow.

More importantly, the West's refusal to leave Berlin, symbolized by the spectacular airlift, had long-range effects on the future of Germany west of the Elbe, for it marked the beginning of the German nation's re-emergence on the international scene. This development was evidently underestimated in Moscow. Germany could have been prevented from becoming a major factor in Europe only so long as a degree of unity prevailed among the wartime Allies. The Berlin Blockade signaled the end of that unity, and with the formation of the North Atlantic Treaty Organization in April, 1949, the East-West realignment was completed. There is no way of knowing whether such a development was foreseen in Moscow, or indeed whether the Soviet leaders realized at the time the paucity of options open to them.

On a different plane, it is doubtful that the imposition of a total blockade was (as the Soviets claimed) merely a response to the introduction of the new DM currency. If such was the case, the move made little sense. By June 24 both currency reforms had been completed and the argument that the Soviet zone would be inundated with old notes was no longer valid. In Berlin itself, the free communication between the sectors continued, and both currencies circulated side by side. There was no way to offset the natural disadvantage of the Eastern vis-à-vis the Western mark except through a compromise. From the Soviet point of view, it would have been better to accept a separate Berlin currency under a four-power sponsorship. But Moscow played for higher stakes and, in this instance, lost.[41]

41. The Soviet government has maintained ever since that the currency reform in West Germany was a violation of the Potsdam agreements (which it was) and presented it as a justification for the Berlin Blockade. In the discussions which the United States initiated in Moscow—the first government-to-government note was sent to Stalin on July 6—Stalin told Smith " in no uncertain terms that the Western Powers no longer had a juridical right to occupy Berlin, implying that we had forfeited this right . . . by introducing the new Western currency in Berlin." Stalin offered to lift the blockade immediately if the Allies would accept the Soviet zone marks as the sole currency in the whole city of Berlin, with the

The currency reform greatly benefited West Germany and West Berlin, as well as the Western Allies, who by then had been contributing nearly $600 million a year to prevent the starvation of the Germans.[42] At the same time, the reform hurt Soviet economic interests in that it stopped the outflow of the "cheap" Eastern marks and the inflow of goods, and left the Soviet administration with the necessity of taking care of the East German economy. The currency reform spurred the remarkable recovery of the West German economy. A very great role in this recovery was played by the restoration of confidence among the Germans, confidence not only in money, but also in their present and future existence as a nation. The Western Powers' determination to stay in Berlin was undoubtedly a key element in this process.

The effect of the currency reform on the economy of the Western zones cannot be overemphasized. In retrospect, it appears fortunate that the reform was a separate one. In the first place, it was an explicit recognition of the fact that Germany was divided and that this reality could no longer be ignored. Second, anything that could have emerged out of a quadripartite agreement would have had much less far-reaching effects and would necessarily have contained various punitive features which would probably have made the economic recovery of West Germany much less spectacular. If by paying such a price the Western Allies could have ensured lasting Soviet cooperation, such an agreement might have been worth considering. But such was clearly not the case; by 1948 the East-West conflict was already developing well beyond German borders and a return to the spirit of Yalta, or even Potsdam, was inconceivable.

Although nobody viewed it that way at the time, the success of the currency reform was partly due to the fact that the economic situation had become desperate. No palliative would have worked;

implied recognition of Berlin's economic incorporation into the Soviet zone. Smith, *My Three Years in Moscow*, pp. 246–47. See also Millis, *The Forrestal Diaries*, pp. 469–70, and The Department of State's *The Berlin Crisis*, Department of State Publication 3298 (Washington: U.S. Government Printing Office, 1948).

42. Herbert Hoover, *The President's Economic Mission to Germany and Austria* (Washington, 1947). For their needs the Allies took from Bank Deutsche Laender 600 million new marks which were equally divided among the three powers. No more requests for cash followed, although the German authorities (first, Laender, and later the Federal Government) continued to pay for various occupation costs. In order to get cash, the Allies had to change their currencies into marks through the banks.

the reform had to be drastic. It sharply reduced the economic power of those who had manipulated and exploited an unstable postwar economic situation and released the positive forces of the German nation which carried forward with the task of economic resurrection.

The danger of allowing the monetary situation in an occupied country to deteriorate too far was pointed out with regard to Italy as early as the fall of 1943 by the Foreign Economic Administration mission. In its report, the mission warned that " it is hard to see how the Italian government, now or in the future, can stabilize its own currency," and indicated that the only possibility for effective stabilization was in the appropriate Allied action.[43] The Allied occupation administration considered a monetary reform in the summer of 1944 but abandoned the idea, concluding that the decision to put such a program into effect rested with the Italian government. But by the time the Italian government was allowed to assume sovereignty it was being subjected to a multitude of pressures from entrenched interests preying upon inflation and opposing any reform which could have endangered the sources of their power. These newly emerged interests had acquired sufficient influence to paralyze the government. In the redistribution of wealth caused by this inflation, the prime losers were members of the middle class and intelligentsia, as well as the old owners of major economic assets, with their broad business connections, management experience and a sense of responsibilty which, insufficient as it was, was still greater than that of the *nouveaux riches.* The Italian government soon concluded that " the administrative and political difficulties " involved in effecting a radical monetary reform were insurmountable.[44]

43. Adlai E. Stevenson, " Report of the FEA Survey Mission to Italy " (unpublished MS, 1943), p. 31.

44. Kamarck, " Allied Financial Policy in Italy " (unpublished MS, Harvard University Library), pp. 96–98. Cf. UNRRA, Italian Mission, *Survey of Italy's Economy* (Rome, June 1947), pp. 9–10. It should be recorded that the communists were also in active opposition to currency reforms in Western Europe. Murphy (*Diplomat among Warriors*, pp. 236–37) recalls how the efforts of René Pleven, French Minister of Finance, to effect a currency reform in France were thwarted by the communist members of the government mainly because a sizable part of the immense Party treasury consisted of bank notes in large denominations which had been seized in various financial institutions during the chaotic days just before and after the liberation of France. A more general explanation of the communist attitude toward currency reforms, of course, is that they view as

This brings us to another factor which contributed to the " German miracle ": the absence of a sovereign German government at the time of the currency reform. In other West European countries the consequences of the postwar inflation were perhaps less severe. But they were permitted to take hold because the weak governments of these countries had to reckon with the new political forces born of the inflation. Weak as these governments were, they were also sovereign; there was no outside power—in the form of an occupation authority—capable of forcing through a drastic reform without regard to internal political repercussions.

The occupation of West Germany continued after the occupation currency vanished in the reform of 1948. But it continued in a different climate, which made the transition to the full sovereignty of West Germany possible. The establishment of new relations between the Germans and the West was delayed by many factors, some of which are felt sporadically both in Germany and Western Europe even today. Yet, in time, other more powerful factors came into play. Partly by the conscious effort on both sides, and partly as a result of internal as well as international developments, West Germany was brought into the Western camp as a fullfledged and willing member.

---

undesirable any measures which lead to the stability of " capitalist " societies. This does not seem to contradict their professed concern for the well-being of the toiling masses which—as the communists insist—are major victims of inflation.

Chapter XII

HIGHLIGHTS AND OBSERVATIONS

The German and Allied experiences with occupation currencies in World War II and after demonstrates that these currencies can be used to serve a variety of purposes: as a means of exchange for the victorious army, to transfer occupation costs to the vanquished, and to manipulate, for good or evil, the economies of the occupied country. In this final chapter I shall first summarize and compare the occupation finance policies and experiences of Germany and the wartime Allies, then review some of the unplanned consequences of these policies, and, finally, offer some over-all observations.

The crucial elements of the various finance policies and experiences which merit direct comparison are the overvaluation of the victor's currencies vis-à-vis those of the occupied country; the enforcement or nonenforcement of price, wage, and market controls; the encouragement or discouragement of troop spending; the transfer of occupation costs to the defeated country; and the relative merits of direct versus indirect rule.

Overvaluation

The victorious powers generally tended to overvalue their own currencies vis-à-vis those of the occupied countries. The German overvaluation averaged about 25–30 per cent; its purpose was to give Germany the initial advantage in importing goods from the occupied countries. The Soviets, in order to secure economic and political advantages, overvalued the ruble up to 4,000 per cent.

The Americans and the British also established rates of exchange which favored the dollar and the pound. In Italy and Germany the overvaluation was about 200–300 per cent. In this the American economic planners were motivated primarily by a desire to punish Germany, while the military were anxious to augment artificially the Congress-approved appropriations and to put additional purchasing power into the hands of the troops. The Soviets were also motivated by a desire to give the troops an extra bonus through the overvaluation of the ruble.

PRICE, WAGE, AND MARKET CONTROLS

Economic controls existed in all the countries of Europe during the war and played a key role in checking inflation. In most countries under German domination, the freezing of wages and prices and the rationing of civilian supplies did not always work, but such measures did serve to ensure at least subsistence standards of living. By and large, price inflation was controlled effectively.

The period of Allied occupation came toward the end of the war when economic productivity was at its lowest. After the Allied victory, normal trade channels and civilian supply systems quickly disintegrated. The Allies made no effort to reinstate economic controls and, in any case, would have had no way of enforcing them. In the wake of mass purges conducted by them in the occupied areas, the local government and administrative machinery almost completely broke down. Fixed prices were preserved only for rationed foods, which were distributed (at a rate of 1,000–1,500 calories a day per person) to the civilian population to prevent famine, disease, and disorder.

Under conditions of such acute shortages, the development of a black market was unavoidable. With prices sometimes fifty times higher than the " fixed " prices, the black market inevitably attracted the meager supplies designed for the rationed distribution. It put disproportionately large sums of money into the hands of relatively few, creating a higher demand for scarce goods and thus pushing the prices up further.

The black market was least developed in the German-dominated countries of Western and Central Europe. It was most active under Soviet occupation in Eastern Europe and under Anglo-American rule in Italy and Germany. The flourishing of the black market was in direct proportion to the disintegration of the old administrative and law enforcement machinery.

TROOP SPENDING

The pressure of large numbers of occupation troops was a major inflationary factor in all occupied countries. The Germans, who were keenly aware of its importance, tried to diminish its effects in a variety of ways. They kept their soldiers' wages low and encouraged savings. They also introduced disciplinary measures and other controls to prevent the troops from drawing upon the local market for their supplies; in some places, the soldiers were paid in special money which could be used only in the army canteens.

The impact of Soviet troop spending on local economies was substantial, not so much because the soldiers' wages were high—in fact their wages were the lowest of all victorious powers—but because of their great numbers and because they generally lived off the land. A similar situation existed in the French zone of Germany.

The effects of American troop spending were the most spectacular of all, especially since the areas they occupied were the poorest. American soldiers were the best-paid and their purchasing power was quadrupled by the rate of exchange decreed by the Allies in Italy and Germany. Unlike the British, the American Command placed no restrictions on troop spending, mainly because they considered such restrictions harmful to the soldiers' morale. Although the Americans were interested only in particular kinds of goods, wherever they were stationed in large numbers their spending invariably pushed up the general price levels. Still more important was the fact that the Americans actively participated in the black market.

Occupation experiences in World War II illustrate the serious economic problems (political and social problems aside) which are involved in stationing generously supplied and highly paid troops in poorer foreign countries. Whereas a country like Switzerland can easily absorb the impact of troop spending of several American divisions without fear of a black market, a Thailand or a Korea is bound to suffer, unless the foreign military community is almost totally isolated in an economic sense.

OCCUPATION COSTS

All victorious powers made the vanquished pay the costs of occupation, but the techniques they followed were different. Except in Poland and Russia, the Germans had their occupation costs paid by local quisling governments, which delivered cash, goods, and services with relative efficiency and minimal disorganizing effects. The Soviets adopted a similar approach, except that the governments they created were much less efficient; in addition, great disruptions were caused by haphazard direct requisitions and inept, politically motivated, interferences with the economy.

The British and Americans made occupied Italy and Germany supply the occupation armies with free housing, labor, transportation, and other services. The cost of the military government was passed on to these countries through occupation currencies which were declared a responsibility of the defeated nations. The issue of the occupation currencies was also supposed to pay, at least in part, for the cost of maintaining the armies of occupation, but here the calculations proved wrong. The American and the British troops received most of their supplies from home, and these could not be paid for in occupation currencies. Thus the transfer of costs to the occupied country was limited by economic circumstances which were beyond the control of the occupation finance planners.

REQUISITIONS

Requisitioning of goods and services was practiced by all belligerents. Its scope was, for the most part, determined by military necessities, although not infrequently the military and civilian officials took personal advantage of their privileged status. The question of payments for the requisitioned goods and services was resolved differently by different armies in different areas. The solution with the best results seems to have been to let local authorities take care of requisitions and of the necessary payments. From the economic point of view, it was advisable to defer the payments and, at any rate, keep them to a minimum, so as not to pump additional sums of money into already inflated economies. Politically, however, such practices were not always possible or even desirable, since outright confiscations adversely affected the relations between the victorious forces and the native populations. The distinctions between various compensation techniques were not sufficiently pronounced to warrant comparisons.

DIRECT VERSUS INDIRECT RULE

Indirect rule was always more successful in World War II than direct rule. The military leaders of all belligerent powers universally supported indirect rule, and most of their governments, including the Soviet government, also appreciated its advantages. These advantages were several. First, indirect rule eliminated a necessity for occupation administrations and there was less need for " area specialists." Second, the existence of a functioning local government had political advantages in that it provided a native target for public discontent. Third, such a government was usually more efficient in utilizing local resources while at the same time it protected the economic interests of the native population to the greatest possible degree. The efficiency of the occupation regimes in German-dominated Europe can be attributed to a large extent to the existence of relatively loyal quisling governments. Except for Poland, Russia, and the war zones in the Balkans, the Germans ruled indirectly; local autonomy was in direct proportion to the degree of cooperation offered by the occupied country.

The Soviets, in their occupation of Eastern Europe, also attempted to work through regimes which they created and which they supported with military and police power. Because the Soviet conquest was characterized by the violent excesses of Soviet troops and by induced social revolution, the effective authority of these new regimes tended to be in inverse proportion to their " friendliness " toward the Soviet Union. But since long-range Soviet aims were essentially political, the purges of the old governmental and administrative machinery served rather than hampered Soviet interests in Eastern Europe.

Direct military rule was sometimes unavoidable. In the areas where the population was universally hostile to the invador (as in German-occupied Poland), or where active military operations made the establishment of an authoritative local government impossible, the military had to assume all responsibility for civil affairs. In the Allied case, a resort to direct rule in Germany and, to some extent, in Italy was not dictated by such considerations and was adopted against the judgment of the military. The American and the British governments had chosen this course for political reasons, not dissimilar to those of the Soviets. Their objectives included a revolutionary transformation of the German and Italian societies through purging the nazis and fascists, a transformation which was implicit in the doctrine of unconditional surrender. Unlike the Soviets, the Western Allies had no program for replacing the old regimes with new governments which would bind the reformed societies to the cause of democracy. Although Anglo-American direct rule clearly represented a burden on the victors, it was considered justifiable both because the Western Allies did not have to depend on the occupied countries' economic resources for their war effort and because it symbolized more than anything else the total subjugation of the enemy nations, thus satisfying the craving for their punishment of the domestic public opinion.

The effects of Allied occupation in the " liberated " countries of Western Europe were roughly comparable to what developed under German occupation in the satellite countries governed by quisling regimes. The economic impact of Allied occupation was considerably cushioned by the bilateral " reciprocal aid " (or " reverse lend-lease ") agreements which the United States and Great Britain concluded with the governments of " liberated " countries, and which provided for orderly supply of the Allied forces with goods and services they required. American credits to these countries were opened shortly after the invasion, which assured a steady flow of supplies from the United States. The local governments reciprocated by supplying the Allied forces with free housing, transportation, labor, fresh food, and some manufactured goods.

Despite these procedures, the mere presence of large numbers of Allied troops and civilians—all of whom enjoyed a privileged status—had a severe impact as a result of troop spending and the black market, which in turn greatly hampered the orderly distribution of essential supplies to the civilian population. These factors aggravated inflation and caused considerable friction between the " liberators " and the local governments and population.

The experiences in the monetary field were equally unfortunate. The Allies did not issue (except, initially, in France) their own military currencies but obtained the supplies of cash they needed from the local governments. The agreements provided for the reimbursement of the local governments in the form of dollar and pound credits for " net " troop pay, i.e., for the money which the Allied personnel spent locally. On the face of it, this procedure was similar to that which the Germans followed in " friendly " countries. However, the amounts which the local governments eventually received were disappointingly small. In the Allied system of accounting " net " troop pay was the difference between the gross pay and the sums which the soldiers spent in the Army PX stores and commissaries and transferred home as savings. Because the Allied personnel made huge profits on the black market, they could save most of their pay and avoid the necessity of obtaining the local currency at the official rate of exchange.

The United States and Great Britain did put their currencies at some disadvantage vis-à-vis local currencies in establishing rates of exchange for the " liberated " countries. This form of indirect subsidy had a salutary effect on the local economies. Nevertheless, the soldiers' pay rates were so high in comparison with local wages that the initial impact of troop spending was universally very strong. Before long inflation made the initial rates of exchange unrealistic. These were renegotiated at the time " reciprocal aid " agreements were settled, and in the end " liberated " Europe found itself heavily in debt to the United States and, to a lesser extent, to Great Britain. By comparison, German economic relations with the occupied " friendly " countries of Europe had resulted in a considerable indebtedness of the Reich's government.

The Allied finance policies had other effects—such as counterfeiting, currency traffic, and the prevalent attitude toward occupation currencies as " cheap " money—which were neither foreseen nor intended and which hurt not only the economic interests of the occupied countries but also those of the victorious powers.

No one foresaw that occupied and occupiers alike would view occupation currencies as " cheap " money for which no one was clearly responsible, and that this attitude would lead to overspending and thus more inflation. In the case of the United States, despite the fact that the occupation currencies were charged against the War Department's appropriations, loose spending combined with careless accounting to increase unduly the cost of the war.

Counterfeiting resulted from the poor quality of the AM lire, AM marks, supplemental francs, and the Military Payment Certificates introduced for American personnel toward the end of 1946. Although the amounts put into circulation by counterfeiters are unknown, they were undoubtedly large and must be added to the ultimate cost of the war.

Currency traffic, which would have been difficult to prevent in any case, was another occupation monetary problem not considered in advance. The dollar became a valuable commodity on the black market in all the occupied countries of Europe. It had a high hoarding value and was always in demand. Notes were brought in by mail and by traveling American officers and officials. These dollars, when sold to the local operators, constituted a claim against the United States, which affected the American balance of payments.

The filtering back of currency into the "home" country of the victor was viewed as dangerous by the Germans, who were mindful of its potential inflationary effects. They did not permit the reichsmark to circulate outside Germany and placed strict regulations on the amount of savings the troops could send home. The British also limited the homeward movement of soldiers' money. But the United States had no such restrictions. Any American could freely convert his lire, francs, marks, and other European currencies into dollars by purchasing postal money orders, U.S. War and Savings Bonds, American Express checks, or by using the facilities of the Western Union. Because so many of them made huge profits on the black market, this inflow of money involved large sums which contributed to domestic inflation. The Treasury Department, however, did not attach much significance to the inflationary impact of this money, and no restrictions were imposed on troop remittances. The controls, when they were eventually instituted, were prompted by different considerations. Because the Army could not legally disburse more than was appropriated by Congress, these remittances, once they exceeded the approved troop pay, formed a deficit which had to be covered by the United States Treasury. The deficit reached a staggering $530,775,400 by the end of 1946. It was only after its dimensions were realized—and threatened to become a political issue in Congress—that effective controls over remittance procedures were introduced.

It is clear that in the field of economics the victor's power to govern by decree is limited. He has a relatively free hand to pursue short-range objectives—to requisition and collect reparations, to dismantle or shut down factories, to seize banks, to curtail local consumption and prohibit transfers of property, and to assure priority for himself in the distribution of available goods—but he cannot make the economy function normally. In Europe the least manageable sectors of the occupation economies were those with the most direct effect on the population's well-being: food and the production and distribution of consumer goods. In these areas the military governments were helpless in direct proportion to the severity of the shortages.

The Germans had the foresight to prepare themselves for occupation by creating administrative cadres. Although certain political and ideological considerations in nazi policy resulted in the waste of human and physical resources in Europe, for the most part the Reich government gave high priority to efficient exploitation. In order to assure maximum productivity locally and the maximum economic integration of that part of Europe under its domination, it was often prepared to forego short-range interests.

The execution of economic policies in German-occupied Europe should be rated as quite efficient. The same cannot be said about the Soviets in Eastern Europe. Although they were also guided by long-range considerations, their interest was mainly in fostering a radical social change; they placed a rather low premium on the operating efficiency of basic government functions.

The Anglo-American approach to the occupation differed substantially from that of the Soviet Union or Germany. Great Britain did not formulate any long-range political goals in Europe until the war was almost over, and the United States did not become fully aware of the extent of its interests in the future of Europe until some two years later. Both Western Powers wanted to make the defeat of the Axis as permanent as possible and worried little, at least after the fighting had stopped, about the efficiency of the occupation administration. While the war was still on the British displayed some interest in getting certain short-range economic advantages from the victory over Italy and Germany. The Americans were by and large satisfied with the victory itself.

The Allies did not choose to study German administrative

techniques. Nor did they benefit from each other's experience either in the countries they occupied alone or in consort. In Germany, with inadequately trained administrative staffs, often unable to cope with their own military, and handicapped by the directives they received from their governments, the zonal administrations were inefficient throughout the critical early period of the occupation.

In the Anglo-American occupation of Italy, military government had to operate in the face of severe economic and political disadvantages. The country's economy was in shambles. The Italians, having joined the Allies in the war against Germany, resented being treated as enemies. Determined to destroy fascism, the victors destroyed in the process the administrative machinery of the old regime. They tolerated an Italian government without permitting it to function as such, thereby denying themselves, and the Italian people, the substantial advantages of indirect rule. In addition, there were serious cleavages between London and Washington on the one hand and the military government on the other. The military government did little more than keep a chaotic situation from getting entirely out of hand.

In Germany, where there was no central or local government, the occupation was based on direct military rule. As in Italy, the occupation administrations were staffed with officials who were ignorant of local conditions and lacking in experience. This did not matter to the Americans—nor at first to the Soviets and the French, who were then also pursuing short-term goals—because their principal objective was to punish the Germans, and anything that increased the civil and economic chaos served this end. Although the British were less interested in the punitive aspects of the occupation, they did follow a similar course.

The changes in the Anglo-American attitude toward Germany after the war were dictated at first almost exclusively by economic considerations. Although a large part of the occupation costs was borne by the German economy, the British and Americans were increasingly forced to import food to prevent mass starvation. Such imports were made necessary by the virtual collapse of the German economy, which was aggravated by the division of the country into four separate zones, by the presence of large occupation armies, and by the apathy of the Germans. Caught in the developing East-West conflict, unable to agree on the formation of a central German government and on the terms of a peace settlement, the Allies found that they could not extricate themselves from the occupation of Germany. The British and Americans attempted to solve the problem of self-sufficiency for their zones by restoring the economic unity of the country. But the effectiveness of such a policy was limited by the resistance to it which came from the Soviet and, to a lesser extent, from the French authorities.

The Western Powers finally chose a separate course of action by merging their zones and freeing the Germans, first of economic controls and later of political supervision. The end of the suppressive period of the occupation was symbolized by a separate currency reform in West Germany in 1948. This reform coincided with the growing militancy of the Soviet Union and was immediately followed by the Berlin Blockade, which made the division of Germany complete and effectively ended the era of Allied wartime cooperation.

Most of the adverse consequences of the Allied occupation finance policies could have been avoided if the planners had better recognized what was involved: that occupation currencies would be the single most effective instrument for manipulating the economies and even the politics of defeated nations, that unless the intention was to do harm their armies had to be isolated monetarily, and that without restraint and careful planning these currencies could hurt the victor as much as the vanquished. There is no question at all that when the victor's intent is to harm the occupied country, the manipulation of monetary circulation will serve his purpose, especially through induced inflation. Runaway inflation leaves permanent social and psychological scars, and the attendant economic problems require massive corrective action, including financial aid, over a long period of time, if the damaged country is to function effectively again.

This is not a verdict against occupation currencies. Their use was fully justified during the early periods of invasion and in the war zones for the duration of the war. But it was questionable to use them as a means of transferring occupation costs to a defeated country, and it was extremely shortsighted to use them to punish former enemies. The American planners of occupation ignored the interdependence of national economies in the modern world;

they refused to realize that they could not make Germany economically impotent without hurting the rest of Europe. What is even harder to understand is that they did not realize the most obvious fact of all: that no occupation can last forever and that the defeated country is bound to emerge again as an independent actor. It soon became evident in the case of Germany that the political and economic costs of a punitive occupation were prohibitive. The problem then became to find the right way, and the right moment, to start transition from punitive treatment to rehabilitation and national resurrection. The victorious Allies did not solve this problem satisfactorily and thereby delayed by several years the economic reconstruction of the wartorn continent, a reconstruction which subsequently cost the United States billions of dollars.

BIBLIOGRAPHY

Primary Sources

Public Documents and Government Publications

Bank for International Settlements. *Annual Reports, 10th–19th.* Basle, Switzerland, 1940–49.

Coles, Harry L., and Weinberg, Albert K. *Civil Affairs: Soldiers Become Governors.* Washington: Office of the Chief of Military History, Department of the Army, 1964.

Corbino, Epicarmo. "Currency and Exchange Policy in the Post-War Years," *Ten Years of Italian Economy: 1947–1956.* Rome, Italy, 1956. (Official publication.)

The Development of Italy's Economic System. Rome, Italy, 1952. (Official publication.)

Donnison, F. S. V. *Civil Affairs and Military Government, North-West Europe: 1944–1946.* London: H.M. Stationery Office, 1961.

Federal Ministry for Expellees, Refugees and War Victims. *The Expulsion of the German Population.* Vols. I–IV. Bonn, Germany, 1955–60. (Official publication.)

Fredricksen, Oliver J. *The American Military Occupation of Germany: 1945–1953.* U.S. Army in Europe, 1953.

Germany Reports. Bonn, Germany, 1955.

Harris, C. R. S. *Allied Military Administration of Italy: 1943–1945.* London: H.M. Stationery Office, 1957.

Hilldring, John H. *American Policy in Occupied Areas.* Washington: U.S. Government Printing Office, 1948.

Hoover, Herbert. *The President's Economic Mission to Germany and Austria.* Washington, 1947.

Loehr, Rodney C. *The West German Banking System.* Historical Division, Office of the U.S. High Commissioner for Germany, 1952.

Ministerstvo Inostrannykh Del SSSR. Ministerstvo Inostrannykh Del ChSR. *Sovetsko-chekhoslovatskiie otnosheniia vo vrem'ia Velikoi Otechestvennoi Voiny 1941–1945 gg.* Moscow 1960.

Notter, Harley A., ed. *Postwar Foreign Policy Preparations: 1939–1945.* Washington: U.S. Government Printing Office, 1949.

Organization of Military Government for Germany, United States. *Economic Data on Potsdam Germany: Special Report of the Military Governor.* September 1947.

Rennell of Rodd, Lord. *British Military Administration of Occupied Territories in Africa.* London: H.M. Stationery Office, 1948.

Sayers, R. S. *Financial Policy: 1939–45.* London: H.M. Stationery Office, 1956.

Supreme Headquarters Allied Expeditionary Forces. *Handbook for Military Government in Germany.* 1944.

United Nations Relief and Rehabilitation Administration, Italian Mission. *Survey of Italy's Economy.* Rome, Italy, June, 1947.

U.S. Statistical Abstract: 1963. Washington: U.S. Government Printing Office, 1963.

U.S. Statutes at Large. XLVII, Part 2; LIX, Part 2; LXI, Part 4.

U.S. Department of State Bulletin.

U.S. Department of State. *The Berlin Crisis.* Department of State Publication 3298. Washington: U.S. Government Printing Office, 1948.

———. *Foreign Relations of the United States. The Conferences at Malta and Yalta: 1945.* Washington: U.S. Government Printing Office, 1955.

———. *Foreign Relations of the United States. The Conference of Berlin, 1945.* 2 vols. Washington: U.S. Government Printing Office, 1960.

———. *Foreign Relations of the United States. The Conferences at Cairo and Teheran: 1943.* Washington: U.S. Government Printing Office, 1961.

———. *Foreign Relations of the United States: 1943.* Vols. 1 and 2. Washington: U.S. Government Printing Office, 1963, 1964.

———. *Germany: 1947–1949.* Department of State Publication 3556. Washington: U.S. Government Printing Office, 1950.

———. *United States and Italy: 1936–1946.* Department of State Publication 2669. Washington: U.S. Government Printing Office, 1946.

———. U.S. Treaties and Other International Acts Series 1648. *Treaty of Peace with Italy.* Department of State Publication 2960. Washington: U.S. Government Printing Office, 1947.

U.S. House of Representatives, Special Committee on Postwar Policy and Planning. Eighth Report. *Economic Reconstruction in Europe.* 79th Congress, 1st Session.

U.S. Senate, Committees on Appropriations, Armed Services, and Banking and Currency. Hearings, June 17–18, 1947. 80th Congress, 1st Session.

U.S. Senate, Committee on Foreign Relations. *A Decade of American Foreign Policy, Basic Documents: 1941–1949.* 81st Congress, 1st Session.

U.S. Senate, Committee on Foreign Relations. *Documents on Germany: 1944–1959.* 86th Congress, 2nd Session.

U.S. Senate, Committee on Government Operations, Permanent Subcommittee on Investigations; Subcommittee on Government Operations Abroad. Hearing, October 20–21, 1953. 83rd Congress, 1st Session.

U.S. Senate, Committee on Government Operations, Permanent Subcommittee on Investigations. Hearing, October 19, 1953. 84th Congress, 1st Session.

U.S. Senate, Committee on the Judiciary. *Interlocking Subversion in the Government Department.* Part 30. 84th Congress, 1st Session.

U.S. Treasury Department. Press Releases, Statements, Annual Reports of the Secretary of the Treasury.

WOODWARD, SIR LLEWELLYN. *British Foreign Policy in the Second World War.* London: H.M. Stationery Office, 1962.

Unpublished Materials

DAVIES, JOSEPH E. Papers. Washington: Library of Congress.

KAMARCK, ANDREW M. "Allied Financial Policy in Italy." Unpublished MS. Harvard University.

STEVENSON, ADLAI E. "Report of FEA Survey Mission to Italy." MS., 1943. (Loaned by the author.)

Stimson Papers. New Haven: Yale University Library.

Personal interviews (see acknowledgments in Introduction) and private letters.

SECONDARY SOURCES

Books

ARON, ROBERT. *France Reborn: The History of Liberation, June 1944–May 1945.* New York: Scribner's, 1964.

BACH, JULIAN, JR. *America's Germany.* New York: Random House, 1946.

BALDWIN, HANSON W. *Great Mistakes of the War.* New York: Harper, 1950.

BASCH, ANTONIN. *The Danube Basin and the German Economic Sphere.* New York: Columbia University Press, 1943.

BENDINER, ROBERT. *The Riddle of the State Department.* New York: Farrar & Rinehart, 1942.

BENNETT, LOWELL. *Berlin Bastion.* Frankfurt a/M: Rudl, 1951.

BENSON, GEORGE C. S. and NEUFELD, MAURICE. "American Military Government in Italy," FRIEDRICH, CARL J., ed., *American Experiences in Military Government in World War II.* New York: Rinehart, 1948.

BENTLEY, ELIZABETH T. *Out of Bondage.* New York: Devin-Adair, 1951.

BLOCH, HENRY SIMON, and HOSELITZ, BERT F. *Economics of Military Occupation.* Chicago: Foundation Press, 1944.

BLOOM, MURRAY TEIGH. *Money of Their Own.* New York: Scribner, 1953.

BLOOMFIELD, ARTHUR I. *Speculative and Flight Movements of Capital in Postwar International Finance.* Princeton: Princeton University Press, 1954.

BLUM, JOHN MORTON. *From the Morgenthau Diaries: The Years of Crisis, 1928–1938.* Boston: Houghton Mifflin, 1959.

———. *From the Morgenthau Diaries: Years of Urgency, 1938–1941.* Boston: Houghton Mifflin, 1965.

BOGOLEPOV, D. P. *Den'gi sovetskoi Rossii.* Leningrad, 1924.

BROWDER, ROBERT PAUL. *The Origins of Soviet-American Diplomacy.* Princeton: Princeton University Press, 1953.

BROWN, LEWIS H. *A Report on Germany.* New York: Farrar, Straus, 1947.

BYRNES, JAMES F. *All in One Lifetime.* New York: Harper, 1958.

———. *Speaking Frankly.* New York: Harper, 1947.

CHAMBERLIN, WILLIAM HENRY. *America's Second Crusade.* Chicago: Regnery, 1950.

CHAMBERS, WHITTAKER. *Witness.* New York: Random House, 1952.

CHURCHILL, WINSTON S. *The Second World War, The Hinge of Fate.* Vol. 4. Boston: Houghton Mifflin, 1950.

———. *The Second World War, Closing the Ring.* Vol. 5. Boston: Houghton Mifflin, 1951.

———. *The Second World War, Triumph and Tragedy.* Vol. 6. Boston: Houghton Mifflin, 1953.

CIECHANOWSKI, JAN. *Defeat in Victory.* Garden City, N.Y.: Doubleday, 1947.

CLARK, DALE. "Conflicts over Planning at Staff Headquarters." in FRIEDRICH, CARL J., ed., *American Experiences in Military Government in World War II.* New York: Rinehart, 1948.

CLAY, LUCIUS D. *Decision in Germany.* Garden City, N.Y.: Doubleday, 1950.

DALLIN, ALEXANDER. *German Rule in Russia, 1941–1945.* London: Macmillan, 1957.

DANIELS, JONATHAN. *The Man of Independence.* Philadelphia: Lippincott, 1950.

DAVISON, W. PHILLIPS. *The Berlin Blockade: A Study in Cold War Policies.* Princeton: Princeton University Press, 1958.

DAWSON, RAYMOND H. *The Decision to Aid Russia: 1941.* Chapel Hill: University of North Carolina Press, 1959.

DEANE, JOHN R. *Strange Alliance.* New York: Viking Press, 1947.

DE GAULLE, CHARLES. *War Memoirs, Salvation: 1944–1946.* New York: Viking Press, 1960.

———. *War Memoirs, Unity: 1942–1944.* New York: Viking Press, 1959.

DEL MAR, ALEXANDER. *Money and Civilization.* London, 1886.

DULLES, ALLAN. *The Craft of Intelligence.* New York: Harper, 1963.

DULLES, FOSTER RHEA. *The Road to Teheran.* Princeton: Princeton University Press, 1944.
EINZIG, PAUL. *Europe in Chains.* New York: Penguin, 1940.
———. *Hitler's "New Order" in Europe.* London: Macmillan, 1941.
———. *The Japanese "New Order" in Asia.* London: Macmillan, 1943.
EISENHOWER, DWIGHT D. *Crusade in Europe.* Garden City, N.Y.: Doubleday, 1948.
FAINSOD, MERLE. "The Development of American Military Government Policy During World War II," in FRIEDRICH, CARL J., ed., *American Experiences in Military Government in World War II.* New York: Rinehart, 1948.
FARAGO, LADISLAS. *The Axis Grand Strategy: Blueprints for the Total War.* New York: Farrar, Rinehart, 1947.
———. *Burn after Reading.* New York: Walker, 1961.
FEILCHENFELD, ERNST H. *The International Economic Law of Belligerent Occupation.* Washington: Carnegie Endowment for International Peace, 1942.
FEIS, HERBERT. *Between War and Peace: The Potsdam Conference.* Princeton: Princeton University Press, 1960.
———. *Churchill, Roosevelt, Stalin: The War They Waged and the Peace They Sought.* Princeton: Princeton University Press, 1957.
FLEMING, D. F. *The Cold War and Its Origins: 1917–1960.* 2 vols. London, 1961.
FOA, BRUNO. *Monetary Reconstruction in Italy.* New York: King's Crown, 1949.
FRIEDMANN, W. *The Allied Military Government in Germany.* London: Stevens, 1947.
FRIEDRICH, CARL J., ed. *American Experiences in Military Government in World War II.* New York: Rinehart, 1948.
FROWEIN, EBERHARD. *Wunderwaffe Falschgeld.* Krenzlingen, 1954.
GANNON, ROBERT I., S.J. *The Cardinal Spellman Story.* Garden City, New York: Doubleday, 1962.
GOLLANCZ, VICTOR. *In Darkest Germany.* London: Gollancz, 1947.
GOTTLIEB, MANUEL. *The German Peace Settlement and the Berlin Crisis.* New York: Paine-Whitman, 1960.
GRAHAM, FRANK D. *Exchange, Prices and Production in Hyper-inflation: Germany, 1920–1923.* Princeton: Princeton University Press, 1930.
HAMMOND, PAUL Y. "Directives for the Occupation of Germany: The Washington Controversy," in STEIN, HAROLD, ed., *American Civil-Military Decisions.* University, Ala.: University of Alabama Press, 1963.
HAZLITT, W. CAREW. *The Venetian Republic, Its Rise, Its Growth, and Its Fall.* 4th edition. London: Adam and Charles Black, 1915.
HILL, RUSSELL. *Struggle for Germany.* New York: Harper, 1947.
HOETTL, WILHELM. *Hitler's Paper Weapon.* London: R. Hart-Davis, 1955.
———. *The Secret Front.* London, 1953.
HOLBORN, HAJO. *American Military Government.* Washington: Infantry Journal Press, 1947.
HUGHES, H. STUART. *The United States and Italy.* Cambridge: Harvard University Press, 1953.
The Memoirs of Cordell Hull. New York: Macmillan, 1948.
HUNTINGTON, SAMUEL P. *The Soldier and the State: The Theory and Politics of Civil-Military Relations.* Cambridge: Harvard University Press, 1957.
IONESCU, GHITA. *Communism in Rumania, 1944–1962.* London: Oxford University Press, 1964.

Israelian, V. L. *Diplomaticheskaia istoriia velikoi otechestvennoi voiny: 1941–1945.* Moscow, 1959.

Jones, Joseph M. *The Fifteen Weeks.* New York: Viking Press, 1955.

Jordan, C. R. *From Major Jordan's Diaries.* New York: Devin-Adair, 1952.

Katzenellenbaum, S. S. *Russian Currency and Banking: 1914–1924.* London: King, 1925.

Kemmerer, Donald L. and Beattie, T. Eugene. *Allied Military Currency in Italy.* New York: Economists' National Committee on Monetary Policy, 1944.

Kennan, George F. *Russia and the West under Lenin and Stalin.* Boston: Little, Brown, 1960.

Kertesz, Stephen D. *Diplomacy in a Whirlpool: Hungary between Nazi Germany and Soviet Russia.* Notre Dame, Ind.: University of Notre Dame Press, 1953.

Keynes, John Maynard. *The Economic Consequences of the Peace.* New York: Harcourt-Brace, 1920.

Klimov, Gregory. *The Terror Machine: The Inside Story of the Soviet Administration in Germany.* New York: Praeger, 1953.

Knappen, Marshall M. *And Call It Peace.* Chicago: The University of Chicago Press, 1947.

Kogan, Norman. *Italy and the Allies.* Cambridge: Harvard University Press, 1956.

Komissarov, V. P., and Popov, A. N. *Den'gi, kredit i finansy evropeiskikh stran narodnoi demokratii.* Moscow, 1960.

Korbel, Josef. *The Communist Subversion in Czechoslovakia.* Princeton: Princeton University Press, 1959.

Krivitsky, Walter G. *In Stalin's Secret Service.* New York: Harper, 1939.

Kronrod, Y. A. *Den'gi v sotsialisticheskom obshchestve.* Moscow, 1960.

Langer, William L. *Our Vichy Gamble.* New York: Knopf, 1947.

Leahy, William D. *I Was There.* New York: McGraw-Hill, 1950.

Lemkin, Raphael. *Axis Rule in Occupied Europe.* Washington: Carnegie Endowment for International Peace, 1944.

Lester, Richard A. *International Aspects of Wartime Monetary Experience.* Princeton: Princeton University Press, 1944.

Loewenthal, Fritz. *News from Soviet Germany.* London: Gollancz, 1950.

Lovell, Stanley. *On Spies and Stratagems.* Englewood Cliffs, N.J.: Prentice-Hall, 1963.

Luethy, Herbert. *France against Herself.* New York: Praeger, 1955.

Lukas, John A. *The Great Powers and Eastern Europe.* Garden City, N.Y.: Doubleday, 1953.

Maclean, Fitzroy. *Escape to Adventure.* Boston: Little, Brown, 1950.

Mackintosh, J. M. *Strategy and Tactics of Soviet Foreign Policy.* London: Oxford University Press, 1962.

Millis, Walter, ed. *The Forrestal Diaries.* New York: Viking Press, 1951.

Moeller, Hans. *Zur Forgeschichte der Deutsche Mark, Die Waerungsreformplaene 1945–1948.* Tuebingen: 1961.

Morgenthau, Hans J., ed. *Germany and the Future of Europe.* Chicago: University of Chicago Press, 1950.

Morgenthau, Henry, Jr. *Germany Is Our Problem.* New York: Harper, 1945.

Morison, Elting E. *Turmoil and Tradition.* Boston: Houghton Mifflin, 1960.

Morray, Joseph P. *From Yalta to Disarmament.* London: Merlin, 1961.

Moyzisch, L. C. *Operation Cicero.* New York: Coward-McAnn, 1950.

Murphy, Robert. *Diplomat among Warriors.* Garden City, N.Y.: Doubleday, 1964.

NETTL, J. P. *The Eastern Zone and Soviet Policy in Germany: 1945–50.* London: Oxford University Press, 1951.

NIZER, L. *What To Do With Germany.* Chicago: Ziff-Davis, 1944.

NORDEN, ALBERT. *Faelscher.* Berlin, 1960.

NORTHEDGE, F. S. *British Foreign Policy. The Process of Readjustment: 1945–1961.* New York: Praeger, 1963.

NUSSBAUM, ARTHUR. *Money in Law, National and International.* Brooklyn: Foundation Press, 1950.

Occupied Europe. London: Royal Institute of International Affairs, 1944.

OPIE, REDVERS. *The Search for Peace Settlements.* Washington: The Brookings Institution, 1951.

PACKER, HERBERT L. *Ex-Communist Witnesses.* Stanford: Stanford University Press, 1962.

PENROSE, E. F. *Economic Planning for the Peace.* Princeton: Princeton University Press, 1953.

PICKLES, DOROTHY. *French Politics: The First Years of the Fourth Republic.* London: Royal Institute of International Affairs, 1953.

POGUE, FORREST C. *George C. Marshall: 1880–1939.* New York: Viking Press, 1963.

PRATT, JULIUS W. *Cordell Hull, 1933–44.* 2 vols. New York: Cooper Square, 1964.

QUINLIN, ROBERT J. "The Italian Armistice," in STEIN, HAROLD, ed., *American Civil-Military Decisions.* University, Ala.: University of Alabama Press, 1963.

RATCHFORD, B. U., and ROSS, WILLIAM D. *Berlin Reparations Assignment: Round One of the German Peace Settlement.* Chapel Hill: University of North Carolina Press, 1947.

REVEILLE, THOMAS. *The Spoil of Europe.* New York: Norton, 1941.

RIESS, CURT. *The Berlin Story.* New York: Dial, 1952.

ROZEK, EDWARD J. *Allied Wartime Diplomacy: A Pattern in Poland.* New York: Wiley, 1958.

R.S.F.S.R. *Social Revolution and Finances.* Moscow, 1921.

RUNDELL, WALTER, JR. *Black Market Money: The Collapse of U.S. Military Currency Control in World War II.* Baton Rouge: Louisiana State University Press, 1964.

SCHACHT, HJALMAR. *My First Seventy-Six Years.* London: Wingate, 1955.

SCHAFFER, GORDON. *Russian Zone.* London: Allen and Unwin, 1947.

SCHUMAN, FREDERICK L. *Soviet Politics at Home and Abroad.* New York: Knopf, 1946.

SHERWOOD, ROBERT E. *Roosevelt and Hopkins: An Intimate History.* New York: Harper, 1948.

SHIRER, WILLIAM L. *The Rise and Fall of The Third Reich.* New York: Simon and Schuster, 1960.

SHUB, DAVID. *Lenin.* Garden City, N.Y.: Doubleday, 1948.

SLUSSER, ROBERT, ed. *Soviet Economic Policy in Postwar Germany.* New York: Research Program on the U.S.S.R., 1953.

SMITH, LAWRENCE DWIGHT. *Counterfeiting: Crime against the People.* New York: Norton, 1949.

SMITH, WALTER BEDELL. *My Three Years in Moscow.* Philadelphia: Lippincott, 1950.

SNELL, JOHN L. *Wartime Origins of the East-West Dilemma over Germany.* New Orleans: Houser, 1959.

———, ed. *The Meaning of Yalta.* Baton Rouge: Louisiana State University Press, 1956.

SNOW, EDGAR. *Stalin Must Have Peace.* New York: Random House, 1947.
SOUTHARD, FRANK A., JR. *The Finances of European Liberation, with Special Reference to Italy.* New York: King's Crown, 1946.
SPAHR, WALTER E. *Allied Military Currency.* New York: Economists' National Committee on Monetary Policy, 1943.
STANDLEY, WILLIAM H., and AGETON, ARTHUR A. *Admiral Ambassador to Russia.* Chicago: Regnery, 1955.
STEIN, HAROLD, ed. *American Civil-Military Decisions.* University, Ala.: University of Alabama Press, 1963.
STIMSON, HENRY L., and BUNDY, MCGEORGE. *On Active Service in Peace and War.* New York: Harper, 1947.
STRANG, LORD WILLIAM. *Home and Abroad.* London: Deutsch, 1956.
STRANSKY, JAN. *East Wind over Prague.* London: Hollis and Carter, 1950.
STRAUSZ-HUPÉ, ROBERT, and POSSONY, STEFAN T. *International Relations.* New York: McGraw-Hill, 1950.
STRONG, ANNA LOUISE. *The Soviets Expected It.* New York: Dial, 1941.
Memoirs by Harry S. Truman. 2 vols. Garden City, N.Y.: Doubleday, 1955.
TRUSCOTT, L. K., JR. *Command Decisions.* New York: Dutton, 1954.
UTLEY, FREDA. *The High Cost of Vengeance.* Chicago: Regnery, 1949.
VASILIEV, LEV. *Puti sovetskogo imperializma.* New York: Chekhov, 1952.
VON BERG, HENDRICK, ed. *Genosse Feind.* Bonn: Bertoverlag, 1962.
VON EINSIEDEL, HEINRICH. *I Joined the Russians.* New Haven: Yale University Press, 1953.
VON PAPEN, FRANZ. *Memoirs.* New York: Dutton, 1954.
WALLICH, HENRY C. *Mainsprings of the German Revival.* New Haven: Yale University Press, 1955.
WELLES, SUMNER. *Seven Decisions that Shaped History.* New York: Harper, 1951.
———. *The Time for Decision.* New York: Harper, 1944.
WESTERFIELD, H. BRADFORD. *Foreign Policy and Party Politics.* New Haven: Yale University Press, 1955.
WHEELER-BENNETT, JOHN W. *The Nemesis of Power: The German Army in Politics, 1918–1945.* New York: St. Martin's Press, 1954.
WHITE, ANDREW DICKSON. *Fiat Money in France.* Toronto: Bridgens, 1914.
WHITE, DOROTHY SHIPLEY. *Seeds of Discord.* Syracuse: Syracuse University Press.
WHITE, NATHAN I. *Harry Dexter White, Loyal American.* Waban, Mass., 1950.
WILLIAMS, WILLIAM APPLEMAN. *The Shaping of American Diplomacy.* 2 vols. Chicago: Rand McNally, 1956.
———. *The Tragedy of American Diplomacy.* Cleveland: World, 1959.
WILMOT, CHESTER. *The Struggle for Europe.* New York: Harper, 1952.
WOLFE, BERTRAM D. *Three Who Made a Revolution.* New York: Dial, 1948.
YUROVSKY, L. N. *Currency Problems and Policy of the Soviet Union.* London, 1925.
ZINK, HAROLD. *American Military Government in Germany.* New York: Macmillan, 1947.
———. *The United States in Germany: 1944–1955.* Princeton: Van Nostrand, 1957.
ZINNER, PAUL E. *Communist Strategy and Tactics in Czechoslovakia: 1918–48.* New York: Praeger, 1963.

Articles

BAFFI, PAOLO. "Monetary Developments in Italy," *Banca Nazionale del Lavoro Quarterly Review,* No. 47 (December, 1958), Rome, Italy.

BENNETT, JACK. "The German Currency Reform," *The Annals of the American Academy of Political and Social Science*, Vol. 267 (January, 1950).

BESS, DEMAREE. "American Viceroy in Germany," *The Saturday Evening Post* (May 10, 1947).

———. "The Cost of Roosevelt's 'Great Design,'" *The Saturday Evening Post* (May 27, 1944).

CASE, JOHN L. "The Development of the Morgenthau Plan through the Quebec Conference," *The Journal of Politics*, XVI, No. 2 (November, 1954).

DAVIS, FORREST. "What Really Happened in Teheran," *The Saturday Evening Post* (May 13, 1944).

DORN, WALTER L. "The Debate over American Occupation Policy in Germany in 1944–1955," *Political Science Quarterly*, LXXII, No. 4 (December, 1957).

FRANKLIN, WILLIAM M. "Zonal Boundaries and Access to Berlin," *World Politics*, XVI, No. 1 (October, 1963).

GOTTLIEB, MANUAL. "Failure of Quadripartite Monetary Reform 1945–1947," *Finanzarchiv*, Band 17 (1956/57), Tuebingen, Germany.

KLOPSTOCK, FRED H. "Monetary Reform in West Germany," *Journal of Political Economy*, Vol. 57 (1949).

KUBEK, ANTHONY. "Harry Dexter White and the War against Japan," *Human Events* (December 8, 1960).

LACH, DONALD F. "What *They* Would Do about Germany," *The Journal of Modern History*, VII, No. 4 (November, 1945).

LA FOLLETTE, ROBERT M., JR. Editorial, *The Progressive* (June 28, 1941).

MORGENTHAU, HENRY, JR. "Our Policy toward Germany," *The New York Post* (November 24–29, 1947).

———. "Postwar Treatment of Germany," *The Annals of the American Academy of Political and Social Science*, Vol. 246 (July, 1946).

MOSELY, PHILIP E. "Dismemberment of Germany: The Allied Negotiations from Yalta to Potsdam," *Foreign Affairs.* XXVIII, No. 3 (April, 1950).

———. "The Occupation of Germany: New Light on How the Zones Were Drawn," *Foreign Affairs*, XXVIII, No. 4 (July, 1950).

PIETRANERA, GIULIO. "Considerations on the Dynamics of the Italian inflation," *Banca Nazionale del Lavoro Quarterly Review*, Vol. I (1947–48), Rome, Italy.

PFLEIDERER, OTTO. "Waerungsreform in Westdeutschland," *Enzyklopaedische Lexikon fuer das Geld-, Bank-, und Boersewesen*, Frankfurt a/M, 1957.

POLK, JUDD. "Freezing Dollars against the Axis," *Foreign Affairs*, XX, No. 1 (October 1941).

SMITH, FRED. "The Rise and Fall of the Morgenthau Plan," *United Nations World*, I, No. 2 (March, 1947).

STOKES, RICHARD L. "The Quarter-Billion Occupation Mark Swindle," *The Freeman* (November 17, 1952).

VON BERG, MICHAEL. "Sowietisches Gold: Production, Verkaufe, Reserven," *Osteuropa Wirtschaft*, Heft 1/1963.

ZEMSKOV, I. "O tak nazyvaemom 'razdele' Yugoslavii na sfery vliianiia," *Mezhdunarodnaia Zhizn'*, No. 8 (August, 1958).

Newspapers and Journals

New York Daily Mirror
New York Times
Pravda
Public Opinion Quarterly
Stars and Stripes
The Wall Street Journal

INDEX